D1461401

WHIP
TO
WILSON

WHIP
TO
WILSON

Edward Short

Macdonald

A Macdonald Book

First published in Great Britain in 1989
by Macdonald & Co (Publishers) Ltd
London & Sydney

Short, Edward *1912-*
    Whip to Wilson.
    1. Great Britain.   Politics. Short, Edward,
    1912-
    I. Title
    941.085′092′4

    ISBN 0-356-17615-0

Typeset by Leaper & Gard Ltd, Bristol, England
Printed in Great Britain by
Redwood Burn Limited, Trowbridge, Wiltshire
Bound at the Dorstel Press

Macdonald & Co (Publishers) Ltd
Headway House
66-73 Shoe Lane
London EC4P 4AB
A member of Pergamon MCC Publishing Corporation plc

CONTENTS

ILLUSTRATIONS

1. Edward Short.
2. The 1965 Christmas party in No. 10 Downing Street.
3. The author at work in No. 12 Downing Street.
4. The Prime Minister with the Government whips in the garden of No. 10.
5. A presentation to the Prime Minister in Newcastle.
6. The author relaxing at Glenridding.
7. On the podium during the Durham Miners' Gala.

I

"A hundred days of dynamic action"

Towards the end of his short premiership Sir Alec Douglas-Home had painted himself well and truly into a corner. Although, even in a full five-year Parliament, the scope for surprise in announcing the date of a General Election is limited, most Prime Ministers contrive to achieve some element of it; but not Sir Alec. As the spring and early summer of 1964 had been allowed to go by the only remaining possibility was the short period between the end of the holiday season – later for Conservative voters than for Labour – and the end of October when inclement weather can be expected.

A Parliament must be dissolved not more than five years from its first meeting and from dissolution to election day is twenty-two days. As the previous election was on 8 October 1959 it was now possible to forecast the election date almost exactly. And, in a speech to the executive of the Conservative and Unionist Party on 3 September, Mr R.A. Butler made it virtually certain that it would be on 15 October, without actually mentioning the date – and Butler was adept at convoluted language. But there was a reason for retaining an element of doubt. The announcement by Sir Alec was delayed until 15 September because of Central Office fears that the cost of a series of large pre-election rallies held the previous weekend would otherwise have had to be counted in the election expenses of Tory candidates.

The delay in making the formal announcement also helped the Labour Party in this respect. We had published our manifesto *The New Britain* on 11 September with a well stage-managed press conference at Transport House followed by a mass rally of eleven thousand of the faithful at the Empire Pool, Wembley on the following Saturday.

As soon as he had taken the inevitable plunge, Sir Alec threw himself into a month-long campaign of meeting the people. As he is an extremely personable and friendly man but no orator, this was probably the right thing to do, rather than publicly defending the Tory record.

Harold Wilson had a very different approach to the electorate. Under him and his predecessor, Hugh Gaitskell, who had died in January 1963, the Labour Party had developed comprehensive policies on almost every predictable aspect of government. Indeed we had, if anything, a surfeit of policy – always one of Labour's weaknesses. He now embarked on a nationwide campaign of mass meetings both to expound these policies – and as an ex-Oxford don he was an excellent teacher – and to demonstrate the indefensibility of the Tory record. He was at this time at the peak of his considerable oratorical powers. His speeches combined sufficient of the university don to stand as definitive statements of Labour policy with sufficient of music hall comic to have his listeners rolling in the aisles from time to time.

It mattered little that the large and enthusiastic audiences were mainly Labour Party members or supporters carefully assembled by our regional officers. The media and indeed the whole world believed that Wilson would win. As a result, his speeches got enormous coverage on television and in the press.

What was not commented upon – and probably not noticed, so skilfully did he do it – was that he had one basic speech which he used everywhere, with sections added to suit a particular locality, to explain some new aspect of policy or to reply to one or other of the more telling points made against us in the campaign. Throughout the whole of his period at No. 10 his speeches were frequently assembled by cannibalising previous ones.

During the campaign, he came to my constituency, Central Newcastle, and spoke at a packed meeting in the City Hall. He was in top form, and Harold at his best was superb. His ability to make everyone present feel confident that we were winning was one of his many gifts as Party leader.

After the meeting, my wife Jennie and I went back with him to the Station Hotel with his wife Mary and Marcia Williams, his secretary. Unfortunately he caught his hand in the car door outside the hotel and was in considerable pain. In the bedroom where we had coffee and sandwiches, he talked (in spite of his fatigue and the pain he was suffering) about the mechanics of taking over, while Mary and Marcia fussed over his hand to his obvious and growing annoyance.

He had no doubt whatever that within a few days he would be in No. 10, nor did I. He confirmed what he had told me some months previously, that he wanted me to be Chief Whip, and he made the job sound as though it would be the linchpin of his administration. In the event, it turned out to be almost exactly as he had portrayed it, because of the minuscule majority; but, usually, it is the dreariest and most frustrating chore in government.

My own result was, as usual, one of the first to be announced because of the small electorate and the fact that the constituency was only a one-mile-long strip along the Tyne. I obtained 70.9 per cent of the votes cast, an increase of 5.1 per cent on the 1959 General Election. No indication of a landslide there! My wife and I sat up most of the night watching the results on television and, as it became obvious that we would probably win – though not by very much – I decided to go to London the following morning. I caught the 10 a.m. plane but, as I knew the die would not finally be cast until the results came in from the shires in the afternoon, I decided not to go immediately to Transport House – never my favourite place – where I had arranged to meet Harold. Instead, I broke my journey from Heathrow at the Israel Embassy in Kensington Palace Gardens to spend a few hours with Arthur Lourie, the Ambassador, and Eppie Evron, his Minister – two of my closest friends in London. I was amazed and pleased at their obvious delight at the prospect of a change of Government. Rightly or wrongly, they believed that there was a lingering anti-Israel bias in British foreign policy. This was partly due to the Foreign Office's long-standing love affair with the Arab peoples, but it was also a hangover from the anti-Israel, indeed anti-Semitic, attitude of Ernest Bevin in the Attlee Government.

Almost all the potential members of a new Labour Cabinet were known to be extremely friendly towards Israel. Harold Wilson himself was almost obsessively so. Indeed, since he resigned the premiership in 1976 he has written a major book on Israel – *The Chariot of Israel* (Norton, 1982). My two Israeli friends left me in no doubt as to the ministers they would like to see in the Foreign Office!

When I eventually reached Transport House at lunchtime, the General Secretary's room resembled an airport lounge full of passengers who had been waiting all night for a delayed plane. Some people stayed put because they were too tired to move, others wandered in and out.

Harold and Mary, who had not gone to bed at the Adelphi Hotel in Liverpool until 4 a.m. were there with their son Giles. Harold's father and sister had also joined them. George Brown, who had played such an energetic part in the campaign was there with Tom Driberg, Ray Gunter, Herbert Bowden, Frank Cousins and Tommy Balogh – one of Harold's economic advisers. Transport House staff plied us with sandwiches and beer (to become part of the Labour Government's standard formula for settling industrial disputes) and appalling coffee.

Marcia Williams must have been even more tired than the rest of us, after the gruelling few weeks she had undergone rushing daily between London and every part of the kingdom. In spite of her fatigue, she seemed to hold the whole group together and know instinctively what had to be done and said. Len Williams, the General Secretary of the Labour Party, was immovably flopped in an armchair like a stranded sea lion.

But the centre of interest was the large TV set churning out the results from the counties which, of course, were rapidly cutting down the overnight lead we had built up in the cities and urban areas. It came to the point where no one could predict what the final outcome would be.

But at 2.47 p.m. we knew we had won the election with 316 seats out of a House of Commons of 630. A Labour Government again after thirteen years in opposition – by a wafer-thin majority!

By 4 p.m. with one result to be announced the following day, we had a majority of four but an effective majority of five as the Speaker, Sir Harry Hylton-Foster, was a Tory – and of course we hoped to re-elect him. The final result was Labour 317, Conservatives 303, Liberals 9, Others 1. But uncertainty remained about the final majority because there were two non-voting Members of Parliament in addition to the Speaker. Obviously we would try to persuade the Tories to take at least one of these, but it was by no means certain that they would agree.

It was the smallest majority for a century and one which all the parliamentary and press pundits said was unworkable. The second Attlee Government had survived for only twenty months with a majority of six. 'It won't be long,' said Martin Redmayne, my predecessor as Chief Whip, when I met him in the corridor at Westminster on the day Parliament reassembled. In fact it was six years.

Such are the vagaries of the electoral system that although we polled 10,000 votes fewer than in 1959 and the Conservative vote fell by 1,750,000, we gained only 59 additional seats. We had not to look far for the explanation. The Liberal vote had almost doubled, although their seats increased only from six to nine. Their intervention in many constituencies had denied us a reasonably secure majority.

As soon as the result was known, Harold, in the apparently leisurely way in which he did everything, strolled out to a small side room to get changed and tidy himself up generally. There was a perpetual problem about his hands, which were almost always begrimed from his pipe. Throughout the whole time I have known him he has constantly cleaned out, stoked up, lit and smoked his pipe, allowing it to go out, then re-lighting it. . . . Mary saw to it that his hands were well scrubbed on this occasion. In the small room where he changed he came face to face with two strangers – security men who were to dog his every step for the next few years.

By now reporters and photographers crowded the front entrance of Transport House and across the road to the steps of St John's Church. The front of the Conservative Central Office on the other side of the square was deserted. Meanwhile Len Williams' secretary sat, hand poised over the phone, waiting for the call from Buckingham Palace. Finally it came – the call that was to change the face of British politics. 'The Queen wonders if Mr Wilson would call at about four,' said Sir Michael Adeane, her secretary.

Two of the endearing qualities of Harold Wilson are his attachment to his family and his unswerving loyalty to his friends. And so, waiting to drive him to the Palace was the driver who had driven him when he was President of the Board of Trade in the Attlee Government.

13

Some quick work by the remarkably competent Marcia had made it possible. But that was not all. For the first time, a Prime Minister going to receive the Queen's commission to form a government took his family to the Palace with him – Mary, his father and sister, and Marcia. He wanted them all to share his moment of triumph, the moment when the boy from Royds Hall Grammar School, Huddersfield, became Prime Minister of the United Kingdom.

One can imagine their pride and perhaps their fears about what lay ahead as they drove in separate cars along The Mall, past the crowds at the gates and into the inner courtyard of Buckingham Palace. They waited in a small room until Harold emerged as the third Labour Prime Minister and, at forty-eight, the youngest Prime Minister since Lord Rosebery in 1894.

He went immediately to Downing Street. Marcia returned to Transport House, where, amazingly, a number of government cars had appeared immediately the call from the Palace had been received. She and I went to No. 10 at once, so I was the first member elect of the new administration to take possession, beating Herbert Bowden by a short head!

When the shiny black door of No. 10 closed behind us I went to the left, through the ground floor of No. 11 into No. 12, the office of the Chief Whip, which, because of our tiny majority, was for the next year and a half to become the nerve centre of the Government's survival tactics in Parliament. The efficiency with which my office functioned would determine whether or not the new Government could govern.

As I turned left, Marcia turned right into the inner fastness of No. 10 to begin her interminable battles with the Civil Servants. She was determined to be responsible for the political and personal side of the Prime Minister's activities, and would brook no interference from the Principal Private Secretary, Derek Mitchell, and the No. 10 Private Office staff, who were responsible for his purely governmental activities.

Derek Mitchell's first objective had been to keep her out of No. 10 altogether. Indeed, before the election he had

14

had a secret meeting in No. 12 with Herbert Bowden under the auspices of Freddie Warren, the Chief Whip's Principal Private Secretary and the terror of every Whitehall Private Office, with the object of keeping Marcia in her place. At this meeting it was decided that if we won the election Herbert Bowden would approach the new Prime Minister and impress on him the need to keep Marcia away from Downing Street.

But when Herbert Bowden plucked up the courage to make the approach he got very short shrift indeed. Both he and Derek Mitchell underestimated the fierce loyalty with which Harold shielded all who had the good fortune to be counted among his friends. Not only was Marcia coming to No. 10, he was told, but she was to have the small room adjoining the Cabinet Room which had previously been used as a waiting room by VIPs coming to see the Prime Minister. She had been a loyal and highly competent secretary and political assistant for many years and he was not going to allow himself to be deprived of her services or to allow her to be pushed into some remote office at the behest of the Civil Servants in No. 10.

Having lost this battle the No. 10 staff caused her endless trouble in getting adequate accommodation for the Prime Minister's political office which she was to head. The first room offered her was ludicrously small, scarcely big enough to hold the filing cabinets. Eventually, after the intervention of no lesser personage than the Secretary to the Cabinet, Sir Burke Trend (later Lord Trend), she was wisely given more space, but at the expense of the Wilsons' private living quarters on the top floor.

Probably because of his attitude towards Marcia, a note of estrangement crept into the relationship between the Prime Minister and his Principal Private Secretary from the start. This was unfortunate because, apart from being a Civil Servant of exceptional brilliance, as his subsequent career has shown, Derek Mitchell was probably as dedicated as anyone in Whitehall to the success of a Labour Government. But the relationship between any minister, prime or otherwise, and his Private Office must be relaxed and free from strain. Two years later, it was Derek Mitchell who went

15

– to become a Deputy Under-Secretary at the Department of Economic Affairs – and Marcia who stayed.

When Harold arrived at No. 10, Downing Street was crowded. The euphoria of his triumph had banished any signs of fatigue and he strode jauntily from his car with cameras flashing and the crowd on the opposite side of the street cheering wildly. How magnificently cocky and confident he was, an almost heroic figure. The little man from Huddersfield who had beaten the fourteenth Earl and now the happy warrior was ready and eager to take up the challenge of leading his country. No one could ever have described Harold Wilson as 'swinging', but maybe his jauntiness helped to create the image of swinging Britain in the sixties. And, like the Beatles, his base was Liverpool.

No highfaluting speech with carefully rehearsed quotes from St Francis of Assisi for him. 'I should like to take this first opportunity of pledging my colleagues and myself to do everything we can to the fullest extent of our abilities in the interest of this country and our people. We are facing very great problems. But there is nothing we cannot do together.' Then he was inside the door of No. 10.

Two floors above him in the Prime Minister's private apartments, Sir Alec and Lady Douglas-Home were packing their bags and, an hour later, they left by the garden gate which opens on to Horse Guards Parade, to spend their weekend at Chequers. This is one of the few agreeable arrangements on a change of government in this country.

Inside the door the sun and the moon fell on the new Prime Minister in the form of Derek Mitchell, Sir Burke Trend, Secretary to the Cabinet, Sir Laurence Helsby, Joint Permanent Secretary to the Treasury and head of the Civil Service, and John Groves, public relations adviser. They were waiting to greet him and were desperately anxious for him to be briefed at the earliest possible moment on his appalling inheritance, to 'see the books' as Harold had put it throughout his election campaign. But his first priority was the appointment of the members of his Government who would be concerned with the menacing economic situation.

He went straight along the corridor to the Cabinet Room, where Herbert Bowden, Marcia and I joined him.

16

He sat down in the Prime Minister's chair in the centre of one side of the huge, green baize-covered table – extremely unhygienic I always thought – took out and lit his pipe, that malodorous instrument which dominated the hundreds of meetings we sat through during those years. He then produced a copy of the Labour Party's manifesto on which he had fought the election and placed it upright in the stationery box in front of him, where it remained until the next General Election, finally he took his pen and started to appoint the Government.

On 15 July he had said: 'What I think we're going to need is something like President Kennedy had when he came in after years of stagnation. . . . He had a programme of a hundred days – and a hundred days of dynamic action'.

In the two or three months before the election, Herbert Bowden and I had spent a considerable time preparing a rundown on every member of the Parliamentary Labour Party as well as new candidates who were likely to be elected, assessing their suitability for ministerial office. We had discussed each one at length and set down the department for which he or she appeared best qualified and the ministerial level we felt was most appropriate – senior minister, minister of state or parliamentary secretary. Almost everyone was included at one level or another, for an MP who could not manage at least the job of parliamentary secretary, considering all the Civil Service support he would receive, had to be very dim indeed.

This preparatory work was done at Harold's request and we saw to it that he had a copy in front of him on the Cabinet table on 16 October. Whether he made any use of it we never knew, but from some of his appointments we suspected he did not! It was clear to us from the first that he had made a great many promises to a great many Members as, indeed, he had to Bowden and me, and that he received advice on appointments from sources other than the Leader of the House and the Chief Whip. It is probably untrue that Marcia influenced ministerial appointment to any great extent, as has often been alleged. In spite of her claim to an encyclopaedic knowledge of the Parliamentary Labour Party it was almost entirely second-hand. She was virtually unknown to the majority of Members of Parliament apart from the small circle who haunted Harold's office when he was Leader of the Opposition. Of these the most prominent was George Wigg (later Lord Wigg), with whom Marcia was very friendly at that time and of whom she has written warmly in the first of her books – *Inside Number 10* (Weidenfeld and Nicolson, 1972). But George Wigg's knowledge of his fellow MPs was limited in the extreme. There were others in the 'kitchen cabinet' who probably gave advice.

Rather remarkably, throughout his premiership, Harold was resistant to pressure from his senior ministers about appointments – and most Cabinet ministers tried to get their (unpaid) parliamentary private secretaries appointed to the Government.

The truth is that he probably relied more on his own hunches and knowledge of his Members' capabilities than most Prime Ministers. For many years he had been a frequent habitué of the Members' tea room in the House of Commons, the place above all others where one can get to know MPs. Day after day he could be seen joining small groups of backbenchers for his tea or for a snack lunch. He was always a great one for small talk, especially about football or cricket, and he always took the trouble to know the local teams of his Members. He loved the parliamentary gossip with which the tea room is always awash and probably knew more about the private lives of his flock than any party leader has ever done.

Perhaps because of his over-generous view of his fellow men, his hunches sometimes proved to be wrong. Of all his many skills, the matching of Members to ministerial office was his least successful. On one of his regular visitations to a regional group of MPs, a trade union Member not noted for either his intelligence or his diligence hogged the discussion. Harold was so impressed that shortly afterwards he appointed him as Minister of State in a complicated department where he had to be carried by the more junior parliamentary secretary.

All his appointments on the evening of 16 October had been promised long before the election. George Brown's was the first. He was to head one of the four new departments forecast in our manifesto. It was to be known as the Department of Economic Affairs and George was to have the rather grand title of First Secretary of State. He was also to answer for the Prime Minister during absences from the Commons, but he was not named as Deputy Prime Minister. Harold refused him this title – as he did Jim Callaghan when he asked for it in 1974 – because he would never countenance the existence of an heir apparent and, in Jim's case, because I was then Deputy Leader of the Party!

Jim Callaghan was to be Chancellor of the Exchequer. I always felt that he would have made a brilliant Secretary of State for Education, probably greater than George Tomlinson in the Attlee Government. He is a man of great compassion, with a genuine love of children and an interest in giving all young people the opportunity to make the most of whatever talents they possessed. This interest was very much in evidence during his premiership (1976-79) when he initiated the great debate on education which, unfortunately, his education ministers allowed to fizzle out inconclusively.

But, of course, Jim had his mind on higher things and he was determined to secure one of the three heights by which the top is usually reached – Treasury, Home Office, Foreign Office. By the time he got to No. 10 in April 1976 he had secured all three in succession.

Any modern Chancellor of the Exchequer must have, as well as financial expertise, enormous reserves of inner staunchness – but particularly a Labour Chancellor, who is assailed vehemently from every side. Whether Jim was really fitted in these respects for the colossal tasks ahead of him was very much doubted by many of us. He had acted as Shadow Chancellor for some time and had worked diligently at fitting himself for the job but, unlike most other ministerial offices, no amount of preparation can make a Chancellor if the right psychological make-up is lacking.

Although he had been defeated in the General Election, Patrick Gordon Walker was still to be Foreign Secretary, as Harold had promised him. It was hardly likely that the Conservatives could raise any objection to this appointment, with the precedent of Sir Alec Douglas-Home becoming

Prime Minister without a seat in the House of Commons so fresh in mind; indeed, he had delayed the recall of Parliament in order to fight a by-election at Kinross.

The first instruction I received from the new Prime Minister was to find a seat for his Foreign Secretary immediately.

Patrick was one of the wisest and most popular senior figures in the Parliamentary Labour Party – the agreeable Oxford don. He was always willing to drop whatever he was doing to help or advise younger colleagues. But he had the fault, if fault it is, which has often turned successful dons into unsuccessful ministers. He was so objective about everything that he had the utmost difficulty in reaching conclusions about anything. And a minister must always be able to make up his mind. Unfortunately, his morale was clearly undermined by his defeat after an extremely unpleasant campaign in Smethwick fought on racial issues. His second defeat three months later at Leyton accelerated the draining away of his confidence. This, I always felt, was one of the saddest episodes in the 1964-70 Parliaments.

Herbert Bowden, Chief Whip in Opposition, was to become Lord Privy Seal, for which there was a salary but few duties, and Leader of the House of Commons, for which there was no salary but heavy duties. I had been his deputy when he was Opposition Chief Whip but, although I had worked closely with him for some years and made a point of having my tea with him every day, I scarcely knew him. He was an upright man who kept himself very much to himself. But I looked forward to continuing my association with him in the Government.

Next morning, when we consulted the Clerk-in-Ordinary to the Privy Council, Sir Godfrey Agnew, about getting the 16 October appointees sworn in before the Queen, we were told that a Privy Council meeting could not be held without a Lord President of the Council, who must take the Oath of Allegiance and kiss the Queen's hand on his appointment before any other ministers could be sworn in. And so Herbert, after being Lord Privy Seal elect overnight, on the Saturday morning was transmuted to Lord President elect.

Denis Healey was appointed Secretary of State for Defence, an office he held until the General Election of 1970 with great distinction and without attracting to himself any of the odium that usually attaches itself to the incumbents of defence ministry offices in Labour circles.

He had always wanted to be Foreign Secretary and knew more about the nitty-gritty of foreign affairs than the rest of the Government put together. I suspected that the Prime Minister really wanted to play a major role in foreign affairs himself, as he did in the negotiations with Ian Smith over Rhodesia, and did not want to be inhibited by a tough, well-informed Foreign Secretary, which Healey would have been. Donnish, quiet, acquiescent figures such as Gordon Walker, and later Michael Stewart, fitted his book much better. When he did appoint a tough foreign secretary in George Brown, trouble between them soon erupted, and George resigned after a succession of threats to do so because, he alleged, of Harold's interference in Foreign Office relations with the United States. Similarly, Herbert Bowden asked to be relieved of the Colonial Office in 1967 because of inter-ference by Downing Street in our relations with Malta.

But the Prime Minister believed that Denis, like other shadow ministers, had given too many hostages to fortune in his pre-election utterances.

Gerald Gardiner, QC, (later Lord Gardiner), that prince among lawyers, was to be the Lord Chancellor. He occupied the Woolsack until the 1970 General Election.

Finally, in the first list of appointments, I was named as Parliamentary Secretary to the Treasury, a sinecure with a salary which enabled me to become Chief Whip, an office which has no constitutional existence. Although I was not technically a member of the Cabinet, the Prime Minister gave instructions that I was to attend all Cabinet meetings, and I was treated as a full member. I never knew whether my opinion was included when the Prime Minister was collecting the voices, as he did when a decision had to be made, because he persisted with the myth that no voting takes place. When in 1974 I became number two in order of Cabinet precedence, I always saw him totting up the two columns when a decision had to be reached.

Having completed the list of seven major appointments, Harold handed it to Derek Mitchell for announcement and turned his attention to the long queue of decisions which await a new Prime Minister, not to mention replying to the congratulations which had been flowing into Downing Street from around the world.

Bowden left for his palatial offices in the Old Treasury Building in Whitehall, which also interconnects with No. 10.

I went through the entrance hall of No. 11 to my office on the ground floor of No. 12, where Freddie Warren, Principal Private Secretary to the Chief Whip, was awaiting me with a glass of sherry with which, I quickly learnt, he plied every visitor and lubricated every difficult situation. Of course, like Herbert Bowden, I had paid a number of visits to No. 12 before the General Election but usually late in the evening so that I would not run across my predecessor, Martin Redmayne. Those pre-election visits are extremely useful but do present problems because they involve Civil Servants serving one administration in discussions which are based on the assumption that their political masters are going to be defeated at the forthcoming election. I also had the advantage of having been Deputy Chief Whip in Opposition and, as such, I was in frequent touch with Warren in those little-known interparty contacts known euphemistically as 'the usual channels', on which the relatively smooth working of Parliament depends so much.

The block of buildings known as Nos. 10, 11 and 12 Downing Street is what remains of private houses jerry-built by Sir George Downing towards the end of the seventeenth century. No. 10 consists of two houses, that built by Downing and, adjoining it, a substantial mansion behind it which overlooks Horse Guards Parade. The two were joined in 1732-35. The rear house now contains the state rooms used mainly for entertaining, though Sir Alec Douglas-Home lived in them, and the Prime Minister's rather poor living quarters above.

No. 12 was burned down in 1879 except for the lower ground floor on garden level and the ground floor on street level. These two floors house the Government

22

Whips' department. Between 1960 and 1963 the Macmillan Government had the three houses reconstructed internally at a cost of a million pounds. This work preserved the historic character of Downing Street down to such details as retaining the original door of No. 10, and resulted in a block of buildings containing over two hundred rooms. Among other changes, No. 12 was restored to its original height to provide three extra floors. Unfortunately none of this extra space was allocated to the Chief Whip, his team of Assistant Whips or his secretariat. All of it was added to the already generous accommodation of the Chancellor of the Exchequer who, unlike both the Prime Minister and his Chief Whip, had no office staff to accommodate in Downing Street.

Having the day-and-night task of processing our ambitious programme through Parliament and, at the same time, preserving the Government from defeat, it seemed to me that if anyone needed to live over the shop it was the Chief Whip. Accordingly I initiated an approach to the new Chancellor on private secretary level to see if he would be prepared to make some accommodation available for the Chief Whip – perhaps a couple of rooms on the top floor which could be reached by a lift. I received a polite but firm refusal as he needed the rooms for his family.

Eventually I had a bedroom created in a spare room off the general office on the lower ground floor where I could spend the night if necessary. Unfortunately, the only washing facilities were across the office and, as this was occupied during working hours by four shorthand typists, I had to be up and away before they arrived in the morning.

I enquired about the cost of installing a shower in the bedroom but, as it was below the level of the sewers in Downing Street, the cost would have been enormous and so, as long as I was Chief Whip, I continued to scurry among the filing cabinets and typewriters to get washed and shaved before the staff arrived, while the Chancellor and his family luxuriated above me in accommodation which Roy Jenkins described as like living in a hotel and doing your own housework.

All ministers had the strictest instructions from the Prime Minister that improvements and decorations in ministerial offices had to be kept to bare essentials. We were all so constrained by this puritan streak in Harold, who abhorred waste of any kind – even of time – that we felt considerable guilt if we had a room or corridor done out with emulsion paint. Imagine our surprise when we returned to office in 1974 and saw the vast amounts which had been spent by the Heath Government on decorations and improvements in Downing Street, Chequers and elsewhere.

The first floor accommodation at No. 12 consisted of a huge, comfortably furnished conference area overlooking St James's Park with three rooms leading off – Warren's office, which overlooked the park, my rather dark room looking into the shabby garden of No. 10 and a gloomy, sinister-feeling room on the Downing Street side which for some unaccountable reason I could scarcely bring myself to enter. To me this room had an unmistakable aura of evil, in spite of all the efforts of the Ministry of Works to furnish it attractively. But I could never find out whether some long-forgotten dark deed had been perpetrated there. I tried to persuade the Assistant Whips to use it as an office, but they also avoided it like the plague.

My room was the original Chief Whip's room, which contained Disraeli's standing writing desk and an armchair used by Churchill during the war. Around the wall were memorabilia of my predecessors, including photographs back to the early years of the nineteenth century. These rather depressing pictorial records of previous incumbents are a feature of most Whitehall departments. On the stairs of both No. 10 and Chequers previous Prime Ministers catch the eye with every step up – or down. It is, I believe, a device used by the Civil Service both to flatter their minis-terial masters and at the same time to remind them of their transitoriness. 'You are only here for a season', they warn from the walls of every Private Office. From now on I was to be stared at reprovingly by long-dead, bewhiskered Chief Whips and by one far from dead who would soon become Leader of the Conservative Party and defeat us in the 1970 General Election – Ted Heath.

The Chief Whip was still referred to in the Commons as the Patronage Secretary, though by my time he had precious little patronage to dispense. In the past, most of the Prime Minister's enormous patronage regarding appointments – for example, of five thousand Civil Servants – and of recommendations for honours and titles, had been exercised by the Chief Whip so that the Prime Minister did not sully his hands in such matters.

He had also taken delivery of the vast amounts of money which were 'donated' to Party funds, and other funds, in return for titles. The selling of honours, with a sliding scale of payments, went on until the Lloyd George scandals precipitated the Honours (Prevention of Abuse) Act of 1925, which effectively stopped it.

In spite of the Macmillan rebuilding and its plush furnishings, the room, indeed the whole of No. 12, always seemed to me to exude an atmosphere of skulduggery and intrigue. What infamous secret bargains must have been struck there throughout the previous century and a half.

In the large conference area there was a collection of interesting small plaster busts of statesmen, mainly Tories, donated by previous generations of Whips. I redressed the political balance by contributing a figure of Keir Hardie. Dominating it was a copy of the weekly whip sent to Members in Disraeli's time.

In a prominent position I hung a painting by a parliamentary colleague, George Rogers (Kensington North), of Lanty Tarn above our house in the Ullswater Valley. In the pressures and appalling fatigue I endured in the following eighteen months, this little picture gave me great solace; but it often made me long to be far from Downing Street and London and on the remote fells where I could smell the peat and hear the curlew and the sad soughing of the wind in the lonely pines.

One most valued exhibit was a painting given to us in 1965. When he was Chief Whip, Ted Heath had been promised one of Churchill's paintings for No. 12 by Lady Churchill. The attractive Canadian lake scene, which could equally have been Ullswater, arrived and I organised a presentation ceremony. I invited previous Chief Whips and the Prime Minister and laid on a splendid afternoon tea. Lady Churchill arrived with her daughter Mary, and I made a speech over which I had taken unusual trouble – quoting, among other things, the song from Camelot about the 'fleeting wisp of glory' and all that ('some wisp' one could imagine Winston saying!). Lady Churchill listened attentively, walked across to the fireplace where the picture was hanging above the mantelpiece, looked up through her lorgnettes and said 'Winston would have liked it there.' End of ceremony.

In my diary for Friday 16 October I recorded that a mountain of paper awaited me on my desk at No. 12. Heaven only knows now what it was all about but it kept me there until midnight. It was almost certainly genuine – and not all ministerial paper mountains are genuine. It is a familiar stratagem used by the Civil Service to keep their ministers fully occupied on harmless trivialities so that they have no time to engage in such dangerous occupations as thinking ahead, policy-making or enquiring too closely into the working of their departments. And, of course, any given amount of paper can be generated by the Civil Service at any given time.

In dealing with this first correspondence I fought and won my first minor battle for independence against the Civil Service. I had dictated a large number of letters to a very shy young shorthand typist who had been allocated to me from the small No. 12 secretariat. When I received the letters back for signature later in the day they were almost unrecognisable. In every case the wording had been altered. I sent for the secretary and asked for an explanation. Mr Warren had altered them all, she told me – whereupon I tore them all up and instructed her to type them again exactly as I had dictated them.

After a number of similar skirmishes, an excellent working arrangement developed between Freddie Warren and myself which grew into a firm and lasting friendship.

When a minister moves to another department a comprehensive assessment of how to get along with him is, I am told, transmitted on the private secretary bush telegraph. I had no more problems of this kind even when I came up against the tough and able Civil Servants in the Department of Education and Science.

26

The next morning, as I was entering No. 12 from Downing Street I met Reggie Maudling, the outgoing Chancellor of the Exchequer leaving No. 11 with his arms full of personal possessions including a stuffed pheasant. We exchanged a few words about the ups and downs of political life and moved on – he out and I in.

Herbert Bowden and I spent most of the morning around the Cabinet table with the Prime Minister on the appointment of junior ministers. Some of his appointments staggered us but revealed how magnanimous he was. In the case of one parliamentary secretary whose job was to be more important than most at that ministerial level, I said: 'But you can't appoint him. Don't you remember all the horrible, defamatory things he has said about you since you became leader of the Party?' Harold looked up, smiled with that impish but enigmatic smile of his, which made me wonder whether he was being magnanimous or very crafty, and said, 'Chief Whip, life is too short to worry about things like that.'

Every British Prime Minister must balance his appointments between the wings of his party. Contrary to popular belief, the extent to which he needs to achieve balance varies with the size of his majority. The greater the majority, the more the internal political problems he will have and the greater the need for balance in appointments. But Harold, with one of the smallest majorities ever known in Britain, achieved a remarkable balance with consummate skill, which was revealing about how he saw the task of leading such a diverse body as the Labour Party. His predecessor, Hugh Gaitskell, a man of rock-like resolve and integrity, believed his task was to fight unceasingly and unrelentingly for what he believed to be right, to model the Party in his own image. Harold Wilson saw it quite differently. To him it was an unceasing search for common ground. In all the hundreds of meetings over which I saw him preside I never knew him fail to find some area of agreement between different – often overtly hostile – points of view. Somewhere, he believed, in every conflict there was a formula, a solution behind which everyone could unite – one of the Wilsonian laws of politics. But, as we were often to discover in the ensuing years, although this government by formulae was relatively peaceful because it avoided the more strident conflicts which disfigure the Labour Party from time to time, it also resulted in policies which were so anaemic and bereft of bite that they commanded little respect and achieved meagre results. The broader the church, the smaller the common ground, and Labour is and has always been a pretty broad church.

It was leadership by consent and compromise as opposed to Hugh Gaitskell's leadership by confrontation and often conflict. Which man would have made the better Prime Minister, we shall unfortunately never know.

In his appointments the new Prime Minister was meticulously careful to represent every point of view, every gradation in the broad spectrum from left to right, often I suspect, to imprison and silence within the Government someone with whom he disagreed. But this was not always the case. For example, there was no appointment offered to Michael Foot (Ebbw Vale), who had been regarded by both the leadership and the Whips as a maverick – well-liked and influential, but still a maverick – and often something of a nuisance. As his subsequent career has shown, he too could have been silenced and tamed by office, but Harold made him no offer and merely told George Wigg to tell him that he would try to bring him into the Government at a later date.

Also, on the left, there was the highly articulate Ian Mikardo (Poplar), a close friend and loyal supporter of Harold who, in my view would have made an excellent minister. Quite a number of anxious moments about divisions would have been avoided had Michael Foot and Ian Mikardo been appointed, and it would have been a better Government. But he would not hear of it. The most I could persuade him to agree – at a later date – was that Mikardo should be appointed chairman of the important Select Committee which monitored the performance of the nationalised industries. This he did supremely well, and as a result, I recommended him for the chairmanship of one of the industries he had investigated – but even this was rejected by No. 10.

And so, although Harold undoubtedly gagged some troublesome voices, he did not carry this practice nearly so far as is often alleged.

On Saturday 17 October the small area outside the Cabinet Room resembled a doctor's waiting room. The appointees had been summoned for interview at ten-minute intervals but, inevitably, as they had to come from all over the country there were both pile-ups and hiatuses when no one was there. Ninety people were interviewed and appointed in five days. All were excited at the prospect of office, but by the time they got to No. 10 the first flush of euphoria had been superseded by anxiety about the ministerial level at which they were to be offered jobs. And all MPs believe they are uniquely fitted to sit in the Cabinet if not to occupy the Prime Minister's chair.

There was one moment of great embarrassment when we noticed a member called Lance Mallalieu, QC, (Brigg) waiting hopefully. We knew immediately that an unfortunate mistake had been made by the Civil Servants. They had been told to summon Lance's brother, J.P.W. Mallalieu (Huddersfield East), who was to be offered the post of Under-Secretary of State for Defence for the Royal Navy. Lance was heavily involved in the World Government movement and the Inter-Parliamentary Union, and for this reason it was felt he would not wish to take on a junior ministerial appointment. Face was saved all round by the Prime Minister's unfailing resourcefulness. He remembered that we needed someone called a Second Church Commissioner, whose only duty was to introduce in the Commons those Church of England measures which required the approval of Parliament. There was no salary, but some prestige and the valuable perk, at that time, of a room in the Palace of Westminster. Lance accepted the appointment and performed his duties admirably.

Our election manifesto *The New Britain* had promised that we would 'set up a Ministry of Technology to guide and stimulate a major national effort to bring advanced technology and new processes to industry.' While the Prime Minister was dealing with the new appointments in Downing Street, a special meeting of the executive committee of the

Transport and General Workers' Union was being held at Transport House at which Frank Cousins, the General Secretary, sought and was granted leave of absence to serve in the Government as Minister of Technology.

There were probably a number of motives behind the appointment. Frank was a leading and highly articulate advocate of unilateral nuclear disarmament; to entice him into the Cabinet would effectively silence him. He was also one of the most influential trade unions leaders in Britain, and could provide the best possible liaison between the Government and the unions. His appointment would strengthen George Woodcock's influence in the TUC and, hopefully, make agreement in the National Economic Development Council easier to achieve. In addition to these tactical considerations he had shown a better understanding than most of the impact which automation (as it was called then) would have on industry, particularly on working practices.

Although he talked too long and too often in Cabinet, he was always a pleasant and helpful colleague. But after a lifetime in trade unionism, including a period at the top of Britain's largest union, he never really fitted into the very different world of Whitehall and he was always ill at ease in the even stranger atmosphere of the House of Commons.

I already had the troublesome problem of finding a seat for Patrick Gordon Walker but, with the appointment of Frank Cousins, I now had to find two seats urgently, for the House of Commons will not tolerate a seatless minister for very long.

Perhaps the biggest bombshell that Harold exploded over Herbert Bowden and me on that Saturday morning was his announcement that, on his way home to Hampstead the previous evening, he had invited sixty-four-year-old George Wigg (Dudley) to become Paymaster General with special duties which were as yet unspecified but which appeared to amount to him being a special assistant to the Prime Minister with a wide-ranging brief to interfere in a great variety of ad hoc matters – a recipe which set all our alarm bells ringing. A formula would have to be drafted to define his duties, the Prime Minister said, because he anticipated a good deal of Tory interest in the appointment – and how right he was. George had long been a member of the kitchen cabinet and had a ferret-like tenacity in pursuing any matter which engaged his attention, and the more the minutiae the better he liked it. Herbert and I felt in our bones that the appointment, whatever the formula, spelled trouble for us – for me in the arena of Party discipline and for him in the business of the House. Like most of us, George had never held ministerial office but he had been an Assistant Whip and had served as Parliamentary Private Secretary to Manny Shinwell, with whom he had a special rapport at this time. To his credit, he had made it his business to learn more than most of us about the ways of the Civil Service.

In his autobiography, *George Wigg* (Michael Joseph, 1972), he said: 'My arrival at No. 10 was neither understood nor accepted by the Private Office." What was true of the Private Office was equally true of most of the Government and remained so until he left office in November 1967. The No. 10 Civil Servants showed their displeasure at his appointment by allocating him a private secretary who was a higher executive officer – a very lowly rank for a minister's secretary. They also gave him a small, inconvenient room, as they had done with Marcia. It was their way of trying to sweep under the mat two of the new Prime Minister's assistants of whom they disapproved. But they greatly underestimated the abilities of both George and Marcia as well as the loyalty of the Prime Minister to his friends. The Paymaster General was quickly found new office accommodation in No. 70 Whitehall, which interconnects with No. 10; just as Marcia, equally quickly, was found rooms on the top floor for her political office. More important, she also moved into the small room off the Cabinet Room, to the extreme annoyance of the No. 10 Civil Servants.

The inevitable parliamentary question about George Wigg's duties came on 12 November, and the Prime Minister replied that it was not the practice to specify these in detail but that Wigg would carry out duties assigned to him from time to time and would answer questions about the coordination of information services. Of course he had furnished himself with all the precedents for the office of Paymaster General being used to employ Prime Ministerial advisers. The Civil Service is superb at finding precedents. As most were Tories, including Lord Cherwell, Earl Winterton and Sir Walter Monckton, the witch hunt against George Wigg, which continued throughout his period in office, got off to a somewhat muted start.

Although I and many other ministers had frequent and just cause to complain about Wigg's interference in matters which lay within our departmental responsibilities, I always felt that his work provided our Government with an extra dimension in the field of security, where he was responsible for major improvements, particularly in the Army. We had no security or indeed any governmental scandals when he was in office. I have no inside knowledge of the former but a good deal about the latter, and I know that he headed off a number of both varieties by scenting them before they materialised and taking the appropriate action. He was known to other ministers as the Spymaster General.

It was valuable to have at least one of the Prime Minister's confidants who possessed a good deal of down-to-earth political nous. George Wigg could give advice in irreverent army language which was the perfect antidote to the also irreverent but often quite different advice he received from Marcia. As the months progressed, Marcia saw herself more and more as a political adviser rather than a personal secretary – indeed in *Inside Number 10* she frequently uses the pronouns 'we' and 'us' in referring to the Government. But she knew little about relations between the Government and Transport House and the efforts we (Herbert Bowden and I) made to keep the Labour Party outside Parliament informed, as she shows in her book.

Unfortunately, the close relationship between George and Marcia of Opposition days quickly disappeared in government and degenerated into near hostility, to the detriment of the Labour Government. He believed that her influence on Harold was 'not always exercised with wisdom or discretion' (*George Wigg*), and he was better placed than most of us to know. My criticism of her was not that she lacked wisdom or discretion but that she was ill-informed on matters on she felt singularly well-equipped to give advice.

*

Three Members who were called for interview on Saturday 17 October were astonished at the appointments they were offered. Both Dick Crossman (Coventry East) and Fred Willey (Sunderland North) arrived at No. 10 expecting to be appointed Secretary of State for Education. Fred had made himself something of an expert on educational policy by carrying out a wide programme of visits to educational institutions, and had set down his ideas in a book on education. He had also been our Opposition spokesman on education. Not unnaturally he expected to take over at the DES. Dick had also been active in the educational field, having floated a number of interesting and radical views on reform which, although he did not appear to realise it, had alarmed both the academic world and Harold Wilson, who was extremely conservative in educational matters. Dick was quite sure he was the man for the job. But Harold had other views. He wanted a safe man in charge of the education system and appointed Michael Stewart, an ex-public schoolmaster who had been spokesman on housing in opposition.

The relationship of Harold Wilson to Michael Stewart during the two Parliaments of 1964-70 was one of great regard and growing reliance – indeed, in the late sixties, as his relationship with George Brown and Jim Callaghan weakened, he probably depended more on his advice than any other minister's. This was a development which almost everyone in the Government welcomed, for Michael Stewart was a man of considerable wisdom and versatility. But he was quiet and unflamboyant, and for this reason that most acerbic of political journalists, Anthony Howard, has dubbed him as part of Labour's second eleven. Any objective assessment of ministerial achievements will show that it is almost always the quiet, self-effacing ministers who are the high achievers. Unfortunately they are disliked by the media, which thrive on flamboyance, and often by their party managers because they do not fully exploit the electoral potential of their achievements.

Dick Crossman, to his surprise and initially his chagrin, was offered Housing. But Harold persuaded him that it was a challenge to his intellect and that success in this department was crucial to Labour's hopes of staying in office and winning the next General Election, which, at that time, everyone believed could not be far off. His first tasks would be to repeal the Rent Act and to initiate a massive house-building programme.

Fred Willey became the non-Cabinet head of the new Ministry of Land and National Resources charged with the colossal, and as it turned out insuperable, task of implementing our manifesto promise to establish a Crown Land Commission 'to end the competitive scramble for building land' and 'to buy for the community land on which building or rebuilding is to take place'.

Dick Crossman never forgave Fred Willey for, as he quite wrongly believed, doing him out of Education. His enmity became only too apparent in the ensuing months when at meeting after meeting he used his considerable dialectical skill to destroy Willey's plans to establish the Commission and, as he was concerned with housing, he had a major say in all the discussions on the Commission proposals. In the end we implemented a mouse of a scheme which achieved nothing and was promptly repealed by the Heath Government. There can be no doubt in the minds of those of us who saw it all that this major plank in our election platform was sabotaged by Crossman. This caused me enormous trouble with both the Parliamentary Labour Party and Transport House, who could not understand our failure to do what we had promised.

Harold takes a more charitable view of Dick's responsibility. He blames the powerful Civil Servants in the Ministry of Housing and Local Government and also, to some extent, blames himself for not having taken a firmer line with MHLG from the start. (*The Labour Government, 1964-70*, Weidenfeld and Michael Joseph, 1971). But the gentlemanly Fred Willey was no match for the Crossman approach, which was compounded of charm and bullying in equal proportions. Furthermore, Fred had not the considerable advantage of a seat in the Cabinet.

The Prime Minister honoured a pre-election promise he had made to Sir Frank Soskice (later Lord Stowe Hill), who had been Solicitor General in Attlee's Government, that he

34

would be Home Secretary – though it is doubtful whether he was fit enough to do the job. He was always a favourite with the Whips, who usually had much more trouble whipping ministers than backbenchers – but never with Frank. No matter how late the division, he was always there.

James Griffiths, a beloved figure in the Party, was, at the age of seventy-four, appointed Secretary of State for Wales – a new office. He brought sorely needed ministerial experience into the Cabinet; only two other members had ever held Cabinet rank previously. It meant a good deal to him that he was to be the charter Secretary of State for his beloved Wales, even on the understanding that it was for a limited period. Among his many attractive public-speaking gestures, Jim used to make his most solemn pronouncements with his two palms spread out on his chest. 'He swears with his hands on both his hearts,' said one of his Welsh parliamentary colleagues.

The redoubtable and often abrasive William Ross became his Scottish counterpart and eventually held the office of Secretary of State for Scotland longer than anyone else had ever done. He was one of the most valuable and balanced ministers in the four Labour Governments of the sixties and seventies until Jim Callaghan decided to dispense with his services when he succeed Harold Wilson in 1976.

Ray Gunter, President of the Transport Salaried Staffs Association, got the Ministry of Labour, which he described to the reporters waiting in Downing Street as 'the bed of nails'. I suspect that any department would have been a bed of nails to Ray. He caused many problems to the Whips because he felt that his job was the most demanding in the Government and that he should be excused from being present at late sittings in the House. I took an entirely different view. I felt that I could not maintain the morale of our members unless senior ministers were seen setting an example in the early hours of the morning. To their credit, I had the fullest cooperation for most of them, especially the Prime Minister, who asked for no privileges of any kind. My acrimonious relations with Ray erupted into a shouting match in my room more than once, but invariably I received an apology from him the next day. On one occasion I even had to complain to the Prime Minister that I was having trouble with Ray again. The broad gist of his response was 'Join the club'.

Two other appointments were of interest because of the subsequent drift of the ministers concerned across the political spectrum in the Party. Anthony Greenwood (later Lord Greenwood) a well-liked, rather glamorous ornament of the left, became Secretary of State for the Colonies and from that moment moved steadily to the right, eventually becoming a highly efficient bureaucrat indistinguishable from a senior Civil Servant.

The other, Anthony Wedgwood Benn (Bristol South East), who was then to the right of centre in the Party, was appointed to the non-Cabinet but prestigious and ancient office of Postmaster General. He moved, at first slowly but in the late sixties and early seventies rapidly, to the far left.

Tony Benn, as he now prefers to be called, was one of the most gifted members of the 1964-70 Governments. He possessed both high intelligence and the rare ability to generate new ideas. He was – and is – I believe, completely without guile, a precious quality among politicians. All the Wilson Governments owed much to the quality of Tony's mind, which illumined and enlivened many an otherwise dull meeting.

The Prime Minister had a limited amount of time to devote to new appointments on the morning of Saturday 17 October because of an urgent meeting with George Brown and Jim Callaghan on the dangerous economic situation. By then all three had read (goodness knows when) the massive Civil Service brief which had been prepared for the new Government and the options it posed. The first Cabinet meeting had been called for Monday, and Brown and Callaghan needed firm proposals to put to their colleagues.

Now that the new ministers had 'seen the books' it was clear that Britain faced a deficit on overseas payments of at least £800 million in 1964 and at least a similar figure in 1965. This was more than twice the figure forecast by Harold in the election campaign – for which he was savagely criticised by the Tories. This barren inheritance from the Home Government overshadowed the five years eight months of our two Governments from 1964-70. It virtually destroyed our chances of carrying out many of the policies on which we had been elected. From now until our defeat in 1970 the first question asked of any minister proposing to implement any part of our manifesto was invariably 'Does it cost anything? And if so, how much?' It led to endless trouble for the Whips and myself explaining to the Parliamentary Labour Party and to the Party outside the House why we could not move as far and as fast as we had hoped and promised.

The Civil Servants had worked out the balance of payment options for our predecessors. But they had taken no action because of the coming election. There were three possible courses of immediate action – devaluation, the restriction of imports by a quota system or additional tariffs on imports.

The argument continues two decades later as to whether or not we should have devalued sterling. The most drastic form of devaluation would have been to let the pound find its own level, which would have reflected the view taken by the rest of the world about the British economy after thirteen years of Conservative rule – a threat which the Prime Minister used on more than one occasion when dealing with the City.

But what is not generally known is that the devaluation option was not really available to us because, well ahead of the election, an understanding had been reached on behalf of the Labour Opposition with Alfred Hayes, President of the New York Federal Reserve Bank, which is part of the Federal Reserve system in the United States, that if we became the Government we would not devalue the pound. In return we received a promise of massive American support for sterling if it should be needed.

This understanding was, I believe, reached without any authority from the Shadow Cabinet but bound the Wilson Cabinet, though I doubt whether most of them knew of its existence.

Apart from this, devaluation in the circumstances in which we took office would have been an extremely dangerous

37

exercise. It might have triggered off competitive devaluation among other exporting countries, with quite unpredictable consequences. It would also have involved severe restraints on domestic consumption.

There had been so much speculation in the press about devaluation that a statement had to be made at once, without waiting for Cabinet approval, saying in the most unambiguous terms that there was to be no devaluation. And so we were committed to defending the pound at a level of 2.80 dollars.

The Saturday morning meeting was left with the proposals on the restriction of imports, the encouragement of exports and severe restraints on public expenditure to recommend to the new Cabinet when it met on Monday.

In the afternoon we had a little light relief from the endless details of taking over the Government and from the economic problems facing us. We had to be legitimised by being sworn in as members of the Privy Council, and where there were any, receiving seals of office from the Queen. The Prime Minister was already a Privy Counsellor but had to be appointed First Lord of the Treasury. The Privy Council was arranged for 4 p.m. at Buckingham Palace but, as most of us were new boys and those who were not had forgotten the procedure, we were rehearsed at three-thirty in the Lord President's room in the Privy Council office by the Adolf Menjou-like Clerk-in-Ordinary, Sir Godfrey Agnew.

The irrepressible good spirits of George Brown made the Council itself an almost hilarious occasion – much to the embarrassment of Sir Godfrey and, I suspect, the amusement of the Queen. The secret Privy Council oath which is read out by the Clerk ends with the words 'So help you God' and part of the ceremony involves new counsellors shaking hands with the existing ones, who stand in line. As I shook hands with George, he said in a whisper which every-one present could hear, 'And God help you, brother.' As Jim Callaghan was receiving his rather weighty seal of office from the Queen, he said – again in a highly audible stage whisper – 'You've got half the gold reserve there, Jim.'

*

38

I left No. 12 at 10 p.m. for north London where I had accommodation. I had never moved my home to London from the North. I was back at 9.30 the following morning – Sunday. I met Herbert Bowden and we went through to No. 10, only to find the Prime Minister had been at work long before us, churning out ministerial appointments. He had left both us and his Civil Servants so far behind that no one knew he had exceeded the numbers laid down in the Parliament Act of not more than 27 senior ministers in the Commons and not more than 73 in all. When he was told about this he airily told Herbert Bowden and myself to go away and find a solution to the problem. 'I am not going to allow Queen Anne to tell me how to appoint my Government,' he said – a truly Wilsonian comment. But Sir Burke Trend pointed out that it was an Act of the Labour Government (of which Harold had been a member) and not of Queen Anne which imposed the limits.

As the newly appointed ministers had all been consulted and accepted their appointments and most of them had been announced, the only possible solutions were either to change the law by Act of Parliament which is a slow process and could certainly not be rushed through Parliament as it would be strongly opposed by the Conservatives, or to cancel a number of appointments. In the meantime a number of ministers could function as such but would not receive their ministerial salaries. Harold said we would legislate in due course and proceeded to appoint even more ministers.

It was not until the Ministers of the Crown Act was passed a few days before Christmas that the appointments became official and ministers were able to receive their salaries. This Act increased the number of ministers who may sit in the Commons from 73 to 91. By this time the administration had grown to 110 – the largest British Government ever. Sir Alec Douglas-Home's Government had 84 ministers. One of the reasons why it was so large – 'ministerial inflation' Selwyn Lloyd called it – was the appointment of a number of junior ministers with specific duties. Denis Howell, for example, was a Parliamentary Secretary in the Department of Education and Science but became known as the Minister of Sport because he was given specific duties regarding sport. He was later to become known as the Minister of Rain! Similarly, Jennie Lee was a Minister of State at first in the Ministry of Public Building and Works and later in the Department of Education and Science, but was known as the Minister for the Arts. And there were others dealing with disarmament, London housing, the United Nations, industrial training and shipping. But our opponents would have none of this! They believed it was to maximise the 'payroll' vote – the votes of ministers who are obliged to vote for the Government of which they are members.

The following day I came up against a rather sad aspect of coming into office. I went across to the Members' cafeteria in the Palace of Westminster for my lunch with Freddie Warren, hoping that we could talk over our problems quietly. However, although Parliament was not to meet until Tuesday of the following week, the place was crowded with excited new ministers and still hopeful Members of Parliament. Not knowing that the Government was virtually complete, they were all extremely friendly towards me. Unfortunately, when the final list of appointments was published later in the day, a number of those who had been passed over and whom I counted among my fairly close friends began to treat me with varying degrees of hostility. Three or four Members, in fact, have not spoken to me from that day to this.

The new Cabinet was due to meet for the first time on the Monday afternoon and I had arranged for Len Williams, the Labour Party General Secretary, to come to see me at No. 12 an hour before the meeting. There were a number of domestic matters to be discussed, chief among which was the problem of finding parliamentary seats for Patrick Gordon Walker and Frank Cousins. I was also anxious to establish an easy *modus vivendi* between Transport House and the Government. Unfortunately he arrived five minutes before the Cabinet was due to begin. Now the one meeting no minister is allowed to miss without the approval of the Prime Minister is the Cabinet. But when I told Len this he went up in blue smoke. For a few moments he was almost beside himself with rage. How dare I treat the National

40

Executive (*L'état c'est moi*) in this way? He stormed out, banging the door behind him. But when we met again he appeared to have forgotten the incident and our relationship became almost friendly.

It is completely incorrect, as Marcia alleges in her book (*Inside Number 10*), that we were negligent or remiss in our efforts to establish a productive and friendly relationship with Transport House. Herbert Bowden, George Wigg and I, as well as most senior ministers, went to enormous and often ridiculous lengths to keep them informed. And, after all, no fewer than twelve ministers were members of the National Executive Committee and one was the chairman.

One would have thought that the job of the NEC was to get a Labour Government elected and, having done so, to let it get on with the job with their goodwill and loyal support. But that was not at all how most officials and some NEC members saw it.

The problem was that the centre of gravity, so far as policy making and decision taking were concerned, had now moved from Smith Square to Whitehall. In spite of all our efforts to inform and consult the officials and the NEC, there was a feeling of alienation and, dare one say it, of jealousy. Whitehall was seeing all the action and they were left out in the cold.

My first brief meeting after the election with Len Williams, like the attitude of some of the unsuccessful aspirants for office, left me saddened.

In spite of all the black clouds which had gathered in the past three days, the first Cabinet had, at least initially, all the atmosphere of a family gathering after a successful holiday. With a few individual exceptions, there was real comradeship in all Harold Wilson's Governments. Of course, the general bonhomie owed a good deal to Harold's never-failing good humour and friendliness.

The seating around the oval table is arranged by the Cabinet Office Civil Servants but is based upon the order of precedence laid down by the Prime Minister. The Lord President, who is fourth in order of precedent after the Royal family in the United Kingdom, sat on the Prime

41

Minister's immediate left. The Secretary to the Cabinet sat on the Prime Minister's right. In the Wilson Government after 1974, when I occasionally took the chair of the Cabinet in the Prime Minister's absence, I learnt how essential it was to have this most competent of Civil Servants within whispering distance. In 1964 I sat between Barbara Castle and Michael Stewart at the end of the table with my back to St James's Park.

The First Secretary and the Chancellor of the Exchequer described the menacing economic situation and outlined their proposals for immediate action. The Cabinet was in no mood to argue – the last time this was the case. The situation was too dangerous to both the country and the new Government to brook delay. The proposals were quickly agreed, though in my diary I recorded that Frank Cousins talked far too much! Later, as they became more experienced, ministers found their tongues and discussions in Cabinet became interminable. It was, of course, a highly intelligent and articulate Cabinet, but Harold himself was partly to blame for its loquacity. He had his own special technique for dealing with difficult situations. When agreement was elusive or when the consensus appeared to be settling in the wrong direction, he would allow the discussion to ramble on until the main issue was obscured and everyone was so exhausted that they would settle for almost anything to obtain release and be able to return to the monastic calm of their Private Offices. He would then sum up along the lines he had wanted from the start. The measures approved included a surcharge of 15 per cent on imports, an export rebate scheme, the setting up of a Commonwealth Exports Council, consultation with both sides of industry on a plan for improving productivity and restraining prices and incomes, including the establishment of a Prices and Incomes Review Body, a strict review of public expenditure and prestige projects such as Concord (still without an 'e' at that time), severance payments to encourage the mobility of labour, and consultations with the IMF on our use of drawing rights.

These decisions were to be embodied in a White Paper to be issued on the 26 October, ten days after taking office. Dynamic action indeed!

Once this urgent business was out of the way, the Civil Servants were asked to leave and we had a discussion on the political situation following the election. As Chief Whip, charged with the task of keeping the Government in office, I found this discussion of great importance in defining our objectives.

Harold emphasised that the small majority would not deter us in any way from doing what had to be done to deal with the economic situation and implement our manifesto *The New Britain*. Getting legislation through Parliament was a matter for the Chief Whip, he said, and all ministers were asked to give me their fullest cooperation and support both in arranging the parliamentary timetable and by their presence in the division lobbies, especially during late sittings.

The Times political correspondent commented on 17 October:

Mr Wilson is too shrewd and agile a politician to prick the bubble of Labour's success by proclaiming with the laurels of victory sitting on his brow, that his Government will find it difficult or perhaps impossible to do the tasks to which the country has called him. His strategy must be in boldness as he knows it.

Unfortunately, Jim Callaghan took Harold's strategy too literally when he introduced one of the longest and most complicated Finance Bills ever known – a long-drawn-out nightmare for the Whips, lasting from the beginning of the Committee Stage on 17 May to the Third Reading on 15 July.

In adopting this posture of firm, confident government the Prime Minister – rightly, in my view – calculated that the electorate would give us credit for vigorous action and would not take obstruction kindly, whether it came from the Tories, who had failed so lamentably and had deceived the nation by concealing the magnitude of our economic problem, or from the Liberals, who would have been destroyed had another election been precipitated. In fact, he argued, we were probably reasonably safe for some time to come. However, he made it clear that he did not want any defeats – even on amendments to Bills – but if they occurred, they would not result in his resignation unless he had specifically said that the vote would be one of confidence in the Government. A defeat on the Second Reading of a major Bill implementing a manifesto commitment would be followed the following day by a motion of confidence.

I stated that my objective was to ensure that the Prime Minister was able to choose the date of the next General Election and not have it forced on him by a defeat in the Commons. There were differing views around the Cabinet table as to whether or not we could stay the course, but Harold radiated that amazing confidence which marked the early years of his premiership and visibly affected even the most pessimistic among us. I often wondered whether he really felt that confidence, which he gave to his colleagues for it was difficult to reconcile with the acute insecurity he often displayed in private.

Everyone went away to apply themselves to the urgent task of preparing their departmental claims to a place in the Queen's Speech. And I soon discovered that the desire for ministerial immortality by way of the Statute Book took precious little account of the priorities which were supposed to be the language of socialism. The State Opening of Parliament was only two weeks away but, before then, the Speech had to be written, printed and in the hands of Her Majesty some days before the event. This meant that instead of the usual few months we had at most ten days to prepare a credible programme which would occupy Parliament for a session (normally a year) – and also provide an attractive shopwindow if the ever-present possibility of defeat materialised.

Among the most urgent problems to which the Prime Minister had to turn his attention was the threatened unilateral declaration of independence in Rhodesia. The British Government had never granted independence to a colony, except on the basis of one man one vote, since 1909, and to agree to the independence of Rhodesia with its existing constitution would have been unthinkable.

Sir Alec Douglas-Home's Government had been firm in their rejection of the strident demands for independence being made by Ian Smith, the Rhodesian premier, who now appeared to hold the view that while a Labour Government would also refuse his demands, it would not resist a unilateral declaration of independence. Smith's plan was first to 'consult' an indaba of tribal chiefs on 22 October in order to secure a bogus stamp of approval for his plan and then to hold a referendum of electors, all of whom were white, on 5 November.

The total unacceptability of these proposals had to be conveyed immediately we came into office. Within two days of his appointment as Secretary of State for Commonwealth Relations, Arthur Bottomley (later Lord Bottomley) wrote an uncompromisingly tough letter to Ian Smith, making it clear beyond doubt that the new British Government supported the stand taken by its Conservative predecessors. He suggested that he should visit Salisbury the following week, after he had attended the independence celebrations in Lusaka.

Smith, with an arrogance which was becoming typical of him, refused to accept the visit if it was to include discussions with the African leaders Nkomo and Sithole – which, of course, it must. And so we were in a situation where a British Cabinet minister was refused permission to visit a British colony except on quite unacceptable terms.

Meanwhile, the indaba of chiefs, all of whom were paid and kept in office by the Rhodesian Government, went ahead on 22 October and produced the predictable result. The following day the Prime Minister invited Smith to London, but he refused, saying he would be prepared to come after his referendum on 5 November.

There were now reliable reports that UDI was imminent – given credence by Smith's dismissal of the commander of the Rhodesian armed forces, Major General Anderson, who angrily declared that he was not prepared to countenance an illegal declaration of independence.

The Prime Minister now demanded a firm assurance from Smith that there would be no such declaration without the approval of the British Government. He also sent the text of a statement which, he said, would be issued to the press and broadcast to Rhodesia on Tuesday 27 October if such an assurance was not forthcoming. Harold's mastery of the art of drafting is almost legendary, but the skill with which this statement was put together marked a high watermark – even for him. It was, of course, aimed at the people of Rhodesia. Without actually threatening, it set out starkly yet subtly the economic and legal consequences of going it alone – using the words 'treasonable' and 'rebellion'. It could be read as hinting at military action. Indeed, the Opposition Leader in Rhodesia, Sir Edgar Whitehead, said of it later, 'You don't talk about rebellion and treason unless you reserve the right to use force as a last resort.'

Massive support for Britain's stand poured in from the Commonwealth and from the State Department in Washington. The day after Harold's letter, an emergency Cabinet meeting was held to discuss the crisis and the one-item agenda was made known to the press. On the same morning, Lord Mountbatten, Chief of Defence Staff, was called to another meeting in No. 10. Wilson's stratagem worked. The press, and the world, assumed that Mountbatten had been called to the Cabinet meeting. To Ian Smith, this was an unmistakable signal that we were planning military action. He climbed down and told his parliament that he had abandoned hope of independence by Christmas.

The Queen's Speech Committee of the Cabinet, of which I was a member, met the day after our first Cabinet meeting under the chairmanship of Herbert Bowden. The third member was Lord Gardiner, but other senior Ministers were called in from time to time to explain the claims of their departments. Preparation of the speech was now the first priority for Herbert and me. My opinion of the Downing Street Civil Servants was already high, but when I saw the preparatory work they had already done on the programme I was amazed. Not only had they trawled through all the departments in Whitehall to prepare a list of desirable and mainly noncontroversial Bills which were already drafted and available to fill any awkward gaps until our own legislation could be prepared, but they had also dissected our manifesto *The New Britain* and prepared a list of our proposals which would require legislation. Of course, not all our proposals had to be enacted; some

46

required Orders under existing legislation and others simply ministerial action. They had also made a careful estimate of the time which would be needed to work out and agree the details of our policies and for the parliamentary draftsmen to embody them in Bills.

A list of possible Bills had been passed to Freddie Warren, who had consolidated it into a possible programme for the first session. We now had to cost each potential Bill in terms of parliamentary time.

We estimated that, by lopping a few days off each recess, the session could have 180 sitting days. This was about 20 days more than in each of the previous three years and, we imagined, would give us more time for our legislation. But, after making provision for the swearing-in of Members after the General Election, the long debate on the Queen's Speech, supply days when the debates were chosen by the Opposition, Consolidated Fund Bills, Government motions, contingencies (always the x factor), private Members' time and adjournment debates before each recess, we were left with, at most, 85 days for Government legislation, including the Budget and the Finance Bill. We were not to know for some months that the Chancellor of the Exchequer was to pre-empt no fewer than 33 of these precious legislation days for his massive Budget, leaving us with 52 days for all the Bills on which the future of the Government would depend. This was fewer than in any year in the ten-year period from 1962/3 to 1971/2. But, not knowing this, we allocated a normally generous 15 days for the Finance Bill. Our legislative programme for the session would have to be tailored to the 70 days remaining.

All this may sound highly organised and tidy but as the months passed it became more and more chaotic – and Jim Callaghan, though the major cause of the chaos, was not the only one. Other ministers were continually producing new Bills and demanding priority for them in the parliamentary timetable. In fact, throughout the whole period of the Wilson Governments I felt acutely that we never really evolved a strategy for planning and using Government time in Parliament according to policy priorities. I sent the Prime Minister a number of memos on this but he was always so occupied with more urgent matters that we were never able to improve the system.

It was at the first meeting of the Queen's Speech Committee that I felt ministers were coming up against the facts of life in Government. And the first of these was that there is a world of difference between putting an attractive vote-winning proposal in an election manifesto on an assurance from the research department at Transport House that it was feasible and workable and, once elected, hammering out a brief for the parliamentary draftsmen to convert into a Bill.

It become increasingly obvious that our manifesto had not been subjected to nearly sufficient expert appraisal as to its cost or, indeed, its feasibility. I do not think we were worse than any other Government coming into office after a period in opposition. It was merely that the kind of appraisal that was needed was very costly and parties in opposition were unable to afford it. I was determined, if ever I had the opportunity to do so, to ensure that parties in opposition would have the resources to engage the best expertise available to examine and cost their proposals. Fortunately I was able to achieve this in 1974 when I was Leader of the House of Commons. All opposition parties in Parliament now have a generous subvention from public funds (the 'Short' money).

Some of our proposals proved to be unworkable, others could only be made to work in a modified form, but fortunately most of them were suitable for legislation, though the Bills often became unbelievably complicated.

The second fact of life in Government which emerged at the initial meeting of the Queen's Speech Committee was the constant, harping demands by the Treasury, in the person of the Chancellor of the Exchequer and his team of three assistant ministers, that no additional public expenditure should be incurred. We were committed to raising social benefits, in particular retirement pensions, all of which had fallen far behind the cost of living; but the Chancellor appeared to hold the view of the Governor of the Bank of England ('Rowlie' he called him) that anything beyond a token increase could be extremely damaging to sterling. It shocked ministers to their socialist cores to be told that if they increased pensions beyond a pittance it would be a sign to the financial world of the profligacy of the new Labour Government and cause a debilitating run on the pound. Fortunately, we had at that time a tough Scottish lady as Minister of Pensions and National Insurance. Peggy Herbison (Lanarkshire North) was more than a match for the Treasury, and agreement was reached later in the week to increase single pensions by over a quarter and married couples' by nearly a fifth.

At this meeting we became aware of a third impediment to our plans: the shortage of parliamentary draftsmen. Training new ones took many years and, while it was possible to employ firms of parliamentary agents to draft minor Bills, our major legislation obviously had to be drafted in house. This ridiculous bottleneck plagued the Labour Government throughout the Wilson years, but at least it did force on us a strict system of priorities in preparing our legislation for Parliament. Another Cabinet committee (the Future Legislation Committee) authorised the drafting of each Bill on a number of criteria – its economic and political importance, the length of time drafting would take, when it would be introduced into the parliamentary timetable in order to complete all its stages by the end of the session, and whether the policy decisions involved had been approved.

Excellent progress was made at this meeting of the Queen's Speech Committee, but there were many gaps and a great deal of uncertainty about items we had pencilled in. The Opening of Parliament was only days away, and we met again the following Tuesday. There was a great deal of jockeying, indeed of infighting, by ministers for legislative commitments in the programme for the session. They were all keen, able and anxious to build their reputation as legislators as quickly as possible. In the week since our first meeting there had been many bilateral discussions and some interdepartmental disagreements had been ironed out. But not all, by any means.

My experience on the Queen's Speech Committee in 1964 marked the beginning of a view which I have come to hold quite firmly: that the Cabinet would be much more efficient

49

and take more objective discussions if it consisted entirely of non-departmental ministers. There are normally eight of these, but any number of ministers without portfolio can be appointed. It would, of course, mean that the most able members of the administration would have to be selected for these offices.

Reading the 1964 Queen's Speech two decades later, the amount of space given to each item corresponds with the degree of toughness and persuasiveness of the ministers concerned, rather than with the Government's priorities.

A week before the Opening of Parliament there were still problems to be resolved between ministers, and the legislative programme in the Speech was still much too long. Herbert Bowden, Lord Gardiner and I had no option but to refer it to the full Cabinet on Thursday 29 October – the day it had to go to the printers. The Prime Minister had expected that Cabinet would only be concerned with giving it formal approval and, maybe, its syntax – Harold's Cabinets were always keen on getting the syntax right. The fact that a surgical operation was required did not please him at all. One of his ground rules for decision-taking was that as far as possible all interdepartmental disputes should be resolved in Cabinet committees.

The difficulty of drafting is directly proportionate to the number of people involved, and a Cabinet of twenty-three highly articulate, lively ministers was not the best body for such a task. However, because of Harold's skill as a draftsman – by far the best I have known – we managed, after what seemed an interminable time, to knock it into shape. Herbert Bowden and I were particularly grateful that he showed more awareness than many of his ministers of the constraints of parliamentary time – good House of Commons man that he was. The Chancellor of the Excheq-uer was equally sensitive about public expenditure. Between them they persuaded the Cabinet to agree to a programme which contained about twenty specific commitments to legislation. These, I estimated, together with others in the pipeline, would involve between sixty and seventy Bills – a workload which was probably rather more than a normal session could carry. And we would have to contend with all the pressures of a tiny majority. When I stressed this point, my colleagues said airily that there was no problem because the session could be prolonged indefinitely beyond the normal early autumn date. No special sanctity about twelve months, they all agreed. But Herbert Bowden and I were particularly anxious to avoid extending the session because this would upset the planning of subsequent sessions. And the great fulcrum of every session is the Finance Bill, which must tie in with both the financial year and the summer recess. In addition, I argued, a Government which might be defeated at any moment would be foolish indeed to forgo or delay the valuable shopwindow of another Gracious Speech from the throne next autumn.

The major hot potato in the speech – in addition to the Finance Bill, which was to be the hot potato to end all hot potatoes – turned out to be the rather cagey reference to steel. We said we would 'initiate early action to re-establish the necessary public ownership and control of the iron and steel industry' – weasel words which at first sight looked as though we intended to renationalise the industry in the coming session but, in fact, merely left open the option to do so. How open I was to discover a few months later. The Cabinet agreed to this wording because, they were told, there was great uncertainty about how long the Bill would take to draft and its passage through the two Houses would be long and hard-fought, so it could only be introduced at the beginning of a session. Another innocent sounding sentence which was to cause us untold trouble and ultimately led to our defeat in 1970 was that we would seek '. . . a closer relationship between the increase in productivity and the growth in incomes in all their forms.' Diffuse words which meant an incomes policy without actually saying so.

The majority of our major manifesto commitments were included – abolition of prescription charges, rent control, a Crown Lands Commission, Regional Councils etc. Overall was the ringing declaration that we would maintain the strength of sterling both by dealing with the short-term problems of the balance of payments and by structural changes in industry.

51

It was a brave programme of a brave Government. Whether we could get it through Parliament or not was less important than the image which it presented of a Government which intended to carry out its election pledges. And if the worst came to the worst it was an attractive manifesto for the next general election.

Throughout the hectic two weeks before the Opening of Parliament I spent a major part of my time trying to find parliamentary seats for Patrick Gordon Walker and Frank Cousins. And there was only one possible bait which would entice an MP to give up his hard won seat. Patrick understood the difficulty of persuading an MP who had won his seat a week ago to relinquish it for a seat-less minister but Frank was rather less understanding and seemed to believe that all I had to do was to select a seat and tell its Member to stand down – for the good of the Party and the Government. I was quite sure that the Members selected would see it rather differently. And, to add to the problem, both ministers wanted seats in the London area.

I had a presentiment of disaster on this matter. I knew that if it went wrong I should be blamed. Because of this I insisted on involving Sara Barker, the Labour Party's national agent, throughout. I was determined that we should decide together which MPs should be approached, and that both the Prime Minister and the National Executive Committee should know it was a joint decision. The nauseating feature of this exercise was that the MPs had to be offered life peerages. There would have been no response whatever without this inducement. There were, of course, very many precedents for offering a peerage to an MP in order to find a seat for a minister; for example, Sir Wavell Wakefield gave up his seat at St Marylebone and accepted a peerage when Quintin Hogg (later Lord Hailsham) renounced his inherited viscounty and aspired to the leadership of the Conservative Party.

Sara Barker and I started our search guided by three criteria – that the Member selected should be getting on in years, that the seat should be winnable in the receding excitement of the post-election period and that the constituency party should, in the opinion of the national agent, agree.

The first Member selected was Will Wilkins, who had held Bristol South with a majority of 11,287. Will had been a respected colleague of mine in the Whips' Office in Opposition, and I felt that if I could persuade anybody to go to the Lords it would be him. He came up to London to see me on Friday 23 October and, to say the least, did not take kindly to the idea. It did not need much consideration for him courteously to decline to give up his seat for either of the seat-less ministers.

I then tried a London member, the Rev. Reginald Sorensen, a seventy-three-year-old who had a majority of 7,926 at Leyton, which had been a Labour seat for very many years, even in the 1931 debacle. He was much more attracted to the idea of going to the Lords and asked for the weekend to consider it. I was only too aware of a major problem which would concern almost anyone I approached. It was the appalling fact that MPs had no pensions but merely a rigorously means-tested charitable fund, and their salaries were so miserably low that few had any savings worth mentioning.

Reg Sorensen came to see me again on the Monday and agreed to make way for Patrick Gordon Walker, who, being Foreign Secretary, we decided should have priority over Frank Cousins. On 22 January he lost Leyton by 205 votes, which I always saw as the electorate's answer to our cynical tampering with the democratic process.

We were left with the problem of the Minister of Technology and, as he was desperately anxious to have a London seat, we decided to approach one of our most congenial and respected Members, George Strauss (later Lord Strauss) Member for Lambeth Vauxhall, who was sixty-three years of age, was known to be well off and had a majority of 6,805. Surely he would agree, I thought, and he would be an asset to the House of Lords. But he did not need any time to think it over. He turned it down at once.

Eventually we were fortunate to find another Member with a safe seat and no financial problems for whom the Lords had a clear appeal. Frank Bowles, MP for

Nuneaton, a solicitor with a majority of 11,702, fitted the bill perfectly. After bringing his constituency chairman to discuss it with me, he accepted with alacrity. Frank Cousins and the local party reluctantly agreed, and in the by-election we held the seat.

News quickly spread among MPs that I was hawking two life peerages and, no sooner had we settled the matter of Nuneaton, than a North-eastern Member came to see me and offered himself as the sacrificial lamb. In the following few days I had six further offers.

On the Friday afternoon, George Wigg, with his leg in plaster from a fracture during the election campaign, hobbled round to No. 12 to see me on a number of matters which, he said, were of mutual interest to us but which appeared to me to fall entirely within the responsibility of the Leader of the House and myself. His visit confirmed the earlier fears of Herbert Bowden and myself that we could expect a good deal of interference from the Paymaster General. Among other things, he told me the Prime Minister had received a letter from Woodrow Wyatt (Bosworth) saying that he could not support the 'old-fashioned nationalisation' of steel. As this could affect a crucial vote in the House, it obviously should have been sent to me at once, not passed to George Wigg. This, I suspected, was Marcia's doing, and I got my private secretary to go to the Private Office at No. 10 and raise the roof about it. I had made it clear to everyone, with the Prime Minister's approval – to Civil Servants, ministers and whips – that any kind of intelligence about voting intentions should be channelled to me immediately. I already knew that Woodrow Wyatt had expressed similar views in the *Birmingham Planet*, a weekly paper he owned.

My private secretary heard that George Wigg had been to see the Clerk to the House of Commons to discuss ways of expediting parliamentary business! Herbert Bowden and I could not possibly organise and process parliamentary business if another senior minister was operating in the same field without informing us, and so we brought up the matter of the Paymaster General's interference at our daily meeting with the Prime Minister – known since Gladstone's day as

54

'Prayers'. The trouble with George Wigg in those early days of the Wilson Government was that he had too little to do in his own small department, while he was bubbling with ideas which extended over the whole field of government – sometimes good ones but more often far from good – and he did not mind cutting corners and treading on his colleagues' toes to try them out. Of course, we never knew when the Prime Minister himself was behind his operations.

Perhaps my most welcome visitor at No. 12 during our first week in office was Sir Samuel Storey, the Conservative MP for Stretford (later Lord Buckton), who came to tell me that he was willing to become Deputy Chairman of Ways and Means – with the agreement of Martin Redmayne, the Conservative Chief Whip. As we had a Conservative Speaker, Sir Harry Hylton-Foster (Cities of London and Westminster), who was only too willing to continue and as Dr Horace King (Labour, Southampton Itchin) had agreed to become Chairman of Ways and Means (in fact, Deputy Speaker), Storey's acceptance meant that two of the three non-voting Members of Parliament would be Conservatives. This was a small gain to the Government but a vitally important one, increasing our voting majority from four to five. Had the Opposition insisted on Labour nominees, our majority would have been reduced to one, and the loss of Leyton three months later would have destroyed the Government.

The alacrity with which the Opposition agreed to this arrangement, clearly advantageous to us, confirmed our view that they did not wish to precipitate an early election – at least so long as the leadership problem in their party was still unresolved. And when the Speaker had an operation in mid-November, they agreed to help us by allowing Sir Harry Legge-Bourke (Conservative, Isle of Ely) to become temporary Deputy Chairman of Ways and Means.

At one of our daily 'Prayers', shortly after the General Election, Harold suggested that I should organise a private service of dedication at the beginning of the session for members of the Government. I invited to No. 12 two old friends and life-long Labour supporters, the Rt Rev. Mervyn Stockwood, Bishop of Southwark, and the Rev. Donald

55

Soper (later Lord Soper). They agreed to take a service in the Crypt of Westminster Hall. I also invited a school friend of Harold's, the Rev. Inglis Evans, who lived on Tyneside, to participate. The result was a movingly beautiful service held on the day after the Opening of Parliament, but fewer than a third of the members of the Government attended. Similar acts of dedication were held at the beginning of the 1966 and 1974 Parliaments, but with fewer Ministers attending each one.

We summoned our newly elected Labour MPs to London for a meeting of the Parliamentary Labour Party at Church House, Westminster, on Monday 27 October. At that time the Palace of Westminster, which is technically a royal palace, was under the control of the Lord Great Chamberlain and there were rigid and archaic rules about the use of its facilities, particularly during the dissolution of Parliament. As the new Parliament had not yet been opened by the Queen, though we met throughout that week for the election of a Speaker and the swearing in of Members, we were not allowed to hold a meeting in one of the many large committee rooms in the House. This was one of the many ridiculous aspects of parliamentary life which we were shortly to change – the Palace of Westminster was on our nationalisation list!

The purpose of the meeting was to adopt our Standing Orders and to elect a leader and deputy leader. Following precedent, I was in the chair. The only candidates were Harold Wilson and George Brown, who were re-elected by acclamation. Harold then gave his troops a pep talk about the smack of firm government and all that. I followed with a deliberately uncompromising talk about what the Whips and I would be asking of the Party in the months or years ahead. I made it clear beyond doubt that pairing, that ancient device which makes parliamentary life bearable, would only be allowed in certain limited circumstances, that all pairs would be under the control of one Whip rather than the regional Whips as in the past, and that no one, not even the most senior minister, could pair without his express approval. I also appealed to Members to take unusual care of their health but to avoid absences for minor ailments. As MPs are a rather high age group and disperse to the four corners of the kingdom each weekend, illness was my greatest worry.

Although this was a private meeting, my remarks about keeping fit hit the headlines the next day. Indeed, the *Spectator* made an actuarially based forecast that there would be five deaths in the Parliamentary Labour Party in the next twelve months!

Finally, and most important, I said that my objective was simply to enable the Prime Minister himself to select the date of the next General Election, and that I would do anything – and I meant anything – to achieve this. The right to choose the date of a General Election is one of the strongest cards held by a British Prime Minister, but this precious privilege is only his so long as he has a majority in the House of Commons.

A pressing task in the second week was beginning the preparation of the twice-yearly list of political honours. It was not until I left No. 12 in the summer of 1966 that the Prime Minister decided to end honours for political service – a decision with which I would never have agreed. I have always taken the view that in a parliamentary democracy such as ours, service to a political party is just as praiseworthy and deserving of honour as any other form of service. I believe it was wrong to end honours of this kind. He did insist, however, that no recommendations for knighthoods should be made for MPs no matter how long they had served or with what distinction. Conservative governments have always showered knighthoods on their long-serving Members of Parliament and, whilst I certainly did not wish to go to such lengths, I felt that the comparison between the two sides of the House was invidious. And it was no use saying, as Harold did, that Labour people should not be interested in honours. Of course they were – and are. The correspondence arriving at both No. 10 and No. 12 Downing Street showed just how keen they were to be decorated. We all have a good deal of the Boy Scout in us.

He also ended the recommendations for hereditary honours – peerages and baronetcies – with which I entirely agreed. This did not deter the Front Bench in the House of Lords from sending a deputation to ask if I would try to persuade the Prime Minister to recommend two Labour peers for viscountcies. Of course he refused, but eventually one of them became a Companion of Honour.

In No. 12 there was an excellent Higher Executive Officer called Miss Dodd – 'Doddy' to all who knew her. She had served successive Chief Whips with utter dedication since 1958. She kept the most meticulously careful record of every event or incident which was likely to recur and could always lay her hands on these records at a moment's notice. She was a tower of strength to me in everything but not least in the messy business of honours. She had an encyclopaedic knowledge of all the people who had been put forward, by whom they had been suggested (often themselves) and how often – and some clearly had organised letter-writing campaigns among their friends to get themselves noticed in Downing Street.

After many hours of sifting through hundreds of recommendations and trying to weigh their respective merits, with the aid of a large-scale map of the United Kingdom spread on the floor, I drew up a tentative list distributing my ration of each grade of honour around the regions of Britain with mathematical fairness. I consulted MPs who knew their areas intimately, regional organisers of the Labour Party and Transport House. Eventually I had a list for submission to the Prime Minister. It was perhaps a tribute to the trouble we had taken in No. 12 that he always accepted my lists without alteration but, occasionally, with additions. The one exception was when he deleted the name of a long-serving secretary which I had included against my better judgment at the request of the Cabinet minister who employed her.

As time passed and I struggled twice a year with the impossible task of fairly weighing one person's merits against another, I developed a great aversion to the present honours system. I expressed this in a minute to the Prime Minister putting forward the outlines of a new system for discussion with the Palace. I suggested among other things abolishing the Order of the British Empire (how silly it is when we no longer have an empire) and various other orders and establishing a comprehensive Elizabethan Order.

58

The name could change with the monarch – and would date the recipient like the registration number of a car. But nothing came of it. It was unfortunate that during our whole period in government Harold was so beset by major problems that he did not get round to matters of this kind. However, he showed great imagination in establishing the Queen's Award for Industry scheme. It was one of the many ideas thrown up by Anthony Wedgwood Benn but the final pattern was Harold's.

Before the Opening of Parliament I had recommended to the Prime Minister the full list of Whips for appointment. The Whips, an essential part of the machinery of parliamentary government, had no place as such in the ministerial scheme of things. Some held sinecure salaried offices which left them free to devote their time to whipping. For example, I was officially Parliamentary Secretary to the Treasury but, apart from signing an occasional document, I had no connection with the Treasury. Five others were Lords Commissioners of the Treasury, again with a few documents to sign from time to time but no duties. Three were officials of the Royal Household – Vice Chamberlain, Comptroller and Treasurer. Their main Household duty was to escort members of the royal family at the annual garden parties but the Vice Chamberlain had another rather special chore. Every sitting day he had to prepare in his own words a report on the day in the Commons – a sort of royal command *Today in Parliament*. This had to be typed and sent to the Queen every evening. A number of attempts had been made in the past to persuade the Palace to end this extremely tedious requirement but the monarch of the day always apparently placed some value on these personal impressions of the House.

A similar situation existed in the House of Lords where some Whips belonged to the Royal Household. The 'Household' Whips received the rather odd perk of an ell of cloth each year, which, fortunately, was sufficient to make a suit!

An innovation in my selection of Whips was the appointment of a woman, the first in the Commonwealth. Whipping had always been regarded as a tough male function and in the months ahead of us was likely to be a good deal tougher. But Harriet Slater (Stoke North) brought a new dimension to whipping. She was a cheerful, motherly woman with an abundance of common sense. During our many all-night sittings in the summer of 1965 she provided tea, camp beds and blankets for the elderly and endless sympathy and understanding in all the human and social problems our Members suffered.

These nine Whips, belonging partly to the Treasury and partly to the Royal Household, received salaries. In addition, there were six Assistant Whips, who were unpaid. As all were accorded the status of ministers, it seemed to me unfair that only some of them should receive salaries – and the Opposition Chief Whip agreed. So I arranged a salary provision for Whips in the Bill which was being prepared to legitimise the Prime Minister's over-large Government, and the Conservatives promised their support.

One change which I made in the organisation of the Whips' Department got me into very hot water with some of my parliamentary colleagues. Previously, each Labour Party region in the United Kingdom had a local Whip who author-ised and recorded the pairs of his Members. But the stakes were now too high to risk any errors about the presence or absence of Members. After all, a couple of errors could bring down the Government! I allocated the most reliable, accident-proof Whips to the regions, irrespective of where their constituencies were. Of course, some were Whips in their own regional groups, but others were not – and this outraged the Members concerned. I had an angry deputation from the East Midlands led by Bernard Taylor (later Lord Taylor of Mansfield), for whom I had a great respect and affection. But I had to stick to my guns.

I appointed Sydney Irving (later Lord Irving), a north-country schoolmaster, as my deputy. He proved to be completely indefatigable and deceptively tough. He supplied some of the steel which I lacked. A new Member, John Silkin (Deptford), a London solicitor and son of a famous father, had entered Parliament at a by-election in July 1963. I regarded him as perhaps the most able of our recent entrants and persuaded the Prime Minister to allow me to appoint him to the Whips' Department. In retrospect this may have been unfair to him and impeded his ministerial career. I only got away with it because our tiny majority made it imperative that I had someone of his ability to take charge of pairing. Over the ensuing months he and Sydney Irving perfected a system of recording the whereabouts of every Labour Member at every moment of every sitting day which was so efficient that their forecasts of the results of divisions were almost invariably accurate. The Labour Government's success in staying the course during the 1964-66 Parliament owed much to their pertinacity – and arithmetic. When I finally left the Whips' Office in the summer of 1966, John succeeded me as Chief Whip.

In the weekend before Parliament reassembled I completed some detailed and comprehensive *Notes for the Guidance of Whips*, on which I had started work during a long illness in the previous year. The term 'Whip' was imported in the eighteenth century from the hunting field, where the job of the whipper-in was to keep the hounds from straying and, so far as our MPs are concerned, that remains the basic function of the Whips in Parliament in the late twentieth century – 'straying' in both the physical and political sense! But there is a good deal more to their work than maintaining discipline in the Party. Whips are also welfare officers who must make themselves aware of the personal problems of their Members and give whatever assistance they can, particularly where attendance at Westminster may be affected. Knowing about these problems can often avert the wrath of other Members when colleagues appear to be getting more than their fair share of time off. When I arrived at No. 12 I was told that it had been the practice to keep a 'dirt book' in which unsavoury personal items about Members were recorded. I gave strict instructions that no such book was to be kept in future.

The Whips, particularly the Chief Whip, are also negotiators with 'the other side' about any matters affecting Parliament on which it is desirable to get interparty agreement. Without these almost daily talks, known as 'the usual channels', between people who profoundly disagree with each other on policy as well as principle, the parliamentary machine could not function as smoothly as it does.

And, of course, each party is in office for a season – though in opposition it may seem like an age. The years since the Second World War have been fairly equally divided between Labour and Conservative Governments. The pendulum swings one way and then the other. It is certain that the two sides in 'the usual channels' will be reversed sooner or later, and so both sides have a vested interest in seeing that civilised rules for the arrangement of business are observed, and this can generally be achieved without compromising one's principles. My experience has been that the Government tends to give more than the Opposition in these negotiations in order to get its business through the House. Of course there have always been backbenchers who have called this a cosy carve-up by the parliamentary establishment – that is, the two front benches. But this is far from the case. The Government Chief Whip is anxious that his Government should succeed; the Opposition Chief Whip is equally anxious that the Opposition should do well. Without some give and take, neither side would achieve much.

In writing my *Notes for the Guidance of Whips* I was breaking with a long tradition – as, indeed, I am in this book – that the methods employed by the Whips must never be explicit. In this it was akin to witchcraft. The rule had always been that whipping like stripping is best done in private. But here also I felt I could take no risks. Every age-old stratagem used over the previous two centuries must be known to all the Whips immediately – and some of them were new to the job. But having set down every trick of the trade, I had to point out that most of what they did would be ad-hocery. New situations would arise every day for every Whip which no notes could cover, however voluminous. I was also running a great risk that my notes would find their way into the press. Political journalists were constantly probing for chinks in our armour, and with the kind of majority we had, the Whips' activities were an obvious place to probe.

My diaries record a stream of press men coming to interview me at No. 12 about how I proposed to keep the Government in office. One of the earliest was Frank Bough, who was then employed by Thomson Newspapers. Some newspapers, such as the *Daily Telegraph*, were predictably highly critical of what they alleged was the over-rigid discipline I imposed on the Parliamentary Labour Party. Their purpose had more to do with creating disaffection among our Members than with presenting the facts of the situation. Fortunately, others took a fairer view of my activities.

On Monday 2 November we had the traditional Eve of Session party in one of the garish staterooms in No. 10 to hear the Queen's Speech read. Well over a hundred people attended – all the ministers, including the Whips, together with Marcia and the rest of the kitchen cabinet. Once we were all assembled and had been given a drink, the Prime Minister gave the traditional instruction: 'Chief Whip – lock the doors.' He then read in full the Gracious Speech, as it had now come to be called. For most of those present it was the first time they had heard the programme which was to be unveiled next day.

It occurred to me that there was here a real problem of communication within the Government. When I became Postmaster General in the summer of 1966 I became even more aware of the isolation of the non-Cabinet head of a Government department who knew very little about what was going on in Government outside his own department. I discussed this with the Prime Minister, and he began holding regular meetings with non-Cabinet ministers.

The programme was received with great enthusiasm and we all remained to consume more of Harold's wine and sandwiches in an increasingly carefree atmosphere. The fact that our existence as a Government hung upon the votes of five of our ageing colleagues looked less and less of a problem.

We had decided quite deliberately to live dangerously, and danger is a great stimulant. Tomorrow the Queen would unveil our programme to the country; we were confident that the country would like it. Who cared what the Opposition thought or said about it! And, if the roof fell in, it was an attractive manifesto for another General Election. 'Brothers, we are on our way,' said George Brown.

At 11 a.m. on Tuesday 3 November, it all began. The first of Harold Wilson's four parliaments was launched with all the pomp and splendour of ancient days. The glittering procession flowed through the Royal Gallery and the Princes Chamber to the chamber of the House of Lords. Accompanying the monarch were all the high officers of state apparelled in their finery, bearing titles from medieval times such as Gold Stick in Waiting, Silver Stick in Waiting, the Clerk of the Cheque, the Harbinger, etc.

But among them was Charles Grey (Durham), now a Whip and Comptroller of the Royal Household. Charlie had started life hewing coal in an east Durham pit, and his presence in all this was a tiny sign that we now had a Labour Government committed to radical change – but in all the glorious flummery it was scarcely discernible. We had won the election; we were now 'in power', as we put it. But here, in the vast British Establishment, was another centre of power which rolled on inexorably like this procession. What happened in elections did not affect it. It was self-perpetuating and supremely self-assured.

But the problems that beset the elected Government in the following five years did not come from this centre of power but from others quite determined to thwart us if we took any action opposed to their interests.

In the chamber the Queen looked a small, lonely figure on the throne – the glittering Imperial State Crown dwarfing her. The judges, resplendent in their robes and wigs, were inelegantly jammed together on the Woolsack like cockerels on a roost. To the right were the foreign Ambassadors and High Commissioners in their gaudy uniforms or evening dress, looking for all the world like the D'Oyley Carte Opera Company taking a final curtain. Peers by the hundred in red and ermine and peeresses in evening dress and tiaras crowded the benches.

Members of the House of Commons, led by the Speaker and the Prime Minister, herded in an indecent crush behind the Bar of the House. Many were unable to get in. This is one of the ludicrous consequences of holding the annual Opening ceremony in the House of Lords chamber, which is much too small, instead of using the more ancient Westminster Hall. But, in spite of our discomfort behind the Bar, it was an impressive sight which had changed little since the first Elizabeth opened her parliaments. And it was a historic occasion for Parliament itself as well as the Labour Party, for the coming session was the seventh centenary of Simon de Montfort's parliament.

After the Opening, the Speaker held a reception in the state rooms of his home at the eastern end of the Palace of Westminster. This marked the end of the ceremonies and pleasantries. Three hours later we were plunged into the parliamentary battle.

Since the election I had been able to work all day in the quiet of Downing Street, but now, on each sitting day, I and my staff moved over to Westminster immediately after lunch. We had three rooms off the Members' lobby – a large one for the Whips, a small one for myself and an even smaller one for Freddie Warren and Miss Dodd. But we also had three shorthand typists who worked at Westminster until late every evening and for whom there was no accommodation. They had their desks in a tiny dark corridor leading to a lavatory. Looking at the enormous edifice, I found it quite impossible to believe that this was the best that could be done for these hard-working girls. Members of Parliament were, it seemed to me, regarded as a necessary evil by the army of officials who held on to all their privileges with great tenacity.

I stormed into the office of the Serjeant-at-Arms (Rear Admiral Gordon Lennox, CB, DSO), where I found him luxuriously housed in one huge room and his deputy in another. I demanded that he accompany me at once to see the dreadful conditions in which my three girls had to work, which, I pointed out, their union (and I was not certain they had one) would most certainly regard as an infringement of the Shops and Offices legislation.

He subsequently made some effort to improve the situation though, in fairness, he could do little to improve the gross imbalance in the allocation of floor space between Members and officials until overall control was taken out of the hands of the Lord Great Chamberlain. The Minister of Works, Charles Pannell (Leeds West) had this in hand as one of his top priorities. A fearless cockney who relished confrontations with high officials, he was the very man for the job.

Two days after the Opening of Parliament the Prime Minister, Herbert Bowden, Charles Pannell and myself met to consider control of the Palace. It had always rankled with MPs and peers of all parties that they had no control over their own parliament building. No meeting or function could take place without the approval of the hereditary Lord Great Chamberlain, and when Parliament was dissolved or prorogued, we had no rights whatever in the building. The housekeeping, including control of the police, doorkeepers and attendants, was in the hands of the Serjeant-at-Arms, in whose appointment neither Parliament nor the Government had any voice. Although before the election we had said we intended to nationalise the Palace, Charles Pannell was persuaded to accept a compromise solution. Westminster would remain a royal palace but control of it would be vested by the Queen in committees of the two Houses. The sole exception was to be Westminster Hall, which would remain the responsibility of the Lord Great Chamberlain.

The Cabinet approved the compromise, but when it was announced in the Commons the Whips had considerable trouble in assuring our Members that they had not been tricked by Buckingham Palace. Lengthy and complicated demarcation discussions followed to define the jurisdiction of each of the two committees. Since that time the facilities for MPs and Peers have improved out of all recognition. It is difficult to understand why an utterly indefensible system which implied considerable contempt for the elected representatives of the people was allowed to continue so long.

In the afternoon after the Opening of Parliament, before the House met to begin the long debate on our programme, I spent a good deal of time in the Members' tea room. This is a long, pleasant room where tea, coffee and snacks are served from mid-morning until the rising of the House. In 1964 backbench Members did not have their own offices.

All their clerical work had to be done in the corridors or the library. One result of this appalling lack of accommodation was that they spent hours each day in the tea room gossiping and devouring newspapers. Every move by Government or Opposition was analysed in detail; every minister and shadow minister was regularly taken apart – with no punches barred. It is still said that no one dares leave a table there because he knows that as soon as he leaves everyone will start to talk about him! The more cohesive regional groups from Wales, Scotland and the North of England had their own tables, where others were not welcome. The tea room was the perfect sounding board for the Whips and ministers whenever a quick view of the reaction of Members was required. Clem Attlee and Harold Wilson went there regularly – Attlee in Opposition used it in the morning to do *The Times* crossword, which he usually completed in twenty minutes, and as Prime Minister in the afternoons to have his tea-time kipper, to which he was very partial – indeed his PPS, Arthur Moyle, was known as Clem's kipper carrier.

When the Whips compared notes afterwards we found the reaction to the Gracious Speech was almost entirely favourable. Woodrow Wyatt and Desmond Donnelly (Pembroke) were against the renationalisation of steel and felt we could only survive by means of a pact with the Liberals which would involve abandoning it; but otherwise we had our party firmly behind us. And that is the first requirement for the success – indeed, for the survival – of any British government.

The Tory reaction was muted. The more experienced of their ministers knew a skilfully assembled Queen's Speech when they saw one.

Press reaction the following day was entirely predictable. The popular press, rabidly pro-Tory with the exception of the *Daily Mirror*, reviled it with all their venom, but *The Times* headed its leading article 'A USEFUL PROGRAMME'.

During the subsequent debate it became clear that the Tories would oppose the creation of a Land Commission, the abandoning of Concorde, the renationalisation of steel and any renegotiation of the Nassau Agreement which committed us to joining a multilateral nuclear force including a mixed-manned fleet. Sir Alec said he wanted to make it clear from the start that it was not their intention to exploit the parliamentary situation in a way 'that good government is made difficult'. That, he stated, was not the function of an Opposition.

As is the custom, I had selected two Labour back-benchers to 'move the Loyal Address' to Her Majesty thanking her for her Gracious Speech – indeed, the whole debate hangs on this motion of thanks. As always, they used the occasion to make noncontroversial speeches about their constituencies. Ernest Fernyhough, the veteran Member for Jarrow, spoke with pride about both the Venerable Bede and Ellen Wilkinson – about the town that was murdered and its more recent resurrection; Gregor MacKenzie quoted the motto of the Burgh of Rutherglen – '*ex fumo fama*' – which, he said, loosely translated as 'chimneys shall smoke briskly' and expressed the hope that under the Labour Government they would smoke even more briskly.

It is common practice for the Opposition to table one or more amendments to the motion thanking the Queen for her address, and we anticipated amendments criticising our more controversial proposals, such as the renationalisation of steel. However, on this occasion the first motion put down was, unexpectedly, a personal motion of censure on the Prime Minister by a group of Tory Privy Counsellors led by Geoffrey Lloyd (Sutton Coldfield), an ex-Minister of Education. Harold, in his opening speech, had taunted Sir Alec Douglas-Home about his failure publicly to disassociate himself from the racialist tactics employed by the Conservatives at Smethwick, where Patrick Gordon Walker had lost his seat. Then he had referred to Peter Griffiths, the successful Tory candidate, as a 'parliamentary leper'. The Speaker was asked whether this was in order and replied, 'I do not think it is out of order. I do always deplore the use of language of that kind because it does not assist anyone.' This was a rebuke which, in my view, no Prime Minister should ever bring upon himself. Manny Shinwell put down an amendment to Lloyd's motion, regretting '. . . that the Leader of the Opposition, after repeated invitations, had failed to dissociate himself from the racialist activities of the Smethwick Conservatives.'

I knew that there would be at least one crucial vote on the Queen's Speech. In the Whips' Office, we had high hopes that one or two Conservatives with small majorities might contract mysterious illnesses which would prevent them from voting. But the 'leper' remark destroyed that chance and injected a quite unnecessary degree of bitterness into inter-party relations in the House which took some weeks to abate. Why Harold went out of his way to hurl this insult across the floor I shall never understand. It may have been merited, but it was out of character for him to do or say anything without thinking out the consequences. His every apparently casual remark was usually carefully calculated not only to lead to result A, but maybe also to B and B to produce C. But the 'leper' remark remains a mystery.

By the evening of that day, 3 November, I had heard that the Opposition were putting down an amendment on steel. I also heard that they had selected Iain Macleod (Enfield West), their most able debater, to speak on it. This was to be their major effort against us, decided no doubt after hearing of our problems with Wyatt and Donnelly. I knew that this vital division would take place at exactly 10 p.m. on the following Monday. Monday is always the most difficult day for an important division because of the possibility of travel delays from the outlying constituencies in Scotland and Wales. In retrospect, I realise that Herbert Bowden and I missed a trick. We could probably have arranged the steel debate on Tuesday, the final day of the debate on the Queen's Speech. Of course, it is by no means certain that the Opposition would have agreed and we wanted to be as reasonable and accommodating as possible in arranging the parliamentary timetable.

This division was to be the first test of our ability to survive. From remarks Jo Grimond, the Liberal leader, had made to the press after the election it was a near certainty that the Liberals would support the Opposition amendment. The 'leper' remark had so incensed the Tories that we calculated they would make a genuine effort to defeat us, probably against their better judgment. Our only safe assumption was that we would be down to our majority of five – and we would only achieve that result if we could muster the whole party.

As the day approached it appeared that fate was intervening on the side of the Opposition. I received a telephone call to say that Brian O'Malley (Rotherham), a Whip, had been rushed to hospital with appendicitis. Sir Geoffrey de Freitas (Kettering) had injured his leg in a car accident and Frank McLeavy (Bradford East) was in hospital with knee trouble. I insisted on both de Freitas and McLeary being brought in by car, especially as I had heard that the Conservative Christopher Soames (Bedford), who was recovering from an operation, was coming in to vote.

I had made it clear to the Parliamentary Party that I intended to bring in sick Members from hospital by ambulance because of the convention that if they are anywhere in the Palace of Westminster they can be nodded through the lobbies by the Whips. On more than one occasion in 1965 I did, in fact – with the consent of their wives – bring in a number of Members who were unconscious and had to be sustained by oxygen. I always pointed out to them afterwards that even if they had died their votes would still have counted, as I understand it is legally impossible to die in the Palace of Westminster! But on this occasion I could not bring in Brian O'Malley from Rotherham a few hours after an appendix operation without endangering his life. We were down to four.

As soon as I got out of bed on the Monday morning and drew the curtains my heart sank. It was a miserable, wet and foggy November day. The radio began to report delays at the airports and on the motorways. My own plane from Newcastle was delayed for three hours and I arrived at No. 12 at twelve-forty. All the Whips spent the day on the telephone tracking down every single Labour MP. Our main problems were, as we had feared, in Scotland. Thirteen of our Members were sitting in Glasgow airport waiting for the fog to clear. I asked them to make other arrangements at once; there was still time to drive to London, though that was a hazardous last resort. Our majority could have been extinguished in an accident on the motorway. Throughout

70

the whole of the 1964-66 Parliament we asked our Members to avoid motorway travel with more than two Members in a car. Four of them decided to come by train and the other nine travelled to Prestwick, which was still open, and were able to book seats on a London plane. One London evening paper carried a banner headline 'LABOUR'S MAJORITY FOGBOUND'; the other 'STEEL VOTE DRAMA'.

In the large Whips' Office in the House of Commons we had on the wall a printed list of all our Members, blown up for us by the Ministry of Works to six feet by four. This was covered with talc, on which we wrote coloured symbols against the names. In this way the Whips recorded information about their Members as it came in, particularly their arrival at Westminster, so that the exact situation could be seen at a glance.

As the day wore on the excitement mounted. It was the kind of build-up that politicians love – not unlike the interest around the TV screens in Transport House as the final General Election results came in. Scores of Members and ministers, even the Prime Minister, strolled in to see what the latest score was. By 7 p.m. we were almost there, but the last stragglers did not arrive until seven-twenty-five. Then the tired but happy Whips flopped into their chairs. We knew we had our majority.

The winding-up speeches by Nigel Birch (Flint West) for the Opposition and William Ross (Kilmarnock) for the Government were made against a background of tension among the backbenchers on both sides, but there was quiet assurance on the Treasury bench. They knew that, barring last-minute accidents, we were home and dry!

At 10 p.m. we crowded through the division lobbies – the first division in the four Wilson parliaments. By a cleverly organised manoeuvre, the Whips always find out during a division how many votes the other side has mustered. Though the doors are locked they are glass doors, and there are spies outside. I knew, before I voted and returned to the chamber, that we had defeated the Opposition amendment by a majority of seven. The next day we discovered that an error had been made and it was six – one more than our overall majority in the House. When the result was announced by the tellers a mighty cheer went up from our benches, and I thought I detected a sigh of relief from the Conservatives. Every seat was filled. Members sat on the steps in the aisles and stood twelve deep behind the Bar of the House to hear the result. It was one of those memorable parliamentary occasions which compensate for the countless hours of often dull debate we have to endure.

Did the Conservatives keep one or two Members out of the division lobby to avoid a Government defeat? We may never know, but I think not – though the absence of three of their Members has never been satisfactorily explained. After the division we tried unsuccessfully to find out why the result was better than it should have been. Of course no party, even with the most skilful Whips, ever knows the strength of its opponents with complete accuracy until the figures are announced, although they collect intelligence about the enemy as avidly as they do about their own troops. The Opposition faced a considerable dilemma. They had to demonstrate to their enthusiastic followers in the country that they were in dead earnest in trying to bring down the Government; at the same time they knew, or the wiser ones did, that if they precipitated another General Election they would be heavily defeated, particularly after our attractive programme had been uncovered.

I dragged a rather reluctant Prime Minister around to the Whips' Office to congratulate my now exultant team on a good day's work. He was reluctant, I think, because he did not want the result to be regarded as out of the ordinary. It would have to be the normal result if he was to remain in No. 10. But on this first occasion I felt we could be forgiven for our elation. The Labour Government had demonstrated its ability to survive and, in the circumstances, that was an achievement which merited at least a tiny pat on the back.

The following day, the last day of the debate on the Gracious Speech, the Opposition put down an amendment which was extremely inept:

. . . but have no confidence that Your Majesty's ministers can implement their proposals without damaging the programme of modernisation

72

already in train and thus imperilling the future wellbeing of Your people.

This was moved by John Boyd-Carpenter (Kingston-upon-Thames) an ex-minister with an episcopal manner of speaking, befitting the grandson of a bishop. He walked with a bouncing gait which earned for him the affectionate nickname of Jumping Jack. He was hard put to it to inject any substance into his rhetoric. However, he was followed by Douglas Houghton (Sowerby), Chancellor of the Duchy of Lancaster, who had a diffuse overlordship over social security and health matters and was chairman of a number of Cabinet committees.

The debate was notable only for the maiden speech of one of our brightest new recruits, Shirley Williams (Hitchin), daughter of Vera Brittain, who had enthralled an earlier generation with her autobiography *Testament of Youth*. Otherwise it was a lacklustre debate on a lacklustre amendment – an anticlimax after the great trial of strength the previous day. And it was a reasonably easy day for the Whips, for we knew that the Liberals would vote with the Government. Throughout most of the 1964-66 Parliament they were courteous enough to let us know whether they intended to support or oppose us, and they always did so long before the divisions were due. This was of considerable help to us, particularly in knowing whether or not we had to bring in the sick. We for our part leant over backwards to maintain the friendliest relations with them.

At the end of the debate we had a majority of twenty-one against the Opposition's amendment. After that the address to the Queen received unopposed support.

One of our Members, Dick Kelley (Don Valley) missed the final vote because, he said, he did not hear the division bells. I had always imagined that their harsh, insistent clanging would awaken the dead. However, we could take no chances, so I got Charles Pannell, the Minister of Works, to have their audibility tested in every part of the building, including the lavatories, the next morning.

The more relaxed day for the Whips was especially welcome as we could now look forward to a further crucial period in a two-day debate on the Chancellor's special Budget, which he was to introduce on Wednesday.

Meanwhile, one of those backbench motions appeared on the Order Paper which enliven our often dull parliamentary papers. These motions are never debated but enable MPs to express and publicise their views on any topic which excites them. On this occasion it was provoked by Ted Heath, who had derisively and rather ungallantly referred to Sir Solly Zuckerman, a distinguished scientist and scientific adviser to the Government as 'an expert on tadpoles and thoroughly unsuited to be an adviser to the Government'. A motion rebuking him was tabled by Manny Shinwell, Michael Foot, Sydney Silverman (Nelson and Colne) and others.

The full Cabinet had not seen the Chancellor's major proposals for his special Budget until the day before he was to announce them. While the reasons for this secrecy were well understood, it still seemed to give the Chancellor a quite disproportionate say in the Government's policy-making. His proposals would probably be discussed with his two senior ministerial colleagues in the Treasury, the Chief Secretary and the Financial Secretary, with the Prime Minister and with certain senior Civil Servants – but not with the Cabinet until a few hours before they were to be revealed to Parliament. Then it was too late to do anything but agree – often, in my experience, with great reluctance. Yet Budget decisions are rightly regarded by the electorate as being the framework of the Government's policy. I was made acutely aware of this in the 1966-70 Parliament when, as Secretary of State for Education and Science, I found myself in a straitjacket by the then Chancellor, but in the creation of which I had virtually no say.

Harold Wilson tried to meet the growing criticism of this Treasury dictatorship in the later years of his premiership by having special Cabinet discussions well in advance of the Budget. By that time, the public expenditure limits were decided on the basis of a long-term rolling programme.

The special Budget proposals included 6d. on the standard rate of income tax, which proved to be one of his wiser decisions; 6d. per gallon on petrol and diesel; an increase of 12s. 6d. per week on most social security benefits; an increase of £1 per week for the 'ten-shilling widow' and the abolition of prescription charges.

The rise in social security benefits was decided by the Cabinet after long and agonising discussions about how the rest of the world would view it and the consequent effect on sterling. The increases were not to take place until 29 March the following year. We were told that was the earliest practicable date, for at that time the records were not computerised. Most of our backbenchers refused to believe this and saw it as a Treasury ruse to save a few million pounds. I spent many hours during the next few weeks trying, without much success, to persuade groups of Members that this was not so.

There was to be a 15 per cent temporary surcharge on imports, excluding food and raw materials, to counter the huge growth in imports over the previous few years.

Ominously for the Whips, there was the promise of both a capital gains tax and the replacing of both the company profits tax and income tax by a corporation tax in the spring Budget. This would mean a huge and complicated Finance Bill.

The statement that the Chancellor was 'creating a climate that will make possible the achievement of an incomes and prices policy' gave a little more definition to the nebulous reference to this subject in the Queen's Speech. Few Members objected to it at the time, but it was the start of a road which was to lead to untold trouble in the party and in our relations with the trade unions.

The reactions in the press and in the Commons were predictable. *The Times* parliamentary correspondent wrote that the Chancellor's proposals hit the Commons like a cold douche. The Chancellor spoke of his 'barren inheritance' and laid the blame squarely at the door of his Tory predecessor, Reggie Maudling. The proposal to increase pensions was warmly applauded on the Government benches but the biggest 'Hear, hear' was the announcement that the widows' earnings rule was to be abolished. The Tories remained glum throughout.

The votes on the increase in the income tax and the price of petrol and diesel took place immediately the Chancellor sat down. The Liberals supported us on the first of these, giving us a majority of 27, but joined the Opposition against us on the second. Nevertheless, it was carried with the handsome majority of 10.

On 24 November the Finance Bill embodying the Budget proposals received a Second Reading with a majority of 32 – our biggest so far. We had successfully weathered both the Queen's Speech debate and the Budget.

On the day on which the Budget was introduced, Herbert Bowden and I first encountered an irritant which complicated our lives a good deal throughout the Parliament. When we went into the Cabinet Room for Prayers, we found Marcia there with the Prime Minister, who told us that as she was his political secretary she would be attending our meetings in future. We were greatly taken aback and, I think, showed it. This was, so far as we knew, the first time that a non-minister had been present at this intimate daily discussion between the Prime Minister and his Leader of the House and Chief Whip which had taken place for the past eighty years or so. It meant that we could not – or were not prepared to – discuss most of the topics for which the meeting had always been used, for example that Minister A had botched up a speech in the House, that Minister B was getting out of touch with backbenchers, that Ministers C and D were getting rebellious about some aspect of Government policy, etc. These intensely personal matters were certainly not the concern of Marcia, excellent secretary though she was. At the end of our rather pallid discussion Herbert said he now had a private matter to raise and looked across the table at Marcia, who, with an unmistakable show of reluctance, took the hint and left the room.

Marcia, in her role as political secretary, saw classified documents and was therefore required to undergo vetting by the security representatives. She took great umbrage at some of the questions she was asked, particularly about her divorce. In my opinion her anger was justified.

During this week we had to make a decision on MPs' salaries – another problem which had been bequeathed to us by our predecessors. At that time it was regarded as extremely damaging electorally – quite wrongly, I believe, for MPs to raise their salaries. MPs were paid £1,750 per annum, but it was estimated their expenses of living in London when the House was sitting, postage, telephone calls, etc. were running at £1,250, leaving them £500 a year to live on. This was an impossible situation, and in December 1963 the Home Government had set up a committee under Sir Geoffrey Lawrence to look into the matter and make recommendations for increases for MPs and ministers. However, there was an all-party agreement that their report should not be presented to the Government until after the election.

We now had the Lawrence recommendations, which were that MPs should receive £3,250 – still low enough, I thought, when all their expenses had to be met from it. The recommendation for their lordships was expressed in more up-stage terms: four and a half guineas a day.

On 11 November the Prime Minister called a meeting of Herbert Bowden, Douglas Houghton, the Earl of Longford (Lord Privy Seal), Lord Shepherd (Chief Whip in the House of Lords) and myself. We decided to recommend to the Cabinet that the Lawrence recommendations for MPs should be accepted and paid retrospectively from the date of the General Election, but that only 50 per cent of the increase for ministers should be agreed and paid from 1 April 1965. The Cabinet approved these suggestions two days later, but not without fierce opposition from Barbara Castle and Ray Gunter and equally vigorous support from George Brown and Frank Cousins, who as a good trade unionist saw it as the rate for the job. I took the view that these long overdue increases must be paid, as I knew that many of our MPs were in real financial difficulty and I did not want the strain of financial embarrassment added to the physical strain which I would have to impose upon them in the coming months.

The Whips had sounded out our members about the Lawrence proposals and found that many were uneasy about getting their increases at once, indeed backdated, while making the pensioners wait until the spring. A group of our backbenchers were trying to organise a campaign in both

77

the Parliamentary Party and in the constituencies to force the Government to bring forward the pension increases. But they were given a severe rebuff by the Prime Minister, who refused to meet them and told them that Manny Shinwell and I would see them.

There were rumblings in the press, which saw the juxtaposition of the delayed pension increases and the immediate parliamentary increases as a heaven-sent opportunity to belabour the Government, and in the party itself. We reviewed the position at Prayers the following Monday, but decided to go ahead with the announcement in the House that day. To our great relief the only Member who raised the matter was the high Tory ex-minister Robin Turton (Thirsk and Malton); but there was some rather fierce criticism at the meeting of the Parliamentary Labour Party later in the week, led by Ian Mikardo. The irrepressible Robert Maxwell (Buckingham) suggested that Members should not accept their increases until the pensioners got theirs, but he got little support, In the weeks that followed, many Members brought back reports from their constituencies of angry comments and resolutions. And the press added fuel to the flames.

The final parliamentary day of the week of the Budget was one which gave me a good deal of personal satisfaction. In the thirteen years in opposition, one of my interests as a backbencher had been in concessionary travel for the elderly, the disabled and children. This was a long tradition in municipal transport, and it was not questioned until 1954, when a ratepayer successfully challenged the Birmingham scheme in the High Court. This put all concessions throughout the country in jeopardy. I then came to their rescue by introducing a Private Member's Bill to legalise all travel concessions. But a Private Member's Bill can only succeed in reaching the Statute Book if the Government gives it parliamentary time and does not use its majority to oppose it. The Eden Government was about to go to the country when, for good electoral reasons, Anthony Eden sent for me and told me that they were not only going to allow my Bill to pass but were going to help it on its way. Unfortunately, in doing so they used their majority to amend it so that all it did was to legalise concessions which had existed at the time of the court decision in November 1954. Since that time there had been many new bus routes, indeed many new communities served by buses, but the undertakings could not extend their concessions in any way.

When we came into office we found a small Bill in the pigeonholes in Whitehall which would, if enacted, give local authorities freedom to institute new concessions or extend or modify existing ones. We decided to introduce this little Bill at the earliest opportunity. It was the first of the hundreds of Bills passed during the Wilson Governments and it gave a great deal of help to the old, the disabled and the children. It received an unopposed Second Reading and passed through all its stages the following week. The Minister of Transport was kind enough to refer to it as the 'Short' Bill.

During the pleasant Friday when the Travel Concessions Bill was introduced, I had an intriguing visit from a Tory MP who had made an appointment to see me. He said if the Government at any time found itself *in extremis* in the House, I should contact him and he would find a reason to stay away. This mystified me until a few weeks later I received an invitation to call at his house in Westminster for a drink. Not wishing to offend a potential extra vote, I duly turned up and found a party in progress but was told that the Member was in bed and had asked for me to be shown upstairs as soon as I arrived. He was propped up in bed looking the picture of health, surrounded by books and magazines and dictating to an attractive secretary. In our talk he told me that there would be vacancies in the near future for ambassadors in a number of our embassies in the Middle East and that he would like to be appointed. Mystery solved!

About this time Sydney Silverman and a number of his friends came to see me about his Private Member's Bill to abolish capital punishment, for which he had fought tirelessly for many years. Almost all Labour and Liberal Members, as well as many Conservatives, had a passionate commitment to end hanging. To many of us it was a kind of touchstone of the more civilised, compassionate society we hoped to create. Support for abolition had grown on each of the many occasions when it had been debated in the past; indeed, it gained majority support in 1957, but the then Conservative Government had only partially implemented the will of Parliament in the Homicide Act, which retained capital punishment for certain offences. Since then at least one innocent person – Timothy Evans – had been hanged.

But a matter of this kind, which aroused deep religious and humanitarian feelings, was not one for the Whips and could best be debated and, I hoped, legislated upon by means of a Private Member's Bill. This is a Public Bill like a Bill introduced by the Government, but it is drafted and introduced by a backbencher. I undertook to implement the promise we had made in the Queen's Speech and provide Government time, but the need to do so had become extremely urgent as a condemned man was awaiting execution. On 6 November at the Home Affairs Committee of the Cabinet, Sir Frank Soskice, the Home Secretary, expressed his horror at the prospect which he was facing of having to refuse a reprieve, and Herbert Bowden and I undertook to find time before Christmas for a Second Reading debate on Silverman's Bill. And a Second Reading, being the clearly expressed view of the House of Commons, could justify the Home Secretary in recommending a reprieve. We did so on 21 December, and the Second Reading was carried with a majority of 170.

The Conservatives then put their Whips on to try to carry a motion that the Committee Stage of the Bill be in a committee of the whole House – not, as is usual, in a small committee upstairs. With Liberal help we defeated this move, which was clearly a delaying tactic. Time is the Opposition's major weapon against the Government. It is also one of the Government's most scarce resources. However, they had another trick up their sleeves. Friday is almost always a day when the business of the House contains little or no party controversy – indeed, on many Fridays in each session it consists of Private Members' Bills or motions for which a ballot is held. For this reason most Members return to their constituencies and ministers catch up on their departmental work. The Whips relax and have no more than a watching role.

Shortly after the Leyton by-election, a Scottish Conservative, Forbes Hendry (Aberdeenshire West) won the ballot for a Friday motion. He was persuaded by the Tory anti-abolitionists – and maybe by their party managers, who were desperate for any kind of victory in the House – to put down a motion that the Murder (Death Penalty) Bill be brought back from the committee upstairs to a committee of the whole House, where the whole laborious Committee Stage would have to start again. Unfortunately I overlooked the fact that an important Conservative Party conference was to be held at Central Hall, Westminster, (five minutes from the House of Commons) on the Friday his motion was to be discussed. Although I had imposed a two-line whip, the Tories refused to register any pairs because, they said, it was merely Private Members' business. In spite of some hours of frantic telephoning from mid-morning onwards when we realised we had slipped up, we could only muster 120 votes against the Opposition's 128.

Naturally the Tories were jubilant, naively believing that this minor coup was a turning point in their fortunes, the beginning of the end, etc. But Herbert Bowden and I had a trump card. We immediately put down a further motion, which said that in order to implement Forbes Hendry's motion the House should meet each Wednesday morning – a hitherto unheard of time to meet – to deal with the Bill. With strict whipping and Liberal support we carried this unusual motion, to the fury of the many Tories who were employed in the City of London in the mornings. On one Wednesday morning in the following March we had a majority of 100!

The Bill eventually passed through all its stages in the Commons on 14 July 1965. The Lords struck a final blow by limiting its operation to five years, unless both Houses agreed by motions at the end of that period to continue it. As we had achieved abolition of hanging for five years, we decided to accept the position rather than become embroiled in a battle with the other House.

81

In the event, with the appalling case of Timothy Evans still in everyone's mind, the motions to make abolition permanent were passed at the end of the five-year period. After strong representations by Labour MP William Malloy (Ealing North) Evans was granted a posthumous pardon and his remains were exhumed from Wormwood Scrubs and reinterred elsewhere.

Most Labour MPs took the view that ending the obscenity of hanging was one of the major achievements of the 1964-66 Government.

We had completed our first two weeks in the House of Commons without undue difficulty and the Whips, at my request, went around the Palace of Westminster exuding confidence. Swan-like we were all serenity on the surface but paddling frantically underneath. For, behind the unfolding parliamentary scene, a grim financial battle was being fought day and night not only to sustain sterling but to save parliamentary democracy and avoid national ruin. An important aspect of this struggle was to demonstrate to the world that the Labour administration was secure and would provide stable government.

Unknown to our backbenchers, senior members of the Government were living from day to day, from hour to hour, in an agony of suspense. Can we make it – or is this the end? they asked each other. The ministers at the eye of the storm were the Prime Minister, the First Secretary and the Chancellor of the Exchequer. But it was the Prime Minister who bore the brunt of its fury, for he alone had the experience, the expertise and the political skill to weather it – and he was an inspiration to us all.

Our fearsome legacy from the outgoing Government was now common knowledge. We had made it so – maybe unwisely. At the end of September our balance of payments deficit for the first six months of the financial year was £341 million and for the full year would be at least £800 million – astronomical figures at that time. Our reserves were dwindling rapidly. We discovered that in the spring the Treasury had warned the then Government that a serious balance of payments crisis would develop later in the year unless steps were taken at once to reduce imports and boost exports. But Sir Alec Douglas-Home had decided to delay the General Election until the autumn, and nothing was done to rectify the worsening situation. Reggie Maudling, the Chancellor, had been given the Treasury's diagnosis of the situation and a number of options for dealing with it, but everything was delayed in the hope that electoral defeat could be avoided.

In the whole history of British democracy there can be few graver examples of dereliction of duty by a Government.

As a result, the Bank of England had to support the pound at its level – unbelievable today – of 2.785 dollars, almost continuously throughout the late summer and early autumn, and the cost of that support rose alarmingly as the days passed. Urgent action was needed to deal with the immediate problem and to restore confidence in the British economy. This was the purpose of the package of proposals announced on 26 October to restrict imports by a surcharge and to encourage the exporting industries. It was also the major objective of the Budget introduced on 11 November. But the Budget also implemented our election promise to increase social benefits and abolish prescription charges and, although we increased both the standard rate of income tax and the social security contributions to pay for these long-overdue measures, they were regarded as grossly extravagant by a number of influential commentators at home and abroad, as well as by the City of London. And so it was not simply a matter of taking remedial measures in the economy like adjusting the controls of a car. In a democracy the Government must justify its actions, but we could only do this by revealing in the clearest terms the state of the economy we had taken over. Unfortunately, each revelation added to the picture of a sick economy, and consequently to our problems.

The strength of sterling, one of the great reserve currencies of the world, depended upon international confidence, which, in turn, depended upon the state of the British economy. We knew it would be only too easy to talk ourselves into an irremediable crisis, dissipating confidence and negating the measures we had taken. But because of our small majority,

83

we wanted what we were doing and why we were doing it to be understood, in case we were forced into an election.

The angry reaction of our EFTA partners in Europe to our 15 per cent import surcharge did not improve matters. In retrospect, perhaps with greater effort we could have carried them with us – though I doubt it. They would have preferred us to impose import quotas, but these could not have become operative immediately and, we knew, would be extremely complicated to organise.

Fred Peart, Minister of Agriculture, and Douglas Jay, President of the Board of Trade, were sent to Geneva to meet our European partners but received a mauling. The Council of Europe, with its membership drawn from seventeen countries, threatened to denounce us, but Anthony Crosland, at that time George Brown's Minister of State at the Department of Economic Affairs, reminded them that we ran a major reserve currency and were entitled to look to them for support. His skilful speech averted a humiliating defeat for the British delegation.

The statement of 26 October had also mentioned the possibility of cancelling the Concorde project. The latest estimate of its cost was £260 million, which we could ill afford. This infuriated the French, who insisted that we honour our agreement with them. We found, to our dismay, that it was no ordinary commercial contract but had the status and force of a treaty.

We got little help or understanding from Europe in our difficulties but we got even less help at home. The Tories, with all the vehemence of which they were capable, opposed all our measures to deal with the threatening situation they had left behind. Sir Alec Douglas-Home said they were irrelevant to the balance of payments problem! Of course they did not vote against the raising of pensions and other social benefits but only against the increases in tax to pay for them. Their record in their first three weeks in Opposition was one of almost unbelievable irresponsibility. The businessmen among them, and there were many, knew that we would not devalue the pound, yet not one of them used his standing in the City of London or elsewhere to say so in unambiguous terms to the speculators who were buying vast amounts of foreign currency, and by so doing were adding to our problems. Their record was, as the Prime Minister pointed out in the debate on defence on 23 November, in striking contrast to the support the Labour Opposition had given to the Macmillan Government's defence of sterling in the aftermath of the Suez fiasco.

Unfortunately, the Opposition speakers in Parliament and the trouble in EFTA and the Council of Europe focussed world attention on Britain's economic problems, and by Friday 13 November the outflow of funds had increased alarmingly. On the following Monday the Prime Minister made a speech at the Guildhall in which every word was carefully calculated to restore confidence. He pledged that we would 'keep sterling strong and see it riding high.' The speech was reasonably well received, but its toughness created an expectation that the bank rate would be raised on the Thursday of that week, the usual day for changes. But when we did not do this, because we knew only too well what the effect of higher interest rates would be on the employment situation, the pressure on sterling intensified ominously.

The Governor of the Bank of England was in constant touch with the Chancellor and the Prime Minister and, expressing the feeling in the City of London as it was his duty to do, brought considerable pressure on them to adopt a massive policy of deflation as Selwyn Lloyd had done in 1961 and Peter Thorneycroft in 1957. But neither Harold Wilson, George Brown nor any other member of the Cabinet could have agreed to this reversion to the hoary old 'stop-go' formula; indeed, we had been elected to replace it by a planned programme of growth.

That weekend the Prime Minister had called a three-day meeting at Chequers of the ministers concerned with defence and the economy, the Chiefs of Staff, including Lord Mountbatten, who was then CIGS, and, unaccountably, George Wigg. The purpose of the meeting was to settle a number of problems in our defence policy strategy and procurement, especially of aircraft, and to brief the Prime Minister for the visit to Washington which he was to make in December. Denis Healey also needed these discussions to enable him to begin work on his first Defence White Paper.

When they assembled in the comfortable great hall on the Friday evening, a shaken Jim Callaghan arrived muttering: 'We can't go on; we shall have to devalue.' (*George Wigg*). The roof, it appeared, was about to fall in.

Faced with this appraisal of the situation by the Chancellor, Harold Wilson and George Brown were forced to agree to a significant 2 per cent increase in the bank rate, and to make the announcement on Monday – the first time since 1931 that it had been raised on a day other than Thursday. The weekend provided time to consult the United States, who decided to put up their own rate at the same time. The closest and most scrupulous co-operation with Washington was practised throughout the Wilson years, even in the difficult days of the Vietnam war, and was a major source of strength to the Labour Government.

The announcement on the Monday triggered a sharp rally of the pound but, quite inexplicably, it very soon resumed its downward slide of the previous week. This was the signal for Lord Cromer, the Governor of the Bank of England, to present the Chancellor with a list of massive deflationary measures. In addition, he suggested we drop all our proposals which were controversial, including capital gains tax and corporation tax. The City of London was twisting the Government's arm as only it knew how. Here was another establishment, the financial establishment, blatantly demanding that the elected government should abandon the policies on which it had been elected. He was told that his proposals were quite unacceptable. Had the City had its way, all our social benefit increases would have been cancelled and, worse, damaging cuts would have been made in every field of public expenditure. In other words, a Labour government could only survive if it did not follow a Labour policy.

On the Tuesday evening, after the worst day yet for sterling, the Chancellor took Lord Cromer to No. 10 to discuss the crisis with the Prime Minister. Lord Cromer repeated his demands and said that, in his view, they were the only way catastrophe could be avoided. But he underestimated the

86

toughness and the financial expertise of Harold Wilson – as others have done to their cost. He was told in forthright language to go back to the Bank and utilise all his goodwill with other central banks to organise a massive international credit of three billion dollars in support of sterling.

Lord Cromer, good public servant that he was, understood that the Prime Minister was his final court of appeal and that he had failed to convince the Government to adopt his remedies. But there was no question of resignation; histrionics were not his style – anyhow, the situation was much too serious. He immediately set about the task of mobilising international support.

Herbert Bowden and I went to see the Prime Minister at 1 a.m., when he told us the details of that dramatic meeting.

For twenty-four hours the telephone lines between the world's major central banks carried a vast network of consultations. By about 7 p.m. the following day Lord Cromer was able to report pledges amounting to £1,070 million from eleven countries. In this colossal effort mounted by Lord Cromer, the US Federal Reserve Bank had played a leading role both by its own contribution and in its influence on other banks.

And so the Labour Government was saved – but it was a close-run thing.

Of course, as the crisis developed, there was growing concern among our backbenchers, fuelled by the rumours flying around the bars and tea room at Westminster. Unfortunately, because of the fragile web of confidence on which sterling depended, they had few hard facts about what was happening; but they sensed that something quite serious was going on.

Each morning at Prayers Herbert Bowden and I agreed with Harold what the Whips could tell their Members. On the Tuesday, at the height of the crisis, he had refused to meet a group of Members from the far left of the Party led by John Mendelson (Penistone). I saw Mendelson the following day and was amazed at his lack of understanding that the Government was trying to cope with an appalling situation. However, most of our Members loyally kept quiet and knew they would have the facts as soon as it was safe to give them.

Fortunately, we now had another channel of communication between the Government and our backbenchers. Manny Shinwell, a very youthful octogenarian, had been elected chairman of the Parliamentary Labour Party, with Arthur Blenkinsop (Newcastle East) and Malcolm MacPherson (Stirling and Falkirk) as his deputies. They, together with the Leader of the House, myself and a small number of elected Members formed a Liaison Committee, which proved to be a valuable two-way means of communication between the Government and its supporters. Manny's vast experience and wisdom lubricated the relationship, which is never an easy one. Throughout the whole of my period as Chief Whip I worked in the closest harmony with him on both communications and disciplinary matters, as did the Prime Minister, until he committed the inexplicable error of making Dick Crossman Leader of the House of Commons. Crossman had such confidence in his own omniscience that he felt he no longer needed Manny to help run the Party and quickly manoeuvred him out of the chairmanship.

I was beginning to get a stream of Members to see me about their commitments outside Parliament. I had not dreamt that so many were so heavily involved in other occupations. The majority were lawyers, a number of whom sat as Recorders. Others were doctors, dentists, opticians, etc. All wanted time off from the House to follow their professions outside, and the parliamentary salaries were so miserably low that I did not blame them. One of our Members who lived in London but represented a Scottish constituency was forced to undertake part-time teaching to make ends meet. We also had a number who were deeply involved in local government. As well as these activities, all Members had to visit their constituencies. I am afraid my response to constituency demands depended to a considerable extent on the Member's majority!

In our thirteen years in opposition there had been no great problem in allowing Members time off to undertake all their engagements, though their absences were always resented by the Members who were present day in day out and manned all the committees. But with the Government's existence depending on a majority of five and so much more being asked of our Members, the position was quite different.

The first step in tightening up was obviously to improve parliamentary salaries. Having done this, we then worked out a rota system in the Whips' Office to allow all Members a fair and equal share of time away from the House, whether they were highly paid lawyers or otherwise. We knew on which days Government business in the Commons allowed a number of Members to be absent, but a three-line whip required everyone to be present with no exceptions under any circumstances except where life would be endangered by bringing a sick Member in – and I required medical proof of this. If no major division was expected, under the Standing Orders we needed only 100 Members to move the closure of a debate; otherwise the Opposition could have prevented us getting our business completed. Equally, 100 Members were required to prevent a closure being moved by the Opposition at a moment which suited them but not us. On days when no divisions were expected we needed only 40 Members to provide a quorum and prevent the House from being counted out.

By a complicated piece of arithmetic we looked at the Government business in the few weeks ahead, calculated the number of days we could distribute and then divided that figure by 317 (our full strength). We then worked out a rota which ensured that each Member was allocated this number of days to see to his outside interests. In doing so we tried, as far as possible, to give them the days for which they had asked. Of course, we could not always succeed, and I had many heated altercations with eminent QCs who had to refuse lucrative briefs because I would not allow them time to attend court. On more than one occasion I had anxious telephone calls from courts throughout the country that Mr X or Mr Y was in the middle of his winding-up speech and might find it difficult to get to Westminster in time for the divisions. I always had to point out that, much as I sympathised with his dilemma, the High Court of Parliament must come first, and that he must be in the division lobby on time.

I was very rarely let down. The judges must often have been very accommodating! The rota allowed Members to be away from Westminster about one day in five and was greatly appreciated – not least by the full-time parliamentarians.

On the day on which sterling was saved by Lord Cromer's mobilisation of the world's central banks, the Queen held a party for the new Government at Buckingham Palace. Lord Plunket, that most excellent of royal aides, asked me to identify the guests and their offices as they came forward to be presented to the Queen and Prince Philip. It was a very large Government and I had difficulty in naming some of the newer MPs and their ministerial appointments. And so on my left I had Sydney Irving, my deputy, who whispered the particulars to me; I then whispered to Lord Plunket, who in turn told the Queen.

Unfortunately, no similar party was held at the beginning of the new parliaments in 1966, 1970 or 1974. I mentioned this to Sir Martin Charteris, the Queen's Private Secretary, when I was Lord President of the Council in 1974. I felt that the monarch should get to know her ministers, as well as MPs, and they her. Regrettably, the only ones she meets are the Prime Minister, the Lord President and a handful of Privy Counsellors. This divorce of the Palace from contact with parliamentarians is a fairly recent development. Before the Second World War ministers and MPs were regularly invited to levees. Monarch, Lords and Commons are all elements in the legislature of the United Kingdom, but in the second half of this century the monarch has moved away from the two Houses.

As the weeks passed we were plagued by an endemic problem in our democratic system of government. Whitehall is a colossal sieve. Throughout all the Wilson Governments we were embarrassed by leaks. It was clear that both Civil Servants and ministers were to blame. Each time a damaging piece of information was made public, the Prime Minister read the Riot Act to the Cabinet and constantly warned that if they made notes in Cabinet they must not, in any circumstances, be taken out of the Cabinet Room. This homily was repeated whenever he saw anyone writing. On one occasion he did so when he saw Barbara Castle scribbling with great concentration. I sat next to her and when I looked over her shoulder I saw her busily engaged on a neatly written shopping list '... 1 lb bacon, $1/4$lb tea....'

Harold's strict rule about note-taking in Cabinet was complicated because he had a Cabinet of inveterate doodlers. Barbara Castle adorned any pieces of paper in front of her with Christmas decorations, especially bells and holly – goodwill everywhere. Since seeing her doodles, I have never believed the theory that doodling is revealing about the personality. William Ross drew the most technically accomplished faces; Harold himself erected elaborate constructions out of absolutely straight lines; Denis Healey drew crude, brutal-looking human figures. I have a collection of their doodles which, at some future date, may enable a psychologist to shed new light on the Cabinet of 1964.

On a number of occasions the Lord Chancellor was asked to conduct investigations into particularly damaging leaks, but as he always failed to find the culprit I decided to create my own back-room machinery in No. 12. Charles Morris (Openshaw), an enthusiastic young Whip, was put in charge of the operation. Each morning he and one or two other Whips scrutinised all the national and major regional newspapers and identified any item which appeared to be a leak. Charles then telephoned the appropriate Whitehall department. If he was assured that it ought not to have been made public, he checked back through the early editions of the newspapers concerned and found the time it was first mentioned. This piece of information, together with the name of the lobby man who had written it, were then compared with the daily diaries of ministers. I always insisted on having copies of their schedules; on more than one occasion they disclosed a contact between a minister and a reporter at the appropriate time. If this comparison revealed nothing, the team of sixteen Whips, who were all-pervasive in the House of Commons, were asked whether they had noticed any discussions taking place between lobby men and any minister from that department.

One leak, not a particularly damaging one, was traced by Charles to a senior minister who was one of the most loyal and likeable members of the Government. When I asked him about it he freely admitted that he had met the lobby correspondent in the corridor and talked to him – unwisely, he now realised.

We had to face the fact that some people are inherently incontinent where classified information is concerned. Some get a sense of power from being able to impart much-sought-after information. Others simply become friendly with the lobby correspondents who haunt the corridors of Westminster gleaning pieces of information, which they are adept at piecing together. Sometimes an innocuous fact is dropped in conversation, but it may be the missing link to complete a damaging story which appears in the press next morning.

On 17 November I attended a meeting of the Legislation Committee of the Cabinet, which had the task of approving Bills as drafted, with a further possible reference to the full Cabinet in the case of Bills on which we could not agree, and which were of major importance or were highly controversial – for example, the Steel Bill. I returned along the corridors of No. 12 extremely pessimistic about the prospects of getting them all through Parliament. Freddie Warren and I estimated that the Bills approved to date would require a minimum of 94 days of parliamentary time, but only 50 days were available for legislation in the present session. We had, therefore, after one month in office, sufficient legislation ready for two sessions – and ministers were still submitting Bills to the committee thick and fast.

It is unfortunate that the constraints of the parliamentary machine are rarely taken into account by political parties in preparing their election manifestos.

The Parliamentary Labour Party met on Thursday evening each week to consider the business of the House for the following week and, in addition, we held an occasional meeting on Wednesday mornings to discuss specific topics. There was constant pressure from some backbenchers to hold the morning meetings every week. There was equal determination by the Prime Minister, the Leader of the

House and myself to avoid this – partly because they would have developed into a permanent backbench monitoring of the Government's performance, with ministers having to justify their every action; and partly because ministers could not afford the time away from their departments. Harold was getting extremely annoyed about this constant pressure for additional meetings and this was exacerbated on Monday 30 November when the *Guardian* reported that pressure groups were determined to have weekly meetings. This was the week of his first real rift with the press and it arose because Bob Carvel in the *Evening Standard* and Peterborough in the *Daily Telegraph* mentioned his lobby meeting of the previous week at which he had mentioned 35 per cent as the rate at which Corporation Tax was likely to be levied. This was a clear breach of the Westminster convention that lobby meetings with the Prime Minister or the Leader of the House should never be mentioned and any information given is always non-attributable. Harold flew into a fury at this and at the press in general, particularly at the suggestions that the Party was getting restive. He was determined to attend the next Wednesday morning meeting – time which he could ill afford. He was, he said, going to give a straight talk which would kill the demand for weekly meetings.

Why he got so worked up about this minor matter, I never knew. Herbert Bowden and I suspected that he was being fed a totally distorted picture about feeling in the Party by George Wigg – and maybe others in the kitchen cabinet. An article in the *New Statesman* of 27 November by Gerald Kaufman, not yet an MP, did not help matters. It mentioned 'disenchantment' among backbenchers and lectured me about improving the Whips' grapevine at Westminster (little did he know how good it was!) and even the Prime Minister about 'mending his fences' at Westminster. We constantly tried to reassure him that, apart from a handful of congenitally difficult ones whom nothing would change, the whole Labour Party at Westminster and outside would eat out of his hand. But it was also the week in which he had decided not to take Marcia with him to Washington – and that added to his irritability.

At the meeting, Harold's pep talk turned out to be extremely mild, for he had calmed down by then. As a result, the left thought they could get away with it and Hugh Jenkins (Putney), supported by Eric Heffer (Liverpool Walton) and others, moved a motion which would have made weekly meetings obligatory. But Manny Shinwell, in the chair, was made of sterner stuff. He used all his skill and wiles to persuade the meeting to move on to the next business.

We were, of course, always willing and indeed anxious to discuss with the Party any real issue which was causing concern and where we were able to be forthcoming in the information we gave. Some matters could not, at this stage, be discussed frankly and openly with the Parliamentary Party for the debates in our meetings became as widely and quickly known outside as a meeting in the Albert Hall. Perhaps the most troublesome of these meetings in our first few weeks in office was on the decision to defer the uprating of social benefits until March. It was raised with varying degrees of vehemence at almost all Party meetings in November and climaxed in the House of Commons on 3 December when the upgrading came up for approval. The Liberals had put down an amendment which, if carried, would have brought forward the date of the increases. Michael Foot, Ian Mikardo and John Mendelson spoke in favour of the amendment but, with the exception of Mendelson, in somewhat muted terms. In the end the Liberals did not press it to a vote; but I knew we would not have been in danger of defeat, because Michael Foot had assured me beforehand that he and his colleagues intended only to stir it up a little but, not to vote for the amendment. I remembered also that elections to the National Executive Committee of the Labour Party were to take place the following week and some electioneering could be expected.

The full extent of the financial crisis was still unknown to our backbenchers because of the knife-edge on which sterling was balanced. There was a widespread but inchoate fear in the Party that the Government had put itself in hock to 'international finance'. It is a remarkable and sad fact that a Labour government is never really trusted by its backbenchers – and even less by our National Executive Committee.

It was also known that there had been an unprecedentedly powerful gathering of ministers and Chiefs of Staff on defence at Chequers. What, the Whips were being asked daily, had been decided there? There was a justified suspicion that Denis Healey was exerting pressure on the Government to abandon the defence policy on which we had fought the General Election. What were we doing, our Members wondered, to reduce the crippling £2400 million defence budget we had inherited?

In opposition we had opposed the proposal of Presidents Kennedy and Johnson for a mixed-manned fleet. Were we still opposing it in Government? And were we still going to insist that there should be no German finger on the nuclear trigger? This was still a highly emotive issue in the Labour Party twenty years after the war. With the Prime Minister's approaching visit to Washington, there was anxiety that he was preparing to reach unacceptable agreements.

Each morning I had a meeting of the Whips in No. 12 and heard all the matters that were troubling their Members. As a result, I knew fairly accurately the views of every Labour MP on each issue. I passed on this information to the Prime Minister and we decided what line the Whips should take in their talks with their regional Members. We also knew exactly which Members could be relied upon to spread information with the greatest speed. This channelling of views and information from individual backbenchers to the Prime Minister and from him to the House of Commons tea room was an essential part of my job in the 1964-66 Parliament.

At the end of November there was more friction between George Wigg and myself. It was clearly understood by everyone in the Government that I was the means of communication between the BBC and the Government. I had regular meetings with the Director General's personal assistant, Harman Grisewood, and occasionally with the Director General himself, about party political broadcasting and the many complaints I received alleging bias in programmes. On 30 November I had a phone call from

95

Trevor Lloyd-Hughes, Harold's Press Secretary – a title borrowed from the Kennedy Administration – to tell me that Wigg had sent him the script of the previous week's *Panorama* programme and asked him what he was going to do about it. I raised this with Harold and he promised to straighten Wigg out on broadcasting matters. But my problem, as so often, was that I did not know to what extent Harold himself was involved.

The Finance Bill which implemented the autumn Budget proposals completed all its stages in the Commons on 9 December, and we looked forward to a peaceful run-up to the Christmas recess and to the end of our first hundred days in office.

The Prime Minister's visit to Washington was a highlight of this period. President Johnson was back in the White House after the election on 4 November and Harold had arranged to visit him early in December, to make his number with the President and to renegotiate the Nassau Agreement made by Harold Macmillan. This agreement, we were told, preserved our status as an independent nuclear power by allowing us to purchase American know-how and Polaris missiles for use in British-built nuclear submarines. It also committed us to joining a multilateral nuclear force which included a mixed-manned fleet of twenty-five surface vessels (MLF). To us, this latter proposal appeared to put a number of new fingers, including the Germans', on the nuclear trigger. It was therefore totally unacceptable to the Labour Party.

Harold had to perform the miracle of appearing to get rid of our so-called independent nuclear weapons while at the same time keeping them! But nothing was beyond the Harold Wilson of 1964. The defence of Britain and the West needed an independent nuclear deterrent, as he and Denis Healey knew, but the Labour Party believed that it would impress neither friend nor potential foe, and that '. . . this nuclear pretence carried with it grave dangers of encouraging the spread of nuclear weapons to countries not possessing them including Germany' (1964 Manifesto).

The Prime Minister persuaded the President to agree to a new British initiative in NATO as an alternative to the MLF. This amounted to an Atlantic nuclear force – our Polaris submarines together with a very minor mixed-manned element. Our bombers and submarines would be committed to NATO for as long as it existed.

Thus he had, as so often, achieved the apparently impossible. In all my long association with him I do not recollect a single occasion when, confronted by two diametrically opposed viewpoints, he could not find a solution. When I heard him explain his US agreement to the Cabinet, I got the impression of a highly skilled conjurer who had thrown his silk handkerchief over our Polaris submarines and, hey presto, they had gone – but he still had them up his sleeve or behind his coat-tails. It was sheer wizardry. He was the cleverest politician for many a long year – by far!

By any standard it was a major achievement. Although it did not amount to abandoning the independent British nuclear deterrent completely, it certainly appeared to do so. At least, it replaced the unacceptable American MLF plan by a British proposal.

But he had paid a price – a high price. He had agreed that the US would have our tacit support in Vietnam. As the war in South-East Asia dragged on month after month, this commitment caused me more trouble and embarrassment in the Party than any other issue.

The American visit was an undoubted success in putting relations between the Johnson Administration and ourselves on an excellent footing. The President and the Prime Minister were both down-to-earth professional politicians with much in common. The tough Texan and the homespun Yorkshireman hit it off famously and initiated an era of Anglo-American friendship which was closer than at any time since the war. And this stood us in good stead in our battles to maintain the value of sterling.

Tired but exhilarated from his visit and cockier than ever, Harold set about selling his ANF proposal to the Cabinet, the Party and the House of Commons. Quite remarkably, he had no trouble with any of them. I knew from the enquiries the Whips had made among their Members that some were, to say the least, sceptical about it; but at the Party meeting and in the House, they kept quiet. Their attitude on the ANF illustrated what I was beginning to suspect: that few Members were prepared to rock the boat so long as we had an almost non-existent majority. From the press cuttings over the following few weeks the only harshly dissident voices were those of John Mendelson and Bill Warbey (Ashfield). Fortunately, they had little following at that time in the Parliamentary Labour Party.

I also had a minor problem with the newly elected Member for Rochester and Chatham, Mrs Anne Kerr, a passionate anti-nuclear campaigner, who absented herself unpaired to take part in a CND rally in Paris.

We arranged a two days' foreign affairs debate – the first day, a supply day at the disposal of the Opposition, and the second a debate on the Adjournment. Our completely irrepressible Prime Minister decided to open the debate and to wind it up. His opening speech lasted for sixty-eight minutes but, in spite of its inordinate length, was one of his best performances of the Parliament. Apart from a mass of detail about his Washington talks (and knowing what to omit was never his strong point), he hinted that massive cuts would have to be made in defence spending, now running at 7.1 per cent of the GNP – a higher percentage than in any western country except the United States. This went down extremely well on our benches, where excessive defence spending was believed to be the reason why we could not build the new schools, hospitals and roads which constituencies throughout the country were demanding. In his winding-up speech at the end of the two days he effectively demolished the carefully nurtured myth that our nuclear deterrent was independent by revealing that we were reliant on the United States for essential elements. 'The fact is that there is no independent deterrent because we are dependent on the Americans for the fissile material for the British war-heads. This is true and he [Sir Alec Douglas-Home] knows it.'

So he had got rid of the British deterrent – but kept it. And then, for good measure, proved that it was not independent anyhow. What an amazing man!

Finally, he had to convince the wider Labour movement that he had not sold the pass. The opportunity came in the following week at the Party's postponed annual conference at Brighton on 12 December, and he achieved another resounding success with a familiar old formula. First, he savaged the Tory press, which had alleged that he had made a secret deal with President Johnson. This was followed by an inspiring call to arms – Dunkirk spirit, a new cutting edge, willingness to modernise, an end to restrictive practices and, to top it all, an echo of his hero John F. Kennedy: 'Our approach must be not what we can take out of the national pool but what we can put in.' He ended: 'Sustained and inspired by our great people, I give you this pledge; that we shall not fail, that from our endeavours we shall build a fairer, a more just society, that from our faith and our ideals, we shall contribute our full need towards creating a world of peace.' It was a memorable speech and he received, and deserved, a memorable ovation.

And so as 1964, his *annus mirabilis*, drew towards its end, I constantly assured him that the whole Labour movement in Parliament and outside was solidly behind him – and that was no mean achievement.

The second landmark in the last days of 1964 was the signing, with all the pomp and circumstance of a major international treaty, of George Brown's Declaration of Intent at Lancaster House on 16 December. George had worked on this agreement with his usual almost demonic energy since the General Election because we hoped to make a favourable impression on world opinion. 'Mr George Brown has achieved in sixty days what eluded Mr Maudling for months', said *The Times*. And, indeed, in two months he had not only organised the Department of Economic Affairs from scratch but had also reached agreement with the TUC, the employers' organisations and his colleagues in Government on a concerted approach to our economic problems and, in particular, to an incomes policy. The Government undertook to establish machinery to monitor continuously the movement of prices and incomes and to use fiscal and other measures to correct an excessive growth in profits. Unions and employers agreed to carry out a sustained attack on obstacles to the efficiency of both workers and management. At the signing ceremony, Lord Collison, Chairman of the TUC, called it 'part of an overall plan for economic expansion and promoting social equality . . . rooted in the view that a planned economy is essential if the country is to prosper and that the growth of incomes should be within the compass of such a plan.'

How very different the record of the Wilson Governments, indeed of the past two decades, might have been if the high hopes of that December morning had been fulfilled. Although the unions co-operated for a time, in the long run they were unwilling to surrender their traditional right to negotiate the best pay deal they could for their members, even to a Labour Government which promised them the earth in return. In fact, more militant leaders, while never ceasing to make speeches about socialism, refused to accept the central theme of socialism: a planned economy.

In the few weeks before Christmas there was a good deal of speculation in the press about the Government's chances of survival. On 7 December *The Times* quoted 'a former senior minister', who said that our majority was not really five but twenty-three votes, for he thought we could count on Liberal support for a long time to come. He also said that whatever the left might do, the one thing they would not do was bring down their own Government. Another 'former Conservative minister' forecast that the Chancellor's deflationary policies would cause growing unemployment towards the end of 1965, and that would be the dangerous period as a Labour government could never afford unemployment.

On the evening of 16 December I held a party at No. 12 for the press gallery and lobby together with some Transport House staff with whom I had been working closely. George Brown came, after a day celebrating the signing of his declaration. His bonhomie overflowed upon everyone present. His words were still intelligible, but only just; his posture was still upright and stable, but barely so. He received a great welcome and assured us all that he loved everyone present, including the press. Harold came, reluctantly, to wish us all a happy Christmas, and eventually

100

Jim sidled in like an elder of the kirk. It was an occasion when we celebrated our survival, and even our opponents among the press – and there were many – could not disguise their admiration for our cliffhanging performance of the past three months.

However, we were not to be allowed to disperse for Christmas without another below-the-belt blow from the Conservative Opposition, who were obviously willing to wound but not to kill. At Question Time on 15 December Jim Callaghan had a number of questions about his proposals for a corporation tax and a tax on capital gains, but he refused to elaborate on them or announce the rates of tax he had in mind. Reggie Maudling roused himself from his famous sloth, which was damaging his chances of winning the leadership of his Party, to make a statement afterwards. 'A very serious situation has been created by the Government's refusal to give more information about the Corporation Tax and Capital Gains Tax. This grave uncertainty is bound to have damaging effects on the strength of sterling,' he said. He and his colleagues knew only too well that sterling had a precarious equilibrium which a careless word could destroy overnight. Yet they were willing to say that word. As Anthony Shrimsley commented: 'If sterling was not jittery before Maudling laid his charge it would certainly have been so when he had finished' (*The First Hundred Days of Harold Wilson*). It was indeed an act of irresponsibility, which cost our reserves an estimated 50 million dollars over the next two days.

George Brown, in one of his monumental furies, issued a statement saying that Maudling 'by his totally irresponsible statement issued recklessly and without apparent regard for the vital interests of the nation . . . has put himself back in the squabble over the succession to the Tory leadership.' If this had been Maudling's motive, it did him little good when the new leader was elected at the end of July the following year.

We also had more trouble between our two trade union leaders in the Cabinet. It arose over our plan to persuade Dr Beeching to undertake a study of national transport, with the object of producing a better-integrated system. Our manifesto had said: 'Labour will draw up a national plan for transport covering the national networks of road, rail and canal communications . . . properly co-ordinated with air, coastal shipping and port services.' Most of us had understood that Dr Beeching had agreed to relinquish the chairmanship of British Rail in January and then undertake the study until June, when he wanted to return to ICI. The choice of Dr Beeching had the strong support of the Prime Minister, who saw in him the archetypal tough, able technocrat who could help turn his election talk of a white-hot technological revolution into reality.

Our none too forceful Minister of Transport, Tom Fraser (Hamilton), wanted Beeching alone to make his survey and his proposals. In this he was supported by Ray Gunter, the Minister of Labour who greatly admired Beeching. But when Frank Cousins saw the relevant Cabinet papers he immediately and vehemently objected on the grounds that Beeching was bound to favour the railways in his recommendations. He would only give his approval if Beeching had a number of assessors to assist him. Beeching immediately rejected this suggestion but remained willing to do the job alone. The impasse between the two went to the Government's arbitrator-in-chief, the Prime Minister. Oddly, he made the wrong decision by supporting the Cousins view, no doubt hoping he could persuade Beeching to accept the assessors. Writing of his strange decision Harold has said: 'It was an occasion when I yielded to sectional Cabinet pressure and, looking back on it, I was wrong'. (*Our Labour Government*.) Dr Beeching took the weekend before Christmas to think it over, but refused to budge. It was agreed that Tom Fraser himself, assisted by a committee, should undertake the study and submit a plan for an integrated transport system. This was a task for which he was temperamentally unfitted. He was much too kind and gentle a man to deal with all the Gunters and Cousinses with which the railways and the road services abounded – and a committee representing all the transport world's powerful special interests could never produce the synthesis we wanted.

102

And so we lost the services of the best brain which had been brought to bear on our transport system in this century. Had the Prime Minister stuck to his guns and allowed Beeching to go ahead with his study alone, our Government would probably have achieved the long-cherished Labour dream of a nationally coordinated transport system. As it turned out, all we did was to tinker with the system and achieve almost nothing.

And another dream was fading. A short entry in my diary a few days before Christmas reads: 'It looks as though the Crown Lands Commission Bill will not see the light of day this session. Crossman is still being obstructive as only he knows how.' Fred Willey, the minister responsible for it, suffered the same kind of difficulties from him as Tom Fraser suffered from Frank Cousins. In each case a quiet, unassuming minister was up against a tough, able and determined opponent.

At our last meeting of the Cabinet before the recess, Harold wished us a happy Christmas and insisted we all go away for a complete break, but not for some years did he get round to giving us a Christmas drink.

I was called back to London for two short meetings during the recess, and on one of these I had a further disagreement with George Wigg, who had persisted in trying to do my job and Herbert Bowden's in addition to his own. We discovered he had sent out a form to all ministers, which they were to complete each week and return to his office, giving details of all their speaking engagements for the following week. As he knew, it was one of the functions of my office to compile a weekly list of ministers' public meetings so that our policy and achievements could be put across in a co-ordinated way. Ministers had got used to this system, which was operated with discretion – there was no question of checking up on ministers who were not pulling their weight in the country, although some undoubtedly were not. Not unnaturally, they greatly resented Wigg's new form, and some rang me up to say they were not going to co-operate.

I was thoroughly fed up with the Paymaster General's extracurricular activities, which were costing me time and energy in placating my colleagues. I got the Prime Minister to call a meeting of George Wigg, Herbert Bowden and myself to settle this ridiculous demarcation dispute. Contrary to my fears, this proved to be an amicable meeting. I suspect that Harold had already spoken to George about it. Herbert Bowden and I established the boundaries of our responsibilities, which were agreed and recorded without acrimony. I had not suspected this magnanimous side of George, and from this meeting to the time he left the Government our relations were friendly – though we kept reasonably clear of each other.

On my second Christmas recess visit to London the Cabinet rejected a proposal by Anthony Wedgwood Benn to increase postal charges. He had overlooked the fact that two vital by-elections, at Nuneaton and Leyton, were to be held in the week he proposed to make the increases!

The recess was overshadowed by the worsening illness of Sir Winston Churchill, who had suffered a serious stroke and was not expected to survive for many days. We had a series of meetings with all concerned with the parliamentary side of the planned state funeral, which we were determined should be appropriate for the great man. Herbert Bowden and I felt it seemly, in view of his condition, that we should cancel all Party political broadcasts. Everyone agreed except George Brown, who was to have done one of them.

On Thursday 21 January there was to be a full-scale debate in the Commons on comprehensive education. On the previous Tuesday, the Cabinet considered a proposal by Michael Stewart, Secretary of State for Education and Science, that he should announce legislation requiring recalcitrant local education authorities to end selection at eleven. In spite of a lucid explanation by Michael, the Cabinet rejected his plea and decided that the case for comprehensive schools should be put to the local authorities in a carefully drafted circular which asked for their cooperation. After an appropriate period of, say, a year, we would be able to judge how far we could move without legislation. But our manifesto had said 'secondary education will be reorganised on comprehensive lines.'

104

And so a third dream receded in almost as many weeks – transport, Crown Lands Commission, comprehensive education. I was extremely apprehensive about the effect of these retreats from the manifesto on our backbenchers and on the Labour Party outside Parliament, for their support and enthusiasm alone could sustain us in office.

On the day before the education debate Leslie Lever (Ardwick) came to tell me he could not support the Government in the division and would abstain. The debate was on an Opposition motion which did not condemn comprehensive schools but asked the Government to discourage local authorities from adopting schemes 'at the expense of the grammar schools'. Of course they wanted the best of both worlds – to give tacit support to comprehensive schools but, at the same time, to be the defenders of the grammar schools, which was a thoroughly illogical posture. 'The destruction of the grammar schools', as he put it, was the theme of Quintin Hogg's speech when he opened for the Opposition. By overstating his case, as usual, he drew the wrath of ardent Labour speakers such as Will Hamling (Woolwich West) that would otherwise have been directed at our own front bench for our failure to announce legislation. His oratory also kept the Liberals out of the division lobby. We had majorities of 27 and 18 and were grateful to Mr Hogg. Unfortunately, our amendment, on which the final vote took place, was almost as illogical as the Opposition motion it replaced. In everything we said on comprehensive schools the Prime Minister was quite adamant that we retain the contradiction which had appeared in our manifesto, also at his insistence, that 'within the new system grammar school education will be extended.' He too wanted the best of both worlds.

But disaster struck us elsewhere on the same day. In spite of opinion poll forecasts showing a swing to Labour of 4-5 per cent, our share of the votes in the Nuneaton by-election fell from 81.1 per cent to 60.8 per cent. Frank Cousins was elected with a greatly reduced majority of 5,241 (11,702 at the General Election). But worse was to come. A recount was announced at Leyton, and later in the evening we heard that Patrick Gordon Walker had lost by 205 votes.

Our majority was now down to three. 'It shows,' said the Leader of the Opposition, 'that the country is ready to turn to a Conservative Government the moment the opportunity offers.' And Quintin Hogg, never at a loss for a colourful comment, saw it as the verdict of an electorate 'who will not be ridden over rough-shod by any would-be Napoleon', ignoring the fact that a Tory MP had resigned from St Marylebone to provide him with a seat.

There were, I believe, three reasons for this miserable result. First, the electors of Leyton resented their MP being 'kicked upstairs' and having someone else foisted on them. Reg Sorensen, their previous Member, had given the impression that he had been summoned to the Lords reluctantly, but this was far from the truth. He was delighted to go! Secondly, although race was not made an issue officially by the Tories, we had many reports of it being raised by their canvassers on the doorsteps. And, thirdly, the unpopular measures we had been forced to take, in particular our failure to raise pensions immediately, had caused us at least temporary unpopularity. The pension issue came up at every public meeting. Some of our backbenchers who had bared their consciences to the world on this issue had a good deal to answer for.

Jo Grimond declared that he knew the reason for our defeat. 'The result,' he said, 'makes nonsense of the Labour Party's proposal to nationalise steel.' But steel had not been mentioned to a single Labour canvasser nor raised at any of our meetings.

George Wigg was convinced that with better organisation we could have won the seat, but I did not believe him.

Quite apart from its depressing effect on the Party in the House, the Leyton result reduced our majority to three, and few thought we could survive much longer. We were in midwinter, a time when illness and sometimes death take their toll. Who could say what blows fate had in store for us in the coming weeks. The press gloated over our imminent demise and the Tories redoubled their efforts to prepare a manifesto for the coming General Election. Ted Heath got himself selected to take charge of this preparatory work, and so stole a march on his rivals for the Conservative leadership.

The Whips redoubled efforts to ensure that the Government did not fall because of any kind of avoidable accident or mischance. I was quite determined to achieve the objective I had set before the Party at the Church House meeting: that the Prime Minister choose the date of the election in his own good time.

The defeat of Patrick Gordon Walker meant that he could no longer remain Foreign Secretary. From the 1979 General Election until the Falklands War, Lord Carrington served as Foreign Secretary with a deputy answering for him in the Commons. But it is extremely doubtful whether the Labour Government could have got away with this arrangement in 1965, when MPs were still extremely interested in foreign affairs – a hangover from our imperial past. Today the emphasis in British politics is on economic affairs. In any case, the Prime Minister believed that the Foreign Secretary should always sit in the Commons. He offered this key post to my colleague Herbert Bowden, who was earning a reputation for steadiness and good sense as Leader of the House – and, Harold told me, he looked like a Foreign Secretary. This strange quirk of Harold's often appeared during his premiership. He liked people to look the part. When Callaghan was angling for the chairmanship of the World Bank during our period in Opposition from 1970 to 1974, Harold told me that he wanted me to become Foreign Affairs spokesman if Jim went, because I looked the way a Foreign Secretary should look!

However, modesty was another of Herbert's many excellent qualities and he turned the Foreign Office down because he felt he was not equipped for it. But I believe the reason he was asked to take it on was because Harold was enthralled by global politics and wanted a Foreign Secretary who would allow him to have the major role.

His eventual choice was Michael Stewart, Secretary of State for Education and Science. The Prime Minister's regard for Michael had obviously grown enormously since we came into office. After Roy Jenkins had refused the job, Tony Crosland, who had already made a considerable

107

name for himself as Brown's deputy at the Department of Economic Affairs, was made Secretary of State for Education and Science. He brought an elegance of deportment, expression and manners which the department sorely needed. His circular inviting local authorities to reorganise their secondary schools proved to be one of the best-constructed documents of all the Wilson years, as well as one of the most memorable and significant in the history of English education. It went some way towards mitigating the Cabinet's failure to take a stronger line on comprehensive schools.

The appointment of Crosland was widely welcomed by our backbenchers, who believed he would take a tougher line with the Treasury on behalf of the schools – and every constituency was crying out for a bigger school building programme. Unfortunately, Ministers of Education are all too often judged by the resources they can extract from the Chancellor of the Exchequer. Tony Crosland understood this and set about achieving objectives which did not involve great cost, such as boosting teacher-training facilities and establishing the polytechnics – though not everyone was happy about the binary system of higher education which developed as a result. Perhaps because he was a Treasury man himself (and they are born, not made), he was less successful with his major education budget. In particular, he had to embark on the changes in secondary education by persuasion, but without making any additional capital expenditure available. As a result, even good Labour local authorities refused to budge without extra capital authorisations. In spite of all the efforts of Tony Crosland and his successors, of whom I was one, the Government's refusal to legislate and the Chancellor's refusal to make funds available meant that comprehensive reorganisation was often a botched-up job from the start.

Michael Stewart's translation to the Foreign Office was welcomed on the right of the Party, but the left had doubts about him and a deputation came to see me to protest about his appointment. I believe he was aware of these doubts and made great efforts, at any rate in the early days, to win wide support for his policies among our backbenchers.

Unfortunately, his unflagging support for the United States was widely resented not only on the left but also across the centre of the Party. Of course, he was doing no more than maintaining the official posture of the Government.

Sunday 24 January was our hundredth day in office – a day, I thought, for celebration. But early in the morning I received a phone call at my house in Glenridding from Freddie Warren to tell me that Sir Winston Churchill had died. I contacted Willie Whitelaw at his Cumbrian home a few miles away. He had succeeded Martin Redmayne as Opposition Chief Whip, and we discussed the arrangements for the state funeral, the tributes in the House the following day and the changes in parliamentary business which would follow. We had already decided that no normal business would be taken in the week preceding the funeral.

Back in London, we met each day to hear the vast number of tributes which poured in from legislatures around the world.

The break from the unrelenting parliamentary vigilance which is the Chief Whip's job enabled me to deal with the backlog of paper which had accumulated over Christmas and to see a number of MPs who had asked for half an hour of my time. But the loss of a whole week of parliamentary time was a serious blow to our hopes of getting the Queen's Speech proposals through Parliament in the current session, let alone the new legislation which the Cabinet was constantly adding to the programme despite the warnings of Herbert Bowden and myself.

But the break also enabled me to see more of the Prime Minister, and in the week after the Leyton defeat we needed time to take stock of our situation. I had a long talk with him late on the Monday evening. He agreed with my view that in spite of our relatively easy survival so far and the brave face we had put upon our prospects, the chances of the Government lasting much longer were not high – and that it would therefore be prudent to try to win some popularity. I had been getting increasingly worried about the attitude of a number of senior ministers who appeared to be sliding into the mentality of the 1945-50 Government, which believed that the electorate were all high-minded citizens who would gladly accept rationing, restraints and higher taxes for the long-term good of all. In fact, they are mainly just ordinary, decent folks whose first thought about every government is how it will affect them and their families. Cynical, maybe – but Harold agreed. He felt the Government was suffering far too many self-inflicted wounds. He thought the Chancellor should do much more to help ministers to improve our image and felt that every department could find proposals which would be popular but not be costly in either cash or parliamentary time – our two commodities in shortest supply.

A similar theme emerged the following morning when the Cabinet met with a nominal agenda so that the Civil Servants could leave after a few minutes. There were two views. The Callaghan view argued that we should follow what he called 'the absolutely honest' course. (Jim always did protest too much.) This meant doing what had to be done to put things right no matter how unpopular, and damn the consequences – even if this meant losing office for many years to come, as it had in 1951. The Brown view, on the other hand, was that we would soon be facing the electors again. The election of a new Conservative leader to replace Sir Alec could not long be delayed. After that, the Opposition would move heaven and earth to unseat us. (In the event Ted Heath was not elected until 28 July.) Having taken our initial remedial action on the economy and safeguarded the poorest members of the community, we should now think of whatever time remained to us in terms of an election. We should therefore not only avoid unpopular measures but undertake popular ones. After all, George argued, three months of largely self-inflicted wounds followed by ten or twelve years in Opposition without the power to do anything would be of little help to the electors who supported us.

There was general agreement that all ministers had been so immersed in getting to know their departments and in getting their legislation off the ground that they had almost forgotten about politics. A fatal lapse in a democracy! One eye must always be kept on remaining in office, otherwise all one's efforts are in danger of being brought to nought.

All agreed that in 1965 they would act a great deal more politically than they had done since the General Election – without, of course, changing our policies or softening the tough measures we had taken.

One of my most agreeable meetings during the week was with Manny Shinwell, Chairman of the Parliamentary Labour Party, whose work complemented mine. I invited him to go to the annual conference of British, American and Canadian parliamentarians in Bermuda. This kind of invitation was one of the few remaining pieces of patronage the Chief Whip possessed, though I was still referred to in Parliament as the Patronage Secretary – especially by those who felt they were not benefiting from my residual powers. Also, with the Prime Minister's approval, I asked him if he would allow himself to be nominated for a CH; the Companionate of Honour is an exclusive and much valued order limited to sixty-five members. He was visibly touched, surprisingly for one long since inured to honours and flattery, and accepted.

We agreed that the party's posture, so far as we could influence it, should now be one of cheerfulness and confidence that we could continue in office as long as we wished. In the three months since the election, we felt we had got off to a good start. Harold, always an admirer of John F. Kennedy, set great store by our record in those momentous first hundred days. In a series of major speeches he set out our achievements as the dawn of a new era.

On the Wednesday of the pre-funeral week the National Executive of the Labour Party, still resentful that it was not made privy to every decision, set up yet another liaison committee between itself and the Government. It was to consist of the Prime Minister, the First Secretary, the Leader of the House, the Minister of Labour and myself from the Government, and the General Secretary, the Chairman, the Vice Chairman and the Treasurer of the Labour Party.

Meetings of the Officers' Committee, as it was called, were held weekly and penetrated quite far into highly confidential matters. They certainly informed the members of the committee, but whether they informed either the Government or the National Executive is less certain. Indeed, less than a month after it was established the committee was sharply criticised at a meeting of the Executive and Danny McGarvey of the Amalgamated Society of Boilermakers made his famous remark that the Executive was not going to be a cheerleader for the Government. In my view that is exactly what it should be, as the Labour Party exists solely to win and retain the power to implement its policies. The Prime Minister was convinced – I suspect by George Wigg, Marcia and others in his kitchen cabinet – that our liaison with backbenchers and the National Executive was poor, and became very restive. Herbert Bowden and I felt that there was no problem when ministers took the trouble to talk to our MPs in the tea room and bars and to visit their subject and regional groups. We also felt that nothing we did would assuage the resentment of Len Williams and certain trade union members of the National Executive that we and not they were running the country.

Later that day I had a long meeting with the Prime Minister to discuss a number of domestic issues, one of which was his desire to find himself an additional Parliamentary Private Secretary. The PPS is an unofficial, unpaid ministerial assistant, but the appointment is much sought after by ambitious young MPs because they believe, without much justification, that it may lead to a ministerial appointment. In the Labour Government the Prime Minister insisted on approving all PPS appointments made by ministers and he vetted them with great care – almost always asking if I was happy about them. In practice they fell into two categories: the dogsbody type, who fetched and carried for his minister; and the potential minister type, who was included in many departmental discussions and treated almost, but not quite, as a junior minister. Harold had a superb PPS of the first type in the universally popular MP for Jarrow, Ernest Fernyhough, but he now wanted a second one who could produce graceful and lucid prose. We discussed a number of names, and eventually he decided to appoint a promising young MP called Peter Shore (Stepney), a political economist who had been head of the Labour Party research department before the election. He soon proved to be an invaluable adjunct to the staff at No. 10. In the next two decades he rendered many an otherwise indigestible Party

112

or Government document intelligible and even attractive. Had all the kitchen cabinet been of his calibre the actual Cabinet would have been much happier about it. He and Harold developed such a rapport that he became known as the Sorcerer's Apprentice.

During the days when Sir Winston's body lay in state in the sombre splendour of Westminster Hall over three hundred thousand people filed past the catafalque. On the Friday evening the three Party Leaders and the Speaker took over the guard duties from the armed forces for a time, during which I escorted Mrs Wilson into the side of the dimly lit hall to watch the silent crowds move past. There was no sorrow – awe certainly and, perhaps above all, gratitude for the life of this giant of a man whose courage had inspired the world. Many were moved to tears.

Over these few days the Prime Minister had talks with a great many world statesmen who had come to London for the state funeral. He had a ninety-minute meeting with Ian Smith, the Rhodesian premier, who had invited himself to the funeral. Smith insisted on entering and leaving No. 10 through the garden, and actually denied to Lester Pearson and Sir Robert Menzies (the Canadian and Australian premiers) that he had had a meeting with the Prime Minister.

No progress was made on the constitutional problem, but he did agree that Arthur Bottomley, the Secretary of State for Commonwealth Relations, and Lord Gardiner, the Lord Chancellor, could go to Salisbury for discussions. He also reluctantly agreed that they could meet the two African leaders in prison if they wished. This visit took place at the end of February, but little was achieved except that the five principles on which our Rhodesian policy was based became more clearly and publicly defined. This clarification was applauded by all sections of the Parliamentary Labour Party and ensured that I would have no problems with our Members on this issue. Harold was seen – not only by our own supporters but, I believe, by the general public – as making a stand on the irreducible five principles while taking one initiative after another to reach a solution.

At another meeting – with Frank Aitkin, the Irish Foreign Secretary – Harold agreed that the remains of Sir Roger Casement, who had been hanged for treason in 1917, should be returned to Ireland for reinterment, after half a century of refusal to do so by successive British Governments. This took place in the early hours of 23 February and was announced in the House of Commons and the Dáil when the coffin arrived in Dublin. It gave considerable pleasure in the Labour Party, which has always had a close affinity with Ireland. (Indeed, green was still the party colour in 1964 on Tyneside, where I had my constituency, because at the turn of the century the founding fathers were mainly Irish.) It also removed an old irritant from Anglo-Irish relations. Of course, our opponents called it gimmickry – as they did most of the imaginative initiatives Harold took. In the later years of his Government he became hesitant about following his hunches because he felt this charge was trivialising the record of his administration. But, as the results of the 1966 and 1970 General Elections showed, the electorate loved the brainy, try-anything, go-anywhere, Harold Wilson better than the more orthodox version which emerged later.

Sir Winston's funeral at St Paul's brought together the greatest gathering of world leaders ever assembled. There were eight monarchs, and many presidents, princes and ministers from a hundred countries. The mood of the service was set by the rollicking 'Battle Hymn of the Republic' chosen by Sir Winston himself. 'Glory, glory, hallelujah, His soul goes marching on' was a fitting farewell to an age and to the maker of history who dominated it.

Afterwards the great steps before the west door were crowded with long-familiar figures, all waiting in the cold of the January morning for their cars. There were many from the war years, looking older than we remembered them. Eden, Attlee, Menzies, Erhard, Ben-Gurion, Eisenhower, Marshal Koniev – and the monumental figure of General de Gaulle towering over all. It was like a time capsule, a last rollcall this side of eternity of the Churchillian era.

114

II

To the sleepless summer

A few days after Sir Winston's funeral we had another sharp reminder both of our mortality and of the vulnerability of our Government when the Labour Member for Abertillery, the Rev. Llewelyn Williams, died in a Newport street. He had won the seat by a massive majority of 20,231 at the General Election and so there was no fear of losing it now. And fortunately, from a whipping point of view, the Conservative seat of Roxburgh, Selkirk and Peebles was also vacant at this time and the by-election was not to be held until 24 March. This meant that we still had our majority of three – at least until that date – and so we arranged to hold the Abertillery by-election a few days later.

We held Abertillery with a majority only 29 votes fewer than in the General Election. The Conservatives lost Roxburgh, Selkirk and Peebles to the twenty-seven-year-old Liberal, David Steel. As the Liberals voted with us occasionally, this was something of a gain for us.

By far the most troublesome political problem I had to contend with among our backbenchers in the New Year was the Government's nominally neutral but in fact pro-American attitude towards the escalating war in Vietnam. Our reliance on United States support for sterling forced us to refrain from any overt criticism. There was, however, considerable pressure being exerted by the Prime Minister on President Johnson to at least prevent any further escalation – but to little avail. Indeed, after the first bombing raid on North Vietnam – following a severe raid by the Viet Cong near Saigon in which a club used by US servicemen was destroyed – Johnson rebuffed a late-night protest from the Prime Minister in terms that one may have expected from an official of the Teamsters' Union but not from the President of the United States. 'I won't tell you how to run Malaysia and you don't tell us how to run Vietnam,' he stormed at Harold. The conversation is quoted verbatim in *The Labour Government 1964-70*.

These behind-the-scenes efforts by Britain to stop the spreading of the war to the North which were unsuccessful – and to prevent the use of nuclear weapons – which were successful – could not be made known in detail because nothing could be said or done which

117

would upset Washington. Most of our MPs grasped this, but a sizable minority refused to understand, as did the non-ministerial members of the National Executive.

After the bombing of the North an anti-US motion was tabled by Sydney Silverman. The Whips immediately went to work to persuade Members not to sign it but, in spite of all our efforts, it attracted over fifty signatures – not all from the left of the party. In addition, Silverman and others demanded a special meeting of the Foreign Affairs Group of the Party. Unfortunately, the American press tended to equate these rather innocuous study groups with the powerful committees of Congress. Because of this it was important that nothing was decided at this meeting which could be misunderstood on the other side of the Atlantic. The Whips were entirely successful in ensuring this by persuading large numbers of moderate Members to attend the meeting.

Immediately we had averted this danger another one arose. We heard that Konni Zilliacus (Gorton) was collecting signatures for a telegram of protest which he proposed to send to President Johnson. Once more the Whips had to scurry around the corridors of Westminster dissuading possible signatories whom we thought might be amenable to reason (and of course some were not!).

Manny Shinwell and I got together to consider what could be done to restrain Members from this kind of embarrassing activity – not an easy problem in view of their zealously guarded freedom of action. Eventually we persuaded the Party that all notices of motions which our Members proposed to put on the Order Paper should first be left with me for twenty-four hours. To attempt to enforce this 'rule' by disciplinary action would have been a breach of parliamentary privilege, but throughout my whole period as Chief Whip it was meticulously observed by almost every Labour MP.

On 3 March Sydney Silverman brought to me another motion on Vietnam which, though entirely acceptable to me personally, was wholly unacceptable to the Government. The next day, after a few friendly haggles, he allowed me to rewrite it in terms which I had agreed with the Prime

Minister. This was the third left-wing motion I had rewritten under our new procedure.

The following week I was invited to lunch by Al Irving, a First Secretary at the US Embassy in London, who was becoming alarmed at the anti-US rumblings in the Party. Al was an extremely reasonable man, greatly respected and trusted in the Labour movement. I suspected he felt much the same about the American involvement in Vietnam as we did. I left him in no doubt about the ferment beneath the surface of the Parliamentary Party, indeed of the whole Labour Party, and portrayed myself as sitting on the lid of a powder barrel in the interests of Anglo-US relations. I told him that if there was any further escalation, particularly in the use of nuclear weapons, there would be no way of holding the situation.

Not only was there unrest in the Party about our tacit support of the Americans – and it was believed by some that we had entered into certain secret commitments with them – but the left of the Party still saw the war in Vietnam as a patriotic nationalist uprising by the Viet Cong. On 12 March the Prime Minister, in an exchange at Question Time, set out to scotch this view and insisted that it was now a war by North Vietnam on the South, and that this took it beyond civil war. He went on to say that the United States would withdraw their forces from Vietnam 'in the event of a prompt and assured cessation of aggression by Hanoi.' To our left, these words were like a red rag to a bull.

Immediately after Question Time, William Warbey, who was as far to the left as it was possible to be at that time, came knocking at my door demanding to see me at once. He described Harold's performance as 'the end' and accused him of lying on behalf of the United States. Looking back over my diary for those years, I seem to have spent half my time in long, complicated discussions with Mr Warbey. He was passionate but always courteous, though quite impervious to reasoning of any kind. I soon learned that the most effective way to handle him was to listen, allowing the torrent of his anger to pour over me until it was spent, and I think he felt better for it. Indeed, I was the Labour Government's full-time scapegoat, bearing their wrath and their sins on my back out into the wilderness.

I reported Bill Warbey's outburst to the Prime Minister, who neither showed nor expressed any concern at incidents of this kind, but I knew from experience that he felt them all deeply – and remembered them. He invariably began to look for some compensatory action which he could take to neutralise the complaints and, hopefully, the complainants. On this occasion I had not long to wait. Two days later, on his eightieth birthday Manny Shinwell showed me a motion on Vietnam which he proposed to table. It was also signed by Philip Noel-Baker (Derby South) a Nobel Prize winner, and Arthur Henderson (Rowley Regis and Tipton) the son of another Nobel Prize winner, both ex-ministers. Those three names made it as influential and respectable a motion as it was possible to get. But a fourth signatory was Sydney Silverman! My already considerable opinion of Harold's skill and cunning went even higher when I saw this, for the motion not only encompassed the Party establishment but also a pillar of the left wing. Although he did not tell me he was behind it, and I was careful never to ask him, it had Harold's fingerprints all over it. I knew the US Embassy would be very interested in its parentage and, absolutely predictably, the next morning Al Irving came to No. 12 to enquire whether it was officially inspired. I was able truthfully to deny this to the best of my knowledge – though I did not allay his suspicions.

On 22 March there was a report that the Americans were using napalm bombs and gas. This triggered off another anti-US motion from John Mendelson and Tom Driberg (Barking), which, because of the disquiet we all felt, I did not amend or hold up for twenty-four hours.

Before the end of March five parliamentary private secretaries, led by David Ennals (later Lord Ennals), broke ranks by sending a statement on Vietnam to the press. Apart from the rules under which these unpaid ministerial assistants operated, this was a blatant breach of our standing orders. I had to send for David, and dressed him down in the most severe headmasterly manner I could muster.

On 30 March we received a report that the United States Embassy in Saigon had been destroyed by a carload of explosives. We were very apprehensive that American retaliatory action against the Viet Cong would lead to a further escalation of the war, which, it was becoming obvious, the United States could not win. The Cabinet held a special meeting, with Vietnam at the head of the agenda. Mysteriously, this agenda was leaked to the press, indicating the Government's concern at the situation.

At the Liaison Committee meeting the following day, Manny Shinwell complained that a number of senior ministers were not supporting the Government's neutral position on Vietnam, either in private conversations with backbenchers in the tea room or in their weekend speeches. Indeed, there was a deafening silence on the subject each weekend.

Meanwhile, the Chancellor of the Exchequer had been getting down to the daunting task of planning public expenditure and taxation in relation to industrial production estimates for some years ahead. We had inherited a programme of expenditure commitments which bore little relation to the productive capacity of the economy to finance them, and high-spending ministers such as Peggy Herbison (Social Security), Tony Crosland (Education), Dick Crossman (Housing) and Fred Peart (Agriculture) were all desperately anxious to lay their hands on a bigger share of the cake. Peggy had succeeded with the increases in social benefits; Dick was using every trick he knew to get the housing programme increased; and Tony Crosland knew he was unlikely to get very far with the comprehensive school reform unless he won approval for a great deal more capital expenditure on school building. And looming overall was the colossal problem of defence spending.

On the Thursday of the Churchill interregnum week, the Chancellor set out his plans to the Cabinet. The choice was depressing in the extreme. It was what we soon learnt to recognise as typical Treasury blackmail. Public expenditure could be allowed to grow at the rate of 4.5 per cent a year, but this would involve increases in taxation unless defence spending could be cut by at least £100 million in 1965 and more subsequently – which Denis Healey said could not be done, although he achieved prodigious economies as the years went by. Nor was there much to be gained by re-examining and re-casting the programmes we had inherited, with the exception of such costly projects as the TSR 2 plane and Concorde. Many of them were so far advanced that, like Macbeth, 'returning were as tedious as go o'er'.

Two other items added to our gloom at this meeting. Fred Peart was preparing for the annual farm price review and wanted permission to start negotiations with the farmers by offering an additional £10 million, and this after an increase of £30 million the previous year. His proposal would have added ^{1}/2d. to the price of a pint of milk on the doorstep. Needless to say it got short shrift from the Cabinet, which was anxious to hold down the cost of living for the poorer members of the community. However, by 31 March Fred had got his additional £10 million and parliamentary approval for his price review, though the Liberals opposed it. As always, the farmers reacted angrily and announced that they were going to send a live chicken to every MP to call attention to the injustice they had suffered. I made arrangements to send Guy's Hospital any that came to Labour MPs. But none came.

Anthony Wedgwood Benn raised the unresolved problem of Post Office finances and once more proposed substantial increases in most postal rates. The debate on his paper, like the debate on the price of milk, generated a good deal of heat – especially his proposal to put the 3d. letter postage up to 4d. It was vehemently opposed by Frank Cousins, who was implacably opposed to an incomes policy and favoured holding prices. But there was a reluctant majority view that the increases were unavoidable. At a later meeting they were agreed and embodied in an excellent White Paper on the Post Office which was debated on 30 March – the day on which we all attended the memorial service to Herbert Morrison in Westminster Abbey.

The Opposition's motion on which the Post Office White Paper was debated regretted 'the proposals contained therein for dealing with the financial problems of the Post

Office'. What a nerve! They were problems which had been swept under the mat before the General Election. Tony Wedgwood Benn made a splendid speech which aroused all the righteous indignation of our Members against the Opposition, always good for the morale of a party in power.

But on that cold Thursday in early January the Cabinet's dilemma was inescapable – 4.5 per cent annual growth, but only if defence was cut drastically, or if private consumption was cut by an equivalent amount.

After the meeting Jim sat with William Ross and me at lunch. When that happened, there was always a reason for it. Jim did nothing without a purpose. After a few avuncular pleasantries he went out of his way to repeat his argument that he could not avoid a draconian (an adjective often used by Treasury ministers when they wanted to terrorise the Government) increase in taxation unless he got his £100 million defence cut. But he felt sure we two really understood his predicament (this was code for he felt sure we did not) and would support him. Anyhow, he added, a cut in defence spending would be popular in the Party.

Two weeks later the Cabinet returned to Crossman's demand to increase the housing programme by 14,000 houses, which was still opposed by the Chancellor – not, he assured us, because he was against building more houses, but because this piecemeal staking of claims and pre-empting of resources by departmental ministers made any sensible planning of priorities impossible. As the irresistible Dick had met the immovable Jim, the Prime Minister deferred the matter until further details were available about the additional houses. Of course, with another election on our minds, every member of the Cabinet had a lively interest in where it was proposed to build them.

Meanwhile, the Whips and I were fending off innumerable attempts by our backbenchers to raise the housing programme in the Commons. Many, I believe, were inspired by Dick Crossman himself. As always when there was disquiet, I reported to the Prime Minister. As a result, I suspect, Dick got his enlarged programme – but on condition that there would be legislation to curb other, inessential building. For good measure he also got approval for another new town. He had not been in psychological warfare in the Second World War for nothing.

On 14 February Herbert Bowden and I met the Chancellor and agreed that he should introduce his Budget on 6 April. He confirmed what we already feared, that it would be one of the longest Finance Bills ever introduced, with well over one hundred clauses. The prospect of days and nights of mounting fatigue, locked in battle with the Opposition, trying to get the Bill through the House of Commons with our majority of three, appalled Bowden and me. But Jim was quite determined to be more than a run-of-the-mill Chancellor. He wanted major fiscal reforms to his credit in the history books. Indeed, when he announced his intention to introduce a corporation tax – which the Treasury had been trying to sell to successive Chancellors for years – he said, 'It is a landmark in our fiscal history such as we have rarely been able to create in this country.' But what, I wondered, would be the cost of his bid for fiscal immortality to the health of our loyal Labour MPs?

On 22 February he made a statement to Parliament on the Annual Estimates after the Cabinet had considered it only six hours previously.

The Civil and Defence Estimates for 1965-66 showed an increase in public expenditure of 8.9 per cent over the current year, but half of this was attributable to price increases. Defence estimates were up 2.3 per cent in real terms. Growth of public sector expenditure was to be related to the prospective rise in production. This meant, he forecast, that over the next five years public expenditure would rise by 4.5 per cent at constant prices – 'taking one year with another' (a mysterious phrase which became very familiar and which no one ever really understood). But this would mean a corresponding 'containment' of the rise in private consumption. Details of how this ominous x in our equation was to be quantified would have to await the Budget and George Brown's National Plan, which was expected to see the light of day in about a month.

And so nothing had changed since the long and agonised discussions in Cabinet early in January. The Treasury, as always, had got its way. The truth was dawning on us that it is the Chancellor of the Exchequer who makes or breaks a government, provided the alliance between him and the Prime Minister holds. In our case, it still did in February 1965. The fact that they occupy adjoining, intercommunicating houses in Downing Street is no accident. It recognises a basic relationship which lies at the heart of any government in this country.

The following day we got our worst press since coming into office. 'LIVING BEYOND OUR MEANS', was the heading of the leading article in *The Times*. Predictably, its major criticisms were that 'private consumption is to be treated as a mere residual'. Productive investment and exports would also 'have to fight for what is left after the Government have taken their bite', and that the policy 'virtually ignores the fact that in an immediate cash sense Britain is near bankruptcy.' But after this scathing criticism it decided to suspend judgment until the Budget!

Not unexpectedly, after the poor reception of the Chancellor's statement, sterling became very weak again and had to rely on a good deal of Bank of England support but the death of the popular Princess Royal diverted the public's attention from our financial problems for a little while.

I also had my worst bout of grumbling so far from our MPs. The disquiet surfaced immediately after the statement, at a meeting of all PPSs which I had called at No. 12 – and they could always be relied upon to reflect the views of their ministers. And again in the evening, when I went with the Prime Minister to a meeting of the Lancashire and Cheshire Group of Labour MPs, one of a series of visits he was making to all the regional groups. In the six weeks between the Estimates statement and Budget Day, no few than twenty-seven Members asked to see me to express their fears about the Government's strategy. A typical entry in my diary reads: 'Reggie Paget called in to see me to play hell about the Government's economic policy'.

I had to explain to them all, and many were newly elected and inexperienced, that the Estimates really revealed little about the Chancellor's strategy. They would have to wait until the Budget was introduced in early April to see the whole picture. But the more thoughtful of our Members were now becoming apprehensive about the National Plan by which they had set great store. It was beginning to dawn on them that no matter how fine its objectives, they would have to be achieved within the cat's cradle of public expenditure, private expenditure and taxation created by the Treasury and adopted so enthusiastically by the Chancellor.

Had we enjoyed a normal working majority and been assured of a full five years' Parliament, I suspect there would have been no great problem. But, with the probability of a General Election hanging menacingly over our heads, our MPs were fearful that we might be driven out of office before we had any real achievements to our credit.

I was also encountering a number of minor but troublesome matters which are the lot of every Chief Whip. On 9 February Bob Mellish, the down-to-earth Catholic Parliamentary Secretary at the Ministry of Housing, came to tell me that he had heard that two Conservative MPs were going to Pentonville Prison the next day to interview a prisoner who had alleged that another young prisoner was receiving special privileges because of the intervention of Lord Longford.

Lord Longford, Leader of the House of Lords and also a distinguished Catholic, had for many years taken an active interest in the welfare of prisoners and in penal matters generally – as he still does today.

I asked Alice Bacon, Minister of State at the Home Office, to make enquiries. She found no evidence whatever that Lord Longford had used his influence improperly as a senior minister to secure special privileges for the prisoner. Nevertheless, certain Opposition Members were clearly trying to make it appear quite otherwise. Herbert Bowden and I discussed it with the Prime Minister at Prayers a few days later. Harold, always anxious to head off trouble, took an unexpectedly serious view of the activities of these Tory MPs and decided to see Lord Longford with the Home Secretary and Sir Charles Cunningham, Permanent Secretary at the Home Office. I thought that this was rather exaggerating the importance of the matter, but Lord Longford was duly summoned and came to see me in No.

12 to find out what this high-powered meeting was about. It was common practice when a minister was unaccountably summoned to No. 10 for him to call in to see me – in the quite erroneous belief that the Chief Whip always knew what was going on.

When I told him, he was astounded and quite incapable of understanding how his humanitarian interest in a prisoner could be misunderstood and why certain Tory MPs should take such an excessive interest in it. A fortnight later we heard that Brigadier Terence Clarke (Portsmouth West) had also been to Pentonville to interview another prisoner about Lord Longford's activities.

Unfortunately, but inevitably, the matter was leaked to the press and John Gordon commented on it in his vitriolic column in the *Sunday Express*.

Lord Longford was not the only minister who caused me problems about this time. On 1 February the Whips heard that Austen Albu (Edmonton), Minister of State at the Department of Economic Affairs, had arranged for the Economics Group of Labour MPs to meet representatives of Burmah Oil Ltd, who were campaigning vigorously and briefing Opposition peers against a provision in the War Damage Bill – a Government measure which was to come up in the House of Lords for its Second Reading a few days later. The association of a minister with efforts to defeat provisions in a Government Bill, no matter how innocent or well intentioned, could not be tolerated. And it added weight to a view which was gaining ground, particularly in the Lords, that we did not mind very much whether the provisions got through or not. I had to warn Austen Albu that the Government could not function if individual ministers went off at a tangent in this way.

We seemed to have entered a silly season among some of our ministers and backbenchers, and I was constantly having to devote precious time to deal with footling incidents of one kind or another. Maybe it was inexperience; maybe the strain of living dangerously was beginning to tell – especially among our new Members, who were not used to the murderous hours we worked and the unrelenting tension of parliamentary life.

Early in the year I discovered that one of our newly elected lady Members, who was a breeder of dogs, was using the House of Commons address in her advertisements in *Dog World*!

Then I had a few anxious moments with one of my fellow Members from the North-east with whom I was on very friendly terms. On 10 February Ted Leadbitter (the Hartlepools) announced to the press that he was resigning the Labour Whip because (of all things) the Postmaster General had refused to move a telegraph pole from the front of a constituent's house – and this when we had a majority of three! It took me half an hour to persuade Ted to withdraw his resignation and talk to the Postmaster General about it. I also rang up Anthony Wedgwood Benn, the Postmaster General, and told him to remove the so-and-so pole if that was what it took.

Three weeks later Ted erupted again, at a dinner given by an association of coal exporters. He took exception to some remark or other in a speech and noisily stumped out of the function in mid-meal – a gesture which the press loved, but hardly one which a government on a knife-edge majority welcomed.

But the most potentially damaging episode involving Ted came on 3 March when I read in the press that he was to be elected mayor of West Hartlepool in May. I could not, in any circumstances, agree to this. It might have been just possible in a London borough, but not in a town 250 miles away. I asked him to come to my room and told him in the bluntest of language, which only good friends can use to each other, that in no circumstances could he become mayor when the Government's existence depended on a majority of three. But, knowing that I was dealing with a strong-willed Member, I had, as well as this frontal attack, taken the precaution of asking Sara Barker, our National Agent, to ring up the Labour Party agent in Hartlepool and tell him to stop playing the fool with us.

Once he settled down to the demanding life of Westminster, Ted became one of the most able and respected of our constituency Members.

128

Edward Short,
(*Philipson Studios*)

The Polaroid photograph taken at a Christmas party in No. 10, and inscribed on the back by Harold Wilson: 'To a great Chief Whip on the occasion of the three-way split' (see page 208).

The author at work in No. 12 Downing Street.

The Prime Minister with the Government whips in the garden
of No.10, taken in the early summer of 1965.

Standing, from left to right:
Brian O'Malley, Harry Gourlay, John Silkin, Jack McCann,
George Lawson, Ifor Davies, Joseph Harper, Will Howie, Alan Fitch.
Seated:
George Rogers, Charles Grey, Edward Short,
Harold Wilson, Sydney Irving,
William Whitlock, Harriet Slater.

Harold Wilson being presented with a picture by Mrs Bradshaw, MBE
in her home in central Newcastle, as Edward Short looks on.

elaxing at Glenridding after the long hot summer of 1965, with
'icky, a devoted companion.
'umberland News)

On the podium during the Durham Miners' Gala, 1973:
Mrs Wilson, Harold Wilson, Edward Short and Mrs Short.
(Newcastle Chronicle and Journal Ltd)

While this was going on, Jim Johnson (Hull West) showed me a quite outrageous and highly defamatory letter concerning him which his Labour colleague in Hull, Commander Pursey (Hull East), had circulated to all trade unions and ward Labour parties in the town. I sent immediately for the Commander, a colourful character, and told him to go to Hull that day and retrieve every single letter he had sent out and hand them to me the following day for destruction. I said if he did so, he might avert an action for substantial damages for libel which he would certainly lose – though I could make no promises; it would depend entirely on the goodwill of Jim Johnson.

A few days later the young and enthusiastic Member for West Lothian, Tam Dalyell, caused outrage among the ministers in the House of Lords. Tam had been elected chairman of the Party backbench Committee on Education and Science and apparently felt it should be a function of the committee to monitor the activities and speeches of ministers. Lord (C.P.) Snow, Parliamentary Secretary at the Ministry of Technology, had made some fairly innocuous remarks in the House of Lords. Tam took exception and sent him a rather peremptory summons to attend his committee to explain himself. Snow was greatly affronted, as were his ministerial colleagues in the House of Lords. I did not believe a breach of privilege was involved, but it called for the placating of the well-known literary figure turned minister and the gentle restraining, without discouragement, of an excellent young Member of Parliament. We had all assumed that Lord Snow, of all people, would be at home in the 'corridors of power' but he was strangely oversensitive to the countless pinpricks which everyone encounters there.

On 14 February Pat Duffy (Colne Valley), speaking at the annual social evening of the Saddleworth Labour Party, said that some Tory MPs were 'half drunk' and 'disgusting to look at' during a recent debate. 'I only wish some of their constituents knew about this,' he added for good measure. Naturally, this was fully reported in the *Sunday Express*. When interviewed by the press the following day he said he stood by everything he had said.

129

As I expected, these remarks were raised in the House on the Monday – the earliest opportunity, as the rules on privilege matters require. Sir Herbert Butcher (Holland with Boston) asked the Speaker to rule that it was a breach of privilege. The Speaker gave himself the usual twenty-four hours to consider the matter. Later in the evening Pat came to see me and we put together a short statement for him to make the following day which, I hoped, would get him off the hook on which he had impaled himself. However, when the Speaker ruled that his speech was a prima-facie breach of privilege and invited him to make a statement, he did not do so but left the chamber. The House voted to refer the offending words to the Committee of Privilege where the issue is finally decided. Pat was the only Labour MP to lose his seat at the 1966 General Election.

Quite apart from the privilege aspect, I was anxious that our Members should not get involved in personal abuse of this kind. It would not only harm the image of Parliament as a whole but would also increase the vulnerability of the handful of Labour Members whose drinking habits were causing me some concern. In addition, with a majority of three, I did not want Conservative and Liberal Members enraged by irrelevant personal jibes.

But the Government itself often made the relationship between the two sides of the House more difficult than it need have been. While the Conservatives were being rather careful not to precipitate another General Election so soon after the last one, at any rate not until they had settled their leadership problem which, decency directed, could not be done with undue haste, they probed every chink in our armour. And a troublesome small chink of our own making appeared early in the new year.

The boundaries of the County Borough of Northampton had been extended and consequently it was necessary to change the ward boundaries within the borough. Two schemes were put to the Boundary Commission. The first was drawn up by the town clerk and supported by the Labour majority on the council, and the second was prepared for and endorsed by the Conservative minority. The Commission recommended the second of these schemes to the Government and Sir Frank Soskice, the Home Secretary, accepted their recommendation without considering the local politics involved. The Northampton Labour Party was incensed at the decision. It was quite incomprehensible to them that the Labour Government should favour its opponents. The council immediately passed a resolution complaining that the Home Secretary's decision weighed heavily in favour of the Conservative Party and requested him to reconsider his decision.

Many of us, while disagreeing with his decision, believed that Sir Frank should now stand by it. However, at the instigation of a Cabinet committee engineered by Dick Crossman, he wrote to the council a week after its critical resolution, announcing that he was rescinding his decision and ordering a second enquiry.

The inevitable censure motion was put down by the Opposition and debated on 25 February. It accused the Home Secretary of yielding to party political pressure in a matter calling for the impartial exercise of his discretion. We won by eight votes.

The press reaction was what we deserved. The word 'gerrymandering' appeared in almost all the papers – even in the *The Times*. The whole episode was exactly the kind of unnecessary raising of the parliamentary temperature which I was trying to avoid. And it was particularly unfortunate that Sir Frank Soskice, one of the best-liked and most reasonable members of the Government, should be involved. It underlined what we were all beginning to suspect: that he was far from well. But, had it been one of our more truculent, abrasive colleagues, the row would have been all the greater.

These minor alarms and excursions were as nothing compared with the subterranean currents in the Parliamentary Labour Party about our proposal in the Queen's Speech and in our election manifesto to renationalise the steel industry. In spite of these clear commitments, immediately after the General Election the idea began to take root in the minds of some of our Members that our only chance of remaining in office was to abandon the proposal. The Liberals, though they did not want another election any more than we did, had subtly disseminated the impression that they would not gang up with the Conservatives to defeat us on any major matter except steel.

Woodrow Wyatt, the right-wing MP, and his collaborator, Desmond Donnelly, an ex-Bevanite who had now moved far to the right of the party, lost no opportunity to advocate an alliance with the Liberals at the cost of steel renationalisation. Woodrow Wyatt could not be ignored. He was a third of our majority; in addition, he wielded the powerful weapon of a weekly newspaper column.

On 3 February he invited me to lunch with him and Donnelly at his beautiful Regency house in Regent's Park. It was an excellent meal and a pleasant occasion. I reaffirmed the Government's intention to go ahead, no matter what the electoral consequences. I came away convinced that the two of them lacked sufficient steel in themselves to bring down the Government which they had been elected to support. The claim in Wyatt's book, *Turn Again Westminster*, that I offered him a ministerial post and then, when he refused, a 'trip around the world' is entirely apocryphal. I was in no position to make such offers. Equally untrue was the story in the evening papers on 17 March that they had been offered life peerages.

I reported my lunch conversation to the Prime Minister. He was not reassured by my view of their intentions; indeed, he was obviously beginning to have some doubts himself about outright renationalisation. I suspected that George Wigg had been feeding him horror stories about opposition developing within the Parliamentary Labour Party, and I became convinced that he was looking for ways in which the issue could be fudged.

Part of Woodrow Wyatt's tactics to frighten us off had been to allege that two other backbenchers, Dan Jones (Burnley) and Cyril Bence (Dunbartonshire East) would not support us. I interviewed them at once and was not surprised to find that we could count on their loyal support. Like all of us, they were apprehensive about a division on the Second Reading of the Bill to renationalise steel. As it

132

was a cornerstone of our policy, it had to be regarded as a matter of confidence if, as seemed certain, the Liberals voted against us.

What was much more difficult to handle than the Wyatt-Donnelly activity was an underground campaign among our Members to persuade, or force, the Government to abandon any hope of getting such a Bill through the present Parliament. Fred Bellinger (Bassetlaw), a minister in the 1945-50 Government, and at least two other ex-ministers were part of this campaign. We also had some evidence that a Cabinet minister and a minister of state were involved, though they were most careful to cover their tracks. And we heard of a meeting at the house of a minister at which six other ministers were present as well as a number of backbenchers.

The Whips were successful in piecing together all these and other snippets of information so that we had a reasonably accurate picture of what was happening beneath the surface of the Party and, by a series of plain-speaking interviews, I was able to prevent the bushfire from spreading. Any kind of conspiracy alarmed Harold, but in this case I was able to assure him that the matter was well in hand. As the underground rumblings continued throughout February I made it a major priority to track down every rumour to its sources and, by a mixture of persuasion and threats, to keep reluctant backbenchers lined up behind the Government.

But still the Prime Minister grew more alarmed and, on 3 March, he almost casually confronted a group of his Cabinet colleagues with an alternative to outright renationalisation. His idea was to get control of the steel industry by acquiring 51 per cent of the equity in each major company. We heard it without enthusiasm, and Herbert Bowden and I feared that a Bill to give effect to this proposal would almost certainly infringe the rules on hybridity in the House of Commons. We were asked to look into this and our enquiries confirmed our initial fears. A hybrid Bill is one which contains elements of both a public Bill and a private Bill, and a private Bill must be examined by a special committee which hears evidence from any private interests affected by it. But I believe the luke-warm reception of his plan convinced the Prime Minister that it was not really a starter.

On 16 March Harold and I attended a meeting of the West Midlands Group of Labour MPs, and the question of steel was raised by the young and ambitious MP for Sparkbrook, Roy Hattersley – as it was in all the groups we attended in the early months of 1965. Harold assured them all that we intended to honour our promise on steel. And so the matter was left – or so Herbert Bowden and I thought.

In the first week of March, the Prime Minister called into his study in Downing Street the Chancellor of the Exchequer, the First Secretary, the Lord President and me to discuss the timing of the next General Election. Harold was in favour of trying to soldier on until the end of 1966, while George Brown thought we should go to the country in the autumn of the present year and not attempt to live through another winter on our precarious majority. Indeed, if other by-elections went the way of Leyton, we would be forced to go, he argued. Herbert Bowden and I, in spite of all our problems in the House, favoured Harold's view, because by the end of 1966 the Labour Government would have demonstrated its ability to govern the country in a competent and moderate way. This meant we needed another session. In the morning Herbert and I had spent two hours together discussing the parliamentary timetable, and it was obvious to us that there was little hope of getting the whole of the Queen's Speech programme, itself only part of our election manifesto, through Parliament in the present session. The main cause of this depressing conclusion was the Chancellor's grandiose Budget, but the new Bills which ambitious ministers were constantly persuading the Cabinet to feed into the programme contributed to our problem.

Jim Callaghan sat on the fence, not caring much whether the election was in October 1965 or in October 1966 so long as it was enough time for him to earn his place in the pantheon of great fiscal reformers.

As so often happened in the Labour Government, the discussion degenerated into a heated argument about a different but related subject, this time between the

134

Chancellor and the First Secretary on whether or not we should sanction increases in coal prices and postal charges. George Brown, because he favoured an early election, adamantly opposed the increases. Jim Callaghan, putting the orthodox Treasury view that such increases were alternative forms of taxation, was equally strongly in favour of them. As always, the Treasury view prevailed. The inland letter rate went up from 3d. to 4d. on 17 May – an increase which aroused considerable anger among our Members.

Any argument for going to the country in the near future was dashed two months later. On 13 May the local elections were held to elect a third of the councillors in 356 local authorities in England and Wales. The Conservatives made a net gain of 552, Labour a net loss of 374 and the Liberals a net loss of 174. These results cast a pall of gloom over the parliamentary party but, we had to reassure our Members and ourselves, they were not quite as depressing as they appeared; when they were compared with the results three years earlier, when the same councillors were elected, and we had made considerable gains. Nevertheless, the Government now had no option but to carry on.

In mid-March we were confronted with the prospect of a conflict with the House of Lords. Our Chief Whip in the Lords reported to the Cabinet that their Lordships were likely to reject the War Damage Bill, against which Burmah Oil and others had been lobbying. The Prime Minister sent for Herbert Bowden and me and instructed us, with obvious relish, to prepare a very long list of potential life peers so that, immediately after each Government defeat in the House of Lords, he could announce the nomination of ten new life peers to the Queen. There was no problem about assembling such a list as we already had on our files over a hundred names, many self-nominated and others submitted from various sources. We quickly revised the list and selected the first ten. We were ready for battle – and on the whole it was a welcome prospect! Now, of course, this tactic could only have the desired effect if it was known to their Lordships, and so a non-attributable leak was arranged. The press immediately ran the story that we had a hundred names ready for submission to the Palace after our first defeat. The additional nought made our plan sound more uncompromising than it was. When this report appeared I had a deluge of phone calls from hopefuls throughout the country who felt that they were eminently suitable to be included.

But the Other Place, knowing, I suspect, that the Government could always give them a second chance to purge their defiance of the elected chamber by sending their amendments back to them for reconsideration, did in fact defy us and passed an amendment deleting Burmah Oil from the Bill. The Prime Minister, the Lord President and I met the Chief Whip and Leader of the Lords and decided that we would wait to see what happened when the Commons reinserted the amendment and sent the Bill back to the Lords. Eventually, discretion proved the better part of valour and they capitulated – much, I believe, to Harold's regret. What a marvellous diversion from our problems a conflict with the second chamber would have been!

In the last week of March Herbert Bowden and I made a major tactical error. We had noticed for some time that the Paymaster General was organising minor manoeuvres in the House of Commons. Many parliamentary questions and notices of motions were clearly inspired by him; speakers were being organised to speak in debates and, we observed, the Labour benches emptied when certain Opposition speakers were called. Anyone who has been a Member of Parliament long enough to get the feel of the House can sense orchestrated manoeuvres behind the normally unfettered and mildly chaotic flow of backbench activity. We knew George Wigg was operating behind our backs in procedural matters which had no possible connection with his ministerial job specification as laid down by the Prime Minister, but we took no action to restrain him as long as he did not inflame passions in the House. Bearing in mind our dangerously small majority, our constant aim was to live amicably with our opposite numbers on the Conservative front bench and, with William Whitelaw as Opposition Chief Whip, it was not too difficult to do so.

However, on Friday 26 March the House was to debate a Private Member's Bill introduced by Airey Neave, Conservative MP for Abingdon, the purpose of which was to give pensions to the 250,000 elderly people who were not entitled to them under the social security legislation. The Government was urgently considering the plight of some of these old people, but others were well-to-do and had opted not to join the national insurance scheme when it was introduced by the Attlee Government. It was a complicated problem and finding a solution would take some time. We also wished to consider this use of valuable and scarce resources in relation to other social priorities. We felt that our attitude was reasonable; after all, there had been a Conservative Government for the previous thirteen years, during which time nothing had been done to help these old people.

Many of our Members were worried about the odium which we would attract by voting against Neave's Bill. A large number came to urge me that the Government should pre-empt this Tory attempt to legislate, which, they felt, owed more to a desire to embarrass the Government than to tender feelings about the elderly.

The previous day's business was the debate on the Consolidated Fund Bill, traditionally used by backbenchers for a long series of short debates on any issues they care to raise. The debate almost invariably goes on all night, and George Wigg thought he saw an opportunity to deny Airey Neave a debate on his Bill and so relieve our Members of the need to vote against it. Under the rules of the House, if Thursday's debate does not end before 11 a.m. on Friday, the whole of Friday's business is lost. He set about organising sufficient speakers throughout the night to ensure that this happened.

On this occasion both the Leader of the House and I knew what he was doing. Tony Crosland raised it at Thursday's Cabinet meeting, and objected strongly. In retrospect we were quite wrong to go along with this latest piece of Wiggery. And to make matters worse, the press knew that the Government knew about it. *The Times* commented: 'That the front bench connived at this manoeuvre seems likely from the behaviour of Mr Wigg.'

At 9.42 a.m. Selwyn Lloyd moved the adjournment of the debate, and this motion was discussed until just before 11 a.m., when George Wigg intervened and spoke until after Big Ben struck eleven. He made an appallingly rude speech which was completely unauthorised by the Government. Quintin Hogg said of him: '. . . he has behaved with the same insolence and arrogance in power as he showed offensiveness in Opposition.'

George Wigg's own account of his intervention in his autobiography (*George Wigg*) bears little relation to reality. He was, in fact, the architect of the whole sorry incident. It was his first – and last – ministerial speech, which he attempted to justify presumably by describing himself as Paymaster General and Minister Without Portfolio. The latter part of this title was news to Bowden and me. The official list of Members of the Government certainly made no mention of it.

At 11.12 a.m. Airey Neave made a short but effective speech which reflected pain and puzzlement rather than anger at the Government denying him his debate by such methods. Obviously, he now expected a debate to take place on his Bill – though it would not be a Second Reading debate and would have no legislative effect. Peggy Herbison, Minister of Pensions and National Insurance, followed and deployed our perfectly reasonable position on his proposals. Anxious to extricate the Government from this foolish and damaging situation, as soon as Peggy finished her speech, I moved 'That the question be now put', to the fury of the Opposition, who had now returned to the chamber in larger numbers. This was carried by a huge majority.

During the division Tom Iremonger (Ilford), sitting in his seat and wearing the top hat which is kept under the Serjeant-at-Arms' desk for the purpose, raised a point of order. He asked whether it was in order for the Patronage Secretary (a title always used when a Member wishes to be rude to the Chief Whip) to practise a deliberate deception on the House. He was ordered by the Speaker to withdraw his remark, but the following weekend in his Cumberland constituency Whitelaw accused me of contemptible behaviour for having denied Neave a Second Reading debate on his Bill.

This procedural aggression was, in fact, what Herbert Bowden and I had tried to avoid. The incident was particularly unfortunate because of the sensitive nature of the business we had prevented. But we learnt our lesson and were quite determined to prevent any further incursions by George Wigg into our area of responsibility. Unfortunately, we were not entirely successful, either in the day-to-day business of Parliament or in a quite different field.

One of my duties as Chief Whip was to act as the official channel of communication between the Government and the BBC. But the Paymaster General, I believe with the knowledge of the Prime Minister, frequently operated clandestinely in broadcasting matters. I received information from my own sources in the BBC that whenever he heard a radio or TV programme which he believed to be biased, he rang up and demanded a copy of the script, instead of coming to see me about his complaint as all other ministers and MPs did. I had to make a number of complaints about political imbalance in various programmes and, as most of the newspapers were virulently anti-Labour and pro-Tory, the radio programme *What the Papers Say* was, in fact, a daily party-political programme on behalf of the Conservatives.

The Prime Minister was getting increasingly concerned about the attitude of the BBC towards the Government, and on 1 March he held a lunch in his private apartments in No. 10 to which he invited Hugh Carleton Greene – the Director General – his assistant Oliver Whitley, Herbert Bowden, who chaired the all-party committee on broadcasting, Trevor Lloyd-Hughes (later Sir Trevor), who headed the press office in No. 10, and me. In reply to our complaints about bias, the Director General said that he felt the Corporation got it about right because the Opposition complained as much as we did! And, he said, their complaints were not only about bias. During the previous week they had complained about a ministerial broadcast by Harold, not because it was controversial, but because it was 'image forming'. This was an entirely new ground of complaint to us.

The lunch was a convivial occasion but it did not in the slightest degree affect the indifference of the BBC to all our complaints. There was no discernible improvement until the 1966-70 Government, when I, as Postmaster General – with the agreement of the Prime Minister – appointed Charles Hill Chairman. His wisdom, toughness and experience of political life injected a much needed element of discipline into its editorial and production activities.

Meanwhile, rumblings were being heard from the Party about our apparent failure to make any major economies in defence expenditure. Our Members on the Left held the simplistic view that this was the key to finding the resources to implement our social policies. Battles were still being fought in Cabinet committees and in Cabinet itself about the ruinous projects we had inherited from our predecessors. Generally the Treasury was in favour of cancellation, while the ministers in the departments concerned wanted them continued.

The TSR 2 project was one of the most troublesome issues. This extremely advanced tactical-strike and reconnaissance bomber was developed for the RAF, but the original concept had been changed on a number of occasions during its long gestation. When we came into office it was designed to fly at twice the speed of sound and carry a strategic nuclear weapon. It had already flown, but a great many technical problems involving considerable costs remained.

By the beginning of March our long failure to agree on whether to continue with TSR 2 had dragged on for over thirty hours in Cabinet alone, and many more hours in Cabinet committees. The Chancellor of the Exchequer decided that enough was enough and demanded cancellation. But one of the problems was that Harold had made some rather indeterminate promises in Liverpool early in 1964 about employment in the aerospace industry – and he was obsessive about keeping promises. However, he could always be relied upon to leave all the options open. The small print of what he said certainly allowed for closure, though the bold print seemed to indicate otherwise – and most electors and Labour MPs only read the bold print. The Cabinet as a whole was equally obsessive about avoiding any decision which would result in unemployment.

The views of our backbenchers, canvassed carefully by the Whips, fell into the minority, who – like Leslie Hale (Oldham West) – either had parts of the aerospace industry in their constituencies or were on the right of the Party and opposed to any defence cuts, and the majority who were constantly urging cancellation. But the majority, unlike the Chancellor, did not see cancellation as a useful measure of public expenditure restraint. To them the saving of £35 million a year would build many schools, hospitals and advance factories.

At the Cabinet on 1 April the Prime Minister, I believe at the behest of the Chancellor, was determined to get a decision to cancel. Unfortunately, we had to adjourn to go to Westminster Abbey for the memorial service for the Princess Royal. It was not possible to get the whole Cabinet together again until 10 p.m. Labour cabinets, in my experience, always talk far too much, but as the time crept up towards midnight even the most loquacious began to show restraint. At 12.30 a.m. the decision was taken to cancel this imaginative project on which so many hopes had been pinned in the services and the aerospace industry.

A number of factors, apart from the cost, influenced this decision. First, we had an option on an American plane, the TFX, though we had decided not to take it up yet. Both the cancellation of the TSR 2 and the option would be announced to the House by Denis Healey after the Chancellor's Budget speech – an arrangement which caused us a good deal of trouble and which we later bitterly regretted. Second, the decision became almost inevitable after we had informed the French Government on 19 January that we would continue with the prototypes of Concorde, another albatross which we had inherited.

As so often happened, a full report of our midnight decision appeared in the morning press. What a leaky Government we were!

*

141

On the morning of Friday 2 April the Chancellor of the Exchequer invited me to No. 11 for a private preview of his Budget proposals. I think he feared that, in view of the unfavourable reception of his Estimates statement, the Whips would have a major job on their hands to persuade our Members that his strategy was in line with the promises they had made to their electors. He also knew that if I had a few additional days to think over the proposals before Budget Day, I would be better able to deal with immediate criticisms. Jim was an astute politician and he recognised that his first major Budget would have great significance for the Government and for his future ambitions. Our Members were looking to it to define the economic strategy of the Government; its success or failure would determine whether we achieved any of our objectives in the industrial and social fields. Is it going to be the blueprint of a new Britain? they asked – or merely the same old stop-go, tinkering approach of recent governments, which was getting us nowhere? In view of the economic straitjacket we were in I felt it was probably as fair a package as it was possible to devise, though some of its proposals would be difficult to sell to all our supporters. But, equally, other proposals would not please all our opponents in the City of London and in company boardrooms. All the same, I was aghast at the prospect of the whipping problems when they came to be debated in a Finance Bill.

On the following Monday Jim revealed all, or nearly all, to the Cabinet, where it was reasonably well received. Of course, such is the strength of the Chancellor's position in the Government that whether the Budget met with approval or not, it was too late for any changes. This made some of our less docile ministers begin to chafe. The pre-Budget meeting once again demonstrated the utter unassailability of the No. 10-No.11 solar alliance in which George Brown was still a partner. But later in the Government's life, he was to find that he also had to knuckle under when he fell foul of Downing Street. The rest of the Cabinet were either the inveterate sycophants who always supported the alliance in the hope of preferment, or the slightly, but always politely, rebellious.

142

Jim Callaghan's speech was by any standard a superb parliamentary performance, one of the best I have heard in thirty-seven years at Westminster. It was probably the high-watermark of his long and distinguished career. It lasted for two hours and thirty-six minutes (including the resolutions at the end) and was a model of presentational skill, lucidity and courtesy.

True to form, for the first few minutes he depressed everyone by making it clear beyond doubt that he intended both to reduce public expenditure and to increase taxation. To make this announcement at the start was a cunning piece of psychology, for he knew that the House would be expecting severe measures. When he uncovered his proposals, they therefore appeared to be far more moderate than they really were.

It was a Budget with a number of easily understood themes. First, there was the encouragement of industry to be more dynamic and export-conscious. This, he emphasised, was the only possible key to the progress we had to make as a nation. Second, he spelled out his message to the trade unions. In return for sacrificing their traditional right to free collective bargaining and agreeing a prices and incomes policy, which George Brown was developing with them with some success, he would ensure absolute fairness of sacrifice between them, the employers and the City. Measures would include a redundancy payments scheme; a capital gains tax and other anti-tax-avoidance provisions on unearned gains; the disallowance of most business entertaining for tax purposes; and the ending of the initial allowance for company cars.

Third, recognising that his Budget speech was a major opportunity to educate our Members, he reiterated the relationship between public expenditure, personal expenditure and the level of industrial production, spelling it out in simple terms: 'My earnest wish is to see the nation freely and willingly devoting the necessary resources to satisfy the simple needs of ordinary men and women – a home to live in, a school to learn in, a hospital when we are sick and a modest living for the elderly. But the fulfilment of these plans jostles against the need for a healthy balance of payments as well as the desire by all of us as individuals for an increase in our own standards of living.' He was, he said, determined to achieve a planned balance between these social and economic priorities.

The higher taxation which he had so ominously threatened in his opening sentences was, when he reached it, mitigated by the saving on the cancellation of the TSR 2 project – which he made public for the first time – and by the higher postal charges, which would bring in an additional £32 million per annum. The modest increases in duty on cigarettes, beer, wine, spirits and motor vehicles were seen by our backbenchers as troublesome but much lower than they had feared.

There was no enthusiasm on either side of the House for the Corporation Tax proposal, except among a group of our Members who believed that it would show us to be a reforming Government and yet cost nothing in terms of resources. This view gained ground in the two Wilson Governments from 1964 to 1970 as the economic problems became more intractable. The Prime Minister himself was one of its principal advocates. The idea of earning a place in history as a great reforming Prime Minister increasingly appealed to him.

But the majority of our Members thought Corporation Tax irrelevant to the concept of fairness between one section of the community and another. It was a logical next step in the separation of the taxing of company profits from income tax, but its complications were such – and its sensitivity to the Conservative Opposition, with their close links with the City, so great – that most Labour MPs viewed its passage through parliament with little short of horror. 'We'll never get it through', was the comment all the Whips reported from their Members.

Unfortunately, the long debate which followed got off to an acrimonious start. After the customary brief first reaction speech by Sir Alec Douglas-Home, Denis Healey intervened, as the Chancellor had promised he would, to make a speech about the cancellation of TSR 2, and the House was immediately plunged into an appalling row which lasted for sixty-nine minutes. Initially it was on whether or not it was

144

in order to make a statement in the guise of a speech. And they had a point. Not unnaturally, many Members wanted to ask questions about TSR 2, but questions cannot be asked after a speech – though on this occasion the Chair allowed a small number. Herbert Bowden and I were accused of trickery. As they had threatened, the Opposition tabled a motion of censure which not only censured us for cancelling TSR 2, as well as other projects which had been announced previously, but also 'strongly deprecated' the method used for announcing it to the House. As it was an official Opposition motion of censure, the Government was obliged to find precious time to debate it. We were confident that we could defeat their attack as we knew we had the support of the Liberals, but we were concerned about the loss of a whole parliamentary day for a censure debate which, had we insisted on Healey making a statement instead of a speech, we could probably have avoided. The volume of legislation now queueing for parliamentary time was such that we could not afford any slippage in the programme.

We decided to retaliate and recoup our loss by a mean trick. We lopped a day off the Easter recess. When he was announcing the business of the week before Easter, the Leader of the House said: 'In view of the desirability of finding time to debate the Opposition censure motion, it will be necessary to ask the House to return not on Tuesday 27 April but on Monday 26 April.' What he was really saying was that he was going to teach the Tories not to be so trigger-happy with their censure motions. In fact, they had already used a whole day for a censure debate on the aerospace industry on 7th February.

The Budget had a reasonably good reception in the press, except for the *Daily Express* and the *Daily Mail*, and the Stock Exchange registered gains all round.

I spent Easter week with my wife and daughter as a visitor at the annual conference of the National Union of Teachers at Douglas, where the NUT, running true to form whenever there is a Labour Government, were in their most militant mood and rejected a 12 per cent pay increase. The highlight of the conference was a speech by Tony Crosland on his

145

fourteen-point plan for expanding the teaching force. What a credit he was to the Labour Government; what an incalculable loss we suffered by his early death a few years later.

The Prime Minister also was bringing credit to his Government in the United States, where he spoke to the Economic Club in New York on our financial and economic policy and reiterated our determination not to devalue the pound. He received considerable acclaim in the press on both sides of the Atlantic.

It was, in fact, a Government of enormous talent. With the benefit of hindsight, I realise we did not display this to the country or the world often enough.

Parliament reassembled on 26 April and the Prime Minister immediately called a meeting of the First Secretary, the Chancellor of the Exchequer, the Lord President, the Minister of Power and me to decide on the timing of the publication of our White Paper on the renationalisation of steel, which had been prepared on the lines of the manifesto. There was now no possibility of legislation in the current session but we felt we owed it both to our own supporters and to the industry itself to publish firm proposals and win parliamentary approval for them, as a basis for legislation in the next session. Some of our Members feared the debate this would entail and, even more, the eventual legislation; but to the great majority, as well as to the trade unions concerned, a Bill to renationalise steel was almost the Ark of the Covenant. In 1964, steel was an industry with sales of £1 billion, a labour force of 315,000 and a product which was used in at least half the manufactured goods we exported. At that time it had a dominating influence over the whole economy which no Labour Government could ignore. Our proposals had been settled in a Cabinet committee before Easter, but the compensation terms had to be kept secret until as near the point of publication as was technically possible.

We decided to publish the White Paper on Friday 30 April after the close of the Stock Exchange and, in order to minimise the manoeuvring and plotting on our own side of the House, to have the debate on the following Thursday.

As we were still uncertain about Woodrow Wyatt, Desmond Donnelly and, now, George Strauss, who had introduced the Bill to nationalise the steel industry in 1949, this was a calculated risk. To frighten the doubtfuls into submission, we decided to leak a story (from a 'reliable' but impenetrable source) that the Government would stand or fall on the result of the debate. The press rang my office constantly during the week about this rumour, only to be told that steel renationalisation was the most important proposal in the Queen's Speech and they must draw their own conclusions about what a defeat would mean to the Government. We had, of course, decided that if we were defeated, we would table a motion of confidence to be debated the following day, and this would have the support of all our Members whatever their views on steel.

These decisions were approved by Cabinet on 27 April. Desmond Donnelly came to see me alone, wrestling in anguish with his conscience. I was anxious to help him and suggested I send him to a meeting of the Council of Europe the following week, where I could have paired him with an Opposition Member, so that he could avoid the steel debate. He asked for twenty-four hours to think this over and returned the following day to say that he regretfully refused my offer and had decided to abstain from voting in the crucial decision. Woodrow Wyatt came to tell me that he too would abstain. These two abstentions would reduce our majority to one.

The Cabinet did not approve the compensation terms until the day before publication. They were to be based on the Stock Market quotation of the shares of the 14 major companies which were to be nationalised over the 61 months from October 1959 to October 1964. Frank Cousins vigorously opposed what he regarded as overgenerous terms. As Chief Whip, I hoped that this very fair treatment of shareholders would reduce the Opposition temperature in the House of Commons. In addition, we proposed to leave a private sector of 210 smaller companies.

The left of the Party immediately pronounced the settlement far too generous. Ian Mikardo told the press that he might vote against the White Paper, but I understood the code in which Mikardo spoke. I knew he would never, under any circumstances, vote against his own Government on anything as crucial to our credibility as steel. On the Tuesday he called to see me to give me this assurance.

The weekend press bubbled with excitement about our chances of survival now that we had come to the crunch. The proposals in the White Paper were almost submerged and forgotten by the more lurid papers in their obsessions with the parliamentary arithmetic.

I spent the weekend in Newcastle and marched in the May Day parade, which was ruined by the ragtag and bobtail collection of anarchists, communists, Trotskyites, etc., following on behind the Labour and trade union procession and heckling Michael Foot, who made one of his less inspiring speeches.

On the Monday morning I had a phone call from Mrs Hayman, the wife of Frank Hayman (Falmouth and Camborne) to tell me that he was ill and unable to come to London. Leslie Spriggs (St Helens) was seriously ill in the Manor House Hospital in North London and, I was told, could not be brought in to vote. Ellis Smith (Stoke-on-Trent South) was also ill. The Tory newspapers were cock-a-hoop when they heard about these casualties. I wrote to Woodrow Wyatt, Desmond Donnelly and George Strauss telling them that I was counting on their votes in the division lobby on Thursday. George Strauss replied to assure me that he would support the Government. Eventually I had letters from the others in almost identical terms, both making the amazing allegation that I had previously agreed to their abstaining, which was totally untrue.

William Whitelaw and his team of Whips were saying nothing about their casualties. In spite of all the efforts of my Whips, I could not get an accurate estimate of the Conservative sick. I suspected they had a number of Members who were too ill to vote because, as soon as Frank Hayman's illness became known, they offered to pair him with one of their Members. We knew that another Conservative, Anthony Marlowe (Hove), was ill but when we offered to pair him we were told he was going to be brought in at his own request. Shortly afterwards, however,

148

we had a phone call from Marlowe's son to say that he was much too ill to come to Westminster and asking if we would pair him! Of course, we said we would be delighted to do so – provided the Conservative Whips agreed. I began to wonder if perhaps they also had a sizeable sick list – particularly later in the week when the Opposition Whips' Office put out a feeler to my secretary about the availability of Labour pairs, but it was difficult to know whether this was a genuine request or merely a probing of our defences. It could have been the kind of bluff that Whips have used for generations to out-manoeuvre their opponents. However, it was clear that they were making prodigious efforts to get all their Members to Westminster for the vote.

All in all, it was my most trying week since the General Election. On the Wednesday the now defunct *Daily Sketch*, our most right-wing newspaper, sent a reporter to Downing Street to interview me on how I was coping with the pressure. No doubt they hoped the Government's demise was imminent.

The Parliamentary Labour Party held a special meeting on the White Paper. Thanks to an excellent speech by Fred Lee, Minister of Power, it was well received – apart from the compensation terms.

When the debate opened on Thursday 6 May I was still uncertain about the number of Conservatives who were unable to attend because of sickness. I was also still uncertain about Woodrow Wyatt and Desmond Donnelly. Woodrow Wyatt has since said: 'The Government (particularly the Prime Minister) were unable to tell whether I was bluffing or not but feared mightily that I was not.' (*Turn Again Westminster*.) I therefore had no option but to take the biggest risk I had taken since the General Election with the life of a Member. I arranged for Leslie Spriggs to be brought to Westminster in an ambulance with a doctor and nurse in attendance from his hospital in Golders Green. If he came within the confines of the Palace of Westminster his vote could be counted. When I went out to see him in the ambulance in Palace Yard he was unconscious and being sustained with oxygen.

149

Looking back, it was an appalling thing to do, but it was necessary to keep the Government in office. When he was restored to health he told me that I had been absolutely right. Iain Macleod led the Opposition attack with a hard-hitting but closely reasoned speech, as we had come to expect of him. Michael Foot, supporting the Government, warned that if the House of Lords interfered with the measure it would mean 'the end of that House'. Desmond Donnelly called the White Paper 'wrong-headed'; Woodrow Wyatt said he would not vote against it but that he had heard nothing which would induce him to vote for it.

George Brown wound up the debate, and in his closing sentence dropped a bombshell in reply to an interjection from Woodrow Wyatt. Reading from a piece of paper in careful, studied terms which immediately reduced the buzz of conversation to complete silence, he said that if the industry and the Conservative Party came forward with any proposals which would give public control for less than a hundred per cent takeover, we would listen. He then allowed Woodrow Wyatt to intervene, an almost unheard of thing to do in the closing seconds of a major debate, to announce that in view of this undertaking he would now vote for the White Paper. Herbert Bowden and I, as well as all the other ministers sitting on the front bench were dumbfounded at the carefully enunciated formula which appeared to be identical with the idea the Prime Minister had floated before Easter. The White Paper proposals had been approved by the Cabinet as the basis for a Bill, and the purpose of the debate was to secure parliamentary approval for them. But now, at the very last moment before a decision was to be made, the First Secretary was saying we would be prepared to consider a different plan. Had he said it earlier, he would have met a storm of protest from our own benches. As it was, they had scarcely recovered from the shock when the division was called.

We survived with a majority of four, with Woodrow Wyatt and Desmond Donnelly supporting the Government. I found it difficult to forgive them for all the anxiety they had caused the Whips over the previous week and for forcing me to risk the life of a fellow Labour Member.

Woodrow Wyatt lost his seat at the General Election in 1970 and never returned to the House of Commons. Desmond Donnelly later left the Labour Party to form a party of his own, but eventually joined the Conservatives. In 1974 he committed suicide in a Heathrow hotel.

The following day I flew to Newcastle with the Prime Minister and Mrs Wilson in a plane of the Queen's Flight to attend a ceremony at the University of Newcastle. Over breakfast we had the morning papers, all of which headlined George Brown's formula and revealed that Woodrow Wyatt and Desmond Donnelly had had discussions with him previously and agreed the wording with him. Harold, remarkably, I thought, did not appear at this point to take the uproar seriously and told me he had seen George Brown's words before the debate. But later, when a severe storm blew up in the Party over what was seen as trickery, he made no mention of having seen them. Was he a party to the manoeuvre? I suspect he was, but we shall never know.

Such was the severity of the storm that Harold had to call a special Cabinet on the following Tuesday to discuss the crisis in the Party. Brown explained frankly that he had agreed the words with the two dissidents to get their support in the division. He apologised to Fred Lee, the minister in charge of steel renationalisation, for not telling him – though he did not apologise for all the trouble he had caused me. It was arranged that the Prime Minister should speak to a special meeting of the Party the following day; the Cabinet, for the first time since the Government was formed, insisted on seeing what he was going to say and vetting it. Of course, his three-paragraph statement was leaked to the press long before the Party meeting. The second paragraph said:

Reference has been made to a willingness to listen to any representations from the industry. It is axiomatic that if the industry were to come forward with any proposals which stated their acceptance, as a final settlement, of public ownership of the principal individual firms, their willingness to contribute the resources of the Iron and Steel Federation, including their specialised agencies and subsidiaries, then clearly within that context the Government would consider any representations the industry might make. It would have to be made clear that such consideration will not be allowed to delay the Government's time-table.

151

Harold had an amazing Houdini-like ability to extricate himself and his Government from difficulties of this kind and, on this occasion, his old magic did not fail.

The behaviour of Woodrow Wyatt and Desmond Donnelly was raised at the National Executive of the party the following week. There were some unprintable comments, but Ray Gunter, who was in the chair, skilfully avoided a condemnatory resolution being carried.

June and July proved by far the most strenuous time in all my years at Westminster; indeed, it was probably the most demanding period of my life. It was sheer idiocy trying to force through the House of Commons an unbelievably complicated Finance Bill of 94 clauses with an almost nonexistent majority against an Opposition which had regained the confidence it lost after its election defeat, and this was visibly taking its toll on the health and temper of all our Members.

To make matters worse, the Finance Bill absorbed so much time that the Opposition's Supply Days, on which they choose the subject for debate, had to be delayed until the two weeks before the summer recess. We then faced no fewer than three motions of censure.

The inter-party battle was also sharpened by the imminent Conservative leadership election. The old method of selection had been replaced by a process which encouraged electioneering by the candidates. Ted Heath and Reggie Maudling, the frontrunners, were going all out to impress their Members with their suitability to step into Sir Alec's shoes. Ted Heath made the most of the countless opportunities which being in charge of the Finance Bill for the Opposition afforded. Without doubt, his work on the 1965 Finance Bill carried him into the leadership of the Conservative Party. William Whitelaw, in those days a close collaborator of Heath, whipped his troops during the passage of the Bill with a ferocity which was quite out of character. From his appointment as Chief Whip until the end of July 1965 he imposed 53 three-line whips. The Tory press, still trying to explain the Labour

152

Government's refusal to be beaten, were constantly repeating the myth that, of course, the Opposition were not really trying to beat us but that they could do so whenever they wished. In fact, during those hot, sleepless summer weeks they tried every trick in the book to defeat us – but always failed in spite of Liberal support in 90 of the divisions.

An unnecessary twist was given to the battle by a speech Harold made in Glasgow. The speech was an important attempt to create some 'quietus' (as he put it) on sterling speculation before the summer recess by announcing that there would be no General Election in 1965. But, unfortunately, he went on to boast that we had got the Finance Bill through the House of Commons without a single defeat. In fact, at the time, we had only completed the Committee Stage and many days of debate were still to come on the Report Stage and the Third Reading. He has since written that the rash boast was 'dictated more by hubris and a desire to pay tribute to my parliamentary colleagues on the platform' (*The Labour Government 1964-1970*). But it infuriated the Tories and they redoubled their efforts to defeat us.

Between Budget Day on 6 April and the Third Reading on 15 July we spent a total of 26 days of parliamentary time on the Finance Bill – for the greater part on matters which bore little or no relation to our election manifesto. Many ministers and backbenchers felt that we should have been devoting a good deal of this precious time to legislation which would have been of more direct value to the people who elected us.

All our Committee and Report Stage debates started at the end of the daily question time, approximately 3.45 p.m., and ended at the following times.

COMMITTEE STAGE
17 May	11.24 p.m
19 May	11.55 p.m.
20 May	4.36 a.m.
24 May	12.00 midnight
25 May	6.00 a.m.

153

26 May	12.45 a.m.
27 May	12.37 a.m.
31 May	5.55 a.m.
2 June	12.57 a.m.
3 June	11.18 p.m.
15 June	11.53 p.m.
16 June	11.37 a.m.
21 June	3.09 a.m.
22 June	3.14 a.m.
23 June	11.15 p.m.
24 June	9.55 p.m.

REPORT STAGE

5 July	12.43 a.m.
6 July	1.37 a.m.
7 July	12.20 a.m.
8 July	10.40 p.m.
12 July	1.18 a.m.

THIRD READING

15 July	10.44 p.m.

Pacing up and down on the terrace one morning, as dawn was breaking over County Hall and Treasury ministers were still locked in combat with the Heath team, a newly elected Member said to me, 'What a bloody awful way to run the country.' And I had to agree with him.

After our experience on this Finance Bill, Herbert Bowden and I decided to try to get the agreement of the Opposition to commit at least part of future Finance Bills to a committee upstairs – that is, to a small committee instead of to a committee of the whole House. It would, we felt, reduce the physical burden on Members and relieve the parliamentary timetable in the summer months for other matters. Happily it is now common practice.

In 1965 the strain on our Members was considerable, though morale was remarkably high. The thought of the long summer recess just around the corner helped them to keep going. The sick list was growing apace, but mercifully (from the point of view of our survival) on both sides of the House – though an edict had gone out from Whitelaw's office that there must be no loose talk about the number or identities of their sick. Towards the end of July we regularly

154

had seven or eight Labour Members who were not well enough to be present.

To help our older and less fit members we had the Serjeant-at-Arms provide us with a number of beds and blankets. I had appointed a woman Whip, Harriet Slater (Stoke-on-Trent North), who possessed exactly the right qualities to cosset our bed brigade, to see that they had cups of tea and sufficient blankets and were bedded down as early as possible to give them the maximum time to rest before the division bells dragged them into the lobbies yet again. The Labour Government owed a great deal to her womanly care for our Members. We also grew to hate the division bell. And the word 'bell', conjuring up an image of a mellifluous sound, is a misnomer. It is a harsh, insistent clanging. During the passage of the Bill we spent the equivalent of two parliamentary days trudging through the division lobbies.

At the 16 June sitting, which lasted almost until lunch time on the following day, two of our Members had strokes. In a debate on one of the Opposition's censure motions after the Finance Bill, James Hill (Midlothian) had to be brought from Edinburgh and sustained with oxygen in Willie Ross's office. Eric Ogden (Derby West) was brought to Westminster and bedded down in Charles Pannell's room – also with oxygen. Immediately the sitting ended he had to be taken into Westminster Hospital, where he remained for some time. Unfortunately, we needed him again on 29 July, and the Opposition Whips refused to provide a pair for him. Once more he had to be brought from hospital by ambulance and wait in his pyjamas and dressing gown with the now familiar oxygen cylinder until the division was completed. During July we had to bring in, on occasions, up to five Members who were regarded by their doctors as seriously ill.

The Opposition's refusal to pair these Members, forcing us to risk their lives, created a good deal of anger among our backbenchers. They had their own sick who could have been used as pairs, but rather than accommodate us they kept us guessing. The press began to comment adversely on these tactics to the extent that, by the end of July, they had become counterproductive.

We then raised the possibility of an inter-party agreement on proxy voting for Members who were certified by a doctor as unfit to be present at Westminster. Predictably, the Tory press ridiculed the idea; but to me it was quite absurd that I could vote for a sick member if he was lying unconscious on a bed in my room or in an ambulance in Palace Yard but not if he was lying on a bed in Westminster Hospital a few hundred yards away.

In 1959 the Select Committee on Procedure had decided against proxy voting but recommended unanimously that a further effort be made to ensure that Members who were seriously ill should never again be required to attend to record their votes. Unfortunately, no agreement had been reached. In view of our experiences in July 1965 we decided to refer the matter to the Select Committee once more. Willie Whitelaw and I gave evidence to the committee on 2 November and were closely questioned about our pairing arrangements for sick Members and about the occasions when the seriously ill were brought in to vote. Eventually the Committee recommended that 'having heard the evidence of the Chief Government Whip and the Chief Opposition Whip, there seems to be no alternative to such a system [of proxy voting] for the seriously ill. They therefore recommend that such a system be introduced unless the usual channels can agree an alternative acceptable method.'

The Leader of the House and I were under considerable pressure to introduce proxy voting as recommended by the Select Committee, but William Whitelaw was under equal pressure from his Party to resist such an innovation. In these circumstances, we were reluctant to attempt to bulldoze it through the House and face a head-on collision on a procedural matter. There were enough lined up already on vital policy issues. After lengthy discussions which lasted well into the late autumn, we reached what *The Times* called 'a highly refined gentlemen's agreement between the Chief Whips which will achieve the aim of proxy voting without using the formal means.' On 24 November we signed the following agreement:

1   Pairs will be provided for all those sick Members whose presence in the House is undesirable on medical grounds.

2   Cancellation of these arrangements will be considered only in exceptional circumstances and then only after considerable notice has been given.

3   In the event of such a breakdown in pairing arrangements, it will be open to the Government to propose the immediate introduction of proxy voting, as recommended by the Select Committee on Procedure.

4   These arrangements will be reviewed after a period of six months.

Although we said in our covering correspondence that the agreement was a private one between the two of us, it was reported in *The Times* two days later. Our scheme worked satisfactorily and was a major factor in preserving the Labour Government until the Prime Minister was ready to go to the country. It was only the second occasion on which a formal written agreement was ever made between the two Chief Whips. The first, known as the Balcarres Agreement, concerns the moving of writs for by-elections and is still in operation.

But to return to the Finance Bill: there were 95 divisions and, although our average majority was 8.7, some results were hair-raisingly close. In the early hours of 7 July the Opposition decided to play cops and robbers, a tactic which George Wigg had used against them when they were in office in 1952. The Opposition Chief Whip had, we knew, imposed a three-line whip throughout the four and a half days of the Report Stage, but at midnight on 6 July he rather ostentatiously changed it to two lines. Immediately, Tory Members began leaving the building in droves without bothering to solicit pairs from our Members – normally a certain sign that they do not intend to call any further divisions. After getting confirmation of the exodus from all the Whips, I agreed to a large number of our Members being allowed to go home.

But the Tories had gone no further than St Stephen's Club, where there is a division bell, a few minutes' walk from the House. To our surprise a division was called shortly after 1 a.m. and, with Liberal support, we were defeated in two divisions. It was a planned ambush, but on an unimportant matter and we did not subsequently try to reverse it. The first, which we lost by fourteen votes, carried a new clause concerning Capital Gains Tax liability of investors in unit trusts. The second, which followed immediately, added the new clause to the Finance Bill. But, as we no longer had a majority after our defeat, we had to move that further consideration of the Bill be deferred – and provide an additional day for the Report Stage. And so my momentary lack of vigilance cost us a precious day which we could ill afford to lose.

In another vote we tied, and the chairman, Sir Herbert Butcher, gave us his casting vote – following the long-established rule that the chairman's vote should preserve the status quo.

Each morning during the passage of the Bill the Whips had to be at their office telephones from 10 a.m. onwards, no matter how late the previous night's sitting had run. Each Whip was responsible for knowing the exact whereabouts and health of all his Members. The pairing Whip, John Silkin, had to know the overall position and his arithmetic had to be correct throughout the day. The large talc-covered board in the Whips' office was marked up in coloured crayons each day from mid-morning onwards, with different colours for those who were in the building, the missing, the hospital cases, the ambulant sick, those who were abroad – and we always had a number of wanderers in foreign parts – the paired, etc. Even the smallest error could not be tolerated. Had we been counting inanimate objects, this would have been easy to achieve and error would have been inexcusable. The task of maintaining an exact tally of 317 ageing men and women in London was unbelievably difficult, but error was still inexcusable.

One day at lunchtime, in the middle of the battle, the board in the Whips' office disclosed a minority of nine. Rigorous counterchecking confirmed this alarming figure. Was it the end of the line? we wondered. But by a miracle of threats, persuasion and complicated car-ferry arrangements, backed up by skilful intelligence work on the state of the Opposition, we were able to produce a majority when the divisions started in the late afternoon.

Most of our Members cooperated with the Whips magnificently but occasionally we had to resort to methods which we would not normally have employed. I took the view that the survival of the Government was paramount; both the health and finer feelings of our Members had to take second place. On a number of occasions Members went home or to their hotels, believing one of the rumours that there were no more divisions. And if you start a rumour in the House of Commons you can be certain that within half an hour someone will whisper it in your ear in confidence. Although they were often tucked up in bed and asleep, we had no hesitation in insisting that they return to Westminster at once. And they always did.

One of our less reputable ploys when a provincial Member's whereabouts in London were unknown and he had not checked in at his hotel, or had checked out before he was supposed to, was to telephone his home to ask if he was there (knowing, of course, that he was not). We could then rely on his wife to keep a close check on his movements, although, initially, our call probably caused her some worry.

At a meeting of the Parliamentary Labour Party called by Manny Shinwell to enable Members to raise complaints, I expected to be heavily criticised for the tight whipping I had imposed. I was agreeably surprised when Ben Parkin (Paddington North) made a speech congratulating the Whips for the 'human' way in which they had organised the whipping on the Finance Bill. Reporting this secret meeting the following day in the *Guardian*, Ian Aitken said: 'Mr Parkin's views – creating a Parliamentary "man bites dog" situation – produced growls of affectionate approval from the meeting.'

The fatigue and frustrations of the Finance Bill were exacerbated by the seething and growing anger of our Members about the Vietnam war. The Americans were becoming more and more ensnared in the appalling quagmire of South-East Asia, and progressive opinion around the world grew increasingly alarmed. Scarcely a meeting of the Parliamentary Labour Party went by without impassioned pleas

159

for our Government to abandon its neutral attitude, which often appeared to give tacit support, for one of outright condemnation of the United States. This, of course, was impossible because of our reliance on American support in defending sterling, as most of our Members understood. But the humiliation of our position was keenly felt by everyone and deeply resented by many. It caused Herbert Bowden, Manny Shinwell and myself more Party problems than any other issue.

The Prime Minister, as always, was acutely aware of the disquiet in our ranks on Vietnam. He searched constantly for new initiatives which would both demonstrate his sympathy for the outraged feelings of his Members without embarrassing the United States Government and make a contribution towards an honourable solution. One such idea was a Commonwealth mission, but it had not got off the ground by July. Then, he made his most colourful move so far. One of our junior ministers for whom he, and all of us, had a particular affection was the ebullient left-of-centre Harold Davies (Leek), Parliamentary Secretary at the Ministry of Pensions and National Insurance, who in the past had visited Hanoi and met Ho Chi Minh, the North Vietnamese leader. There was at this time an unofficial North Vietnam representative in London disguised as a journalist. At the request of the Prime Minister, Harold Davies made an approach to him to see whether the Vietnamese Government would allow him to visit Hanoi and meet Ho Chi Minh again. As a result it was made known to the Prime Minister that a completely secret visit would be welcomed. Washington also agreed – provided the visit remained secret. They were desperate for any inkling of Ho Chi Minh's thinking on the war.

Harold Davies left immediately American agreement was received, accompanied by a Foreign Office official. As we were deeply involved in the Finance Bill, I had to ask the Opposition Whips to pair him and told them he had gone to investigate byssinosis in Hong Kong – which, it was generally known, needed investigation at that time. However, news of the visit reached the press on Friday 8 July when he was en route. This treacherous leak ended any hopes for the success

160

of the visit. The North Vietnam authorities refused to allow the Foreign Office official to enter the country. He remained in Hong Kong, while Davies went on alone to meet Ho Chi Minh and the Russian and Chinese Ambassadors.

At Westminster the Tories, from whom we might have expected some credit for at least making an effort to contact the North Vietnamese leader, had a field day asking entirely hostile questions. On the Friday morning Maudling and Whitelaw came to see Bowden and me to demand a statement from the Prime Minister. We promised to put the request to him but kept them waiting until the end of the day (always unpopular on a Friday) to tell them that he had refused.

The result of the Davies mission was welcomed by the United States Government and the initiative in sending him to Vietnam delighted our backbenchers. They applauded the Prime Minister for an imaginative if somewhat bizarre attempt to help in a tragic situation and they were furious at the negative, destructive attitude of the Opposition.

It was known that Sir Alec Douglas-Home would resign from the leadership of the Conservative Party, and the use of the Finance Bill by Heath and Maudling for electioneering made the resignation appear imminent. Nevertheless, it came as something of a shock when, on 22 July, Sir Alec announced that he was stepping down. There was a good deal of affection for him on our side of the House, but he was too much of a gentleman to lead the Tories! He was the last Conservative leader to emerge from the old, mysterious, magic circle. The new leader was to be elected democratically by a procedure devised by Sir Alec. The successful candidate was required to obtain 14 per cent more of the votes polled than his nearest rival.

Ted Heath, Reggie Maudling and Enoch Powell were nominated. Ted Heath, though top of the poll, did not get the necessary margin of votes. But his two opponents withdrew and he was declared the new Leader on 20 July – the first-ever elected leader of the Conservatives.

The new Leader made his debut on 28 July. The Prime Minister, invigorated by the thought of his beloved Scilly Isles only a few days away, and by the survival of his

Government through the tortuous paths of the Finance Bill, complimented him at Question Time on his election. He said that he would not inflict on him the traditional courtesy of saying that he hoped he would long enjoy his new office as Leader of the Opposition – because he was sure he would. Always good for a cheer from the troops behind!

The debate on that day, one of the Opposition's Supply Days, was on a motion criticising the Government for the rise in the cost of living since the General Election. Neither the Prime Minister nor Ted Heath took part.

Despite unimpressive speeches from our own Front Bench we had no difficulty in defeating the motion.

But behind these parliamentary battles all was not quite so well. The last few days of July saw a considerable run on sterling, and the Chancellor announced yet another list of austerity measures in the Commons. Only the fact that the long summer recess was almost upon us prevented open rebellion in our ranks as he unfolded his sombre package, which pushed the realisation of so many of our cherished plans even further into the future.

Capital projects were to be delayed and confined within strict limits for each Government department; purchasing by the Government, by local authorities and by nationalised industries was to be deferred; hopes of removing the remaining health service charges were abandoned for the present, as were the income guarantee scheme and the plan to provide mortgages at favourable interest rates for owner occupiers; licensing was to be introduced for privately sponsored construction projects (except housing); hire purchase was to be restricted, etc.

The Times correspondent reported that the Labour Party was seething with unrest. This was, of course, an exaggeration, but there was widespread anger within our ranks. Some Members thought they saw a 1931 situation emerging again and were saying so in the Members' tea room. All the anxiety expressed itself in an angry letter sent by John Mendelson to Manny Shinwell demanding a special Party meeting to discuss the situation. This was held on Monday 2 August but, thanks to Shinwell's unfailing skill in the Chair, was not nearly as difficult as we feared it would be.

The day after the Chancellor's statement was another of the Opposition's delayed Supply Days and we had to meet the challenge of a second censure motion which 'deplored the Government's failure to honour its election pledges'. Now Harold took great – and justifiable – pride in honouring his promises, and to accuse him of not honouring his election pledges was like waving a red rag to a bull. This motion made him furious. He was determined to speak in the debate and set out our record.

Of course he also hoped, by entering the debate himself, to make it impossible for the new Conservative leader to stay out. But Edward Heath did just that and, as a result, was accused of cowardice.

Harold, with great gusto, boasted about the 65 Bills we had passed – more than had been achieved in the previous session by a Government with a majority of 100 – and this was despite the disproportionate amount of time spent on the Finance Bill. I felt that a little boasting on this score was fair enough, but there was a danger of confusing the volume of legislation with the quality of government.

Tony Crosland wound up for the Government. The final speech in these day-long debates must end exactly at 10 o'clock, and most ministers contrive to end their perorations as the first chime of Big Ben strikes. But Tony ran out of notes a few embarrassing minutes early and had to extemporise – which he did appallingly badly.

But spirits were high on our side of the House and Tony Crosland was probably our most popular minister. Nothing could dampen our good spirits. The motion was defeated by a majority of 21.

However, apparently not content with two major defeats, the Opposition decided to launch another attack. They tabled an official censure motion, for which we had to provide a precious day out of Government time. The motion was as follows: 'That this House has no confidence in Her Majesty's Government and deplores the Prime Minister's conduct of the nation's affairs.' This was debated on Monday 2 August.

Edward Heath opened the debate with a speech which by contrast with the Prime Minister's speech of the previous

163

week, to which it was supposed to provide the crushing reply was a poor effort. And not only by contrast. By any standard it was an ineffective speech which sent his party off on their holidays wondering whether they had made the correct choice of Leader.

Reggie Maudling in his opening remarks charged that the Prime Minister 'loves the smear and the innuendo, that he is a mean-minded little man . . . masquerading as a Prime Minister.'

But both the Leader of the Opposition and his deputy were pounded into the ground by Harold at his rudest and most pugnacious, this time winding up the debate against a deafening organised barrage of abuse from the Opposition benches. The motion was rejected by 303 votes to 290. The Liberals abstained, as did Bill Warbey and Reggie Paget, the left and right extremities of the Labour Party. But when our amendment was put to the House (the Opposition motion having been defeated) we only had a majority of four. The explanation was that the Liberals who were present decided, like the Oozlam bird, to fly both ways at once and voted against the Government. Also in this second vote Reggie Paget honoured us by his presence in the division lobby. And so we had now beaten off three frontal attacks within six days – attacks which were, we were told, going to transform the political scene and electrify the Conservative Party.

The *Spectator* warned that sooner or later Mr Grimond must make up his mind that the flirting days were over; either he could offer the Emperor the clothing of his Party of 10, or he could come out in opposition to Mr Wilson and to socialism. If he decided to do that, then the Emperor's days would surely be numbered.

Meanwhile, the run on sterling had not been assuaged by the Chancellor's new measures. But after living with the problem for nine months, Harold and Jim had begun to adopt a more relaxed attitude to the pound's fluctuations. But not Lord Cromer. He demanded to see Edward Heath and Jo Grimond to explain the gravity of the situation. The Prime Minister refused to allow him to do so, as it would almost certainly have become known to the press, and would have been seen both at home and abroad as a signal that disaster was just around the corner. Instead, the Prime Minister suggested that he go away on holiday – which he did.

Harold, Mary and the dog went off to the Scillies. The sun was shining, the Prime Minister and the Governor of the Bank of England had gone on holiday – nothing much could be wrong. And it did the trick!

Members of Parliament shook the dust of Westminster off their feet and went away to enjoy what remained of the hot summer.

III

To our second Christmas

My wife and I spent August at Glenridding, enveloped in the peace of the lakes and fells. It was a month of almost unbelievable tranquillity after a year of prodigious, nonstop activity; a time for winding down. Westminster and all its problems look much smaller and less important from the other end of the country, especially when one is surrounded by mountains.

But on 22 August I received a sharp and sad reminder that I was still the one who bore responsibility for imposing all the harsh whipping to keep the Government afloat – and would soon have to impose it again. The death was announced of Norman Dodds (Erith and Crayford), one of our most loyal and diligent Members of Parliament, for many years the parliamentary champion of gypsies and other travelling folk. He had been ailing for some time but had insisted on turning up to vote at Westminster night after night throughout July. And I, in all my difficulties, had been willing for him to do so. I have no doubt that the strain of the Finance Bill and the series of censure motions contributed to his untimely death, which reduced our majority to two. Fortunately, he had a majority 8,855 and we could expedite the by-election by getting the Speaker to issue the writ during the recess. This could be done simply by posting a notice in the *London Gazette*.

But Norman's death was not the only blow. The second fell less than two weeks later. On 2 September Sir Harry Hylton-Foster, the Speaker, was walking in St James's when he collapsed and died in the street. I cut short my holiday and returned to London at once, determined to do everything in my power to secure the election of another Conservative or Liberal as Speaker.

There was no need to recall Parliament as there was ample time to consider a successor. A point which did worry me as I travelled south was how we could now, without a Speaker, issue a writ to Erith and Crayford so that the vacancy could be filled by the time the House met again. But, as so often, the incomparable Freddie Warren came to our rescue by remembering that in November 1964, when the Speaker was in hospital, the House had set up a caretaker committee to take over his essential duties when he was unable to fulfil

169

them. Fortunately this committee was still in existence and could issue the writ.

Both the Prime Minister and the Leader of the House agreed that we should try at all costs to avoid electing a Labour Speaker. I met Willie Whitelaw, my opposite number on the Conservative benches, who had also travelled down from Cumberland. He prefaced our discussion by pointing out that the election of a Speaker was, of course, a matter for the House to decide. I replied that while this was so, governments had always selected someone whom they believed to be suitably qualified (and few Members are) to nominate to the House, sometimes in agreement with the Opposition parties but more often without. Both Sir Harry and his predecessor, Mr Speaker Morrison, had been selected by the Conservative Government of the day without any agreement with the Opposition – indeed we had nominated a candidate to oppose Mr Morrison.

Neither of us was explicit about the man or woman we wanted, but we both understood that I wanted a non-Labour Speaker because the Speaker does not vote except in the event of a tie, while he wanted a Labour Speaker in the knowledge that this would reduce our tiny majority. We agreed to talk with Eric Lubbock, the Liberal Chief Whip. When the three of us met a few days later I agreed to prepare a short all-party list of about five names, which we would each consider with our colleagues for a week and then meet to try to reach agreement.

Herbert Bowden and I selected the five names. Eric Lubbock agreed them, and Willie Whitelaw did so after one deletion. Prominent on the list was Sir Elwyn Jones, the Attorney General, a genial lawyer and very experienced parliamentarian. Although I felt he would make an excellent Speaker, he was included merely to give our list credibility, for the aim was to avoid a Labour choice. And Elwyn, we hoped, would eventually sit on the Woolsack.

However, the entire Conservative press began tipping Dr Horace King, Chairman of Ways and Means since the General Election. This alarmed me, as his election as Speaker would throw into the melting pot the three non-voting offices (Speaker, Chairman and Deputy Chairman of Ways and Means). Since the General Election two of the three had been filled by Conservatives – an arrangement which was a clear voting advantage to us and which I wanted to preserve. The lobby correspondents were only too well aware of this. They also knew that it was rare at that time for a Chairman of Ways and Means to become Speaker. Unfortunately, it appears now almost to be the standard practice, although a deputy does not necessarily make the best chief. Their major concern was, of course, to embarrass the Government.

Long before the week elapsed, Willie Whitelaw came to tell me that the Shadow Cabinet felt that Dr King had done an excellent job in the Chair during the long sittings on the Finance Bill, and that he was their choice. As far as they were concerned, that was the end of the matter.

In the same week Woodrow Wyatt came out in support of Dr King in his column in the *Daily Mirror* and said that he intended to propose him to the House, whatever the Government did. This lack of concern about the majority of the Government he had been elected to support quite shocked me although, considering his efforts on steel renationalisation, it should not have done.

In view of the Shadow Cabinet's decision and Wyatt's support for Dr King, I decided to carry out a Whips' exercise covering the entire Parliamentary Labour Party about his acceptability to our own Members. This showed that only 10 per cent of our Members wanted Dr King irrespective of the effect his election would have on our majority. But he had majority support provided we would not have to fill both of the remaining non-voting offices. Of course, we could have no such assurance.

Because of this dilemma, I had a talk with Eric Lubbock about the possibility of the Liberal Roderic Bowen, QC, (Cardigan) taking on the deputy chairmanship if Dr King became Speaker. I had reason to believe he would accept if I asked him. Eric was very reluctant, and I wrote to Jo Grimond to tell him that I was proposing to approach Bowen. He replied, quite fairly I thought, to say that he had only 10 Members to represent 3 million Liberal votes and that he would regret the 10 per cent diminution of their

171

voting strength which Bowen's acceptance would entail.

My problem now was whether I should risk losing the small but useful fund of goodwill I had built up with the Liberals over the past year by taking one of their 10 votes, against the wishes of their Leader and Chief Whip.

I decided that the time had come to have a talk with Dr King, who came to No. 12 to see me. He understood our difficulty, but he made it clear that he would accept nomination, whether by Woodrow Wyatt or anyone else. He left me in no doubt that he believed his hour had come and he meant to become the first Labour Speaker, whatever the effect on our majority.

I let the matter rest for a few days, during which nothing changed except that there was a mounting press campaign for Dr King and severe criticism of my supposed machiavellian backstage manoeuvring. Eventually, at Prayers, the Prime Minister, Herbert Bowden and I decided that we really had no option but to nominate Dr King, even if it precipitated the defeat of the Government. I asked him to call on me again on 13 October and told him of our decision, after which I took him through to see the Prime Minister, who, as always, was extremely kind to him. As he was leaving, Horace said, 'Of course, if the Party had not wanted me to take it I wouldn't have done so.'!

Willie Whitelaw now told me that the Conservatives would not fill the deputy chairmanship, as the Chairman would be a Conservative – we had agreed that Sir Sam Storey should step up from Deputy Chairman to Chairman. And, he said with some justice, the three non-voting offices should be shared among the three parties. He felt it would be quite appropriate to find a Liberal who was willing to accept.

I asked Roderic Bowen to call at No. 12 on 20 October. I put him fully in the picture, particularly about the views of Grimond and Lubbock, and offered him the nomination for Deputy Chairman of Ways and Means, making it sound as attractive as possible and hinting that, who knows, it could some day lead to the big Chair itself. He was at this time the Recorder of Swansea, but I had taken the precaution of obtaining an assurance from the Lord Chancellor that,

172

if elected, he need not give up this prestigious and lucrative office. He promised to sleep on it and returned next day to tell me he had agreed to accept. I immediately took him to see the Prime Minister, a procedure now becoming a sort of ritual confirmation of appointments of this kind. Harold could scarcely conceal his delight, and certainly showed his gratitude to Roderic Bowen, who had no doubt displeased the leader of his own Party in accepting. In *The Labour Government, 1964-70*, Harold says that a prominent Conservative MP had come to him and offered to accept the post if we were unable to find a Liberal. Neither Herbert Bowden nor I were told about this at the time.

Anyhow, we kept our majority of three (temporarily reduced to two) and breathed an enormous sigh of relief.

Unfortunately, Roderic Bowen lost his seat at the General Election six months later, as did the Conservative Chairman of Ways and Means, Sir Sam Storey. There was a widely expressed view that he had brought his defeat upon himself and that it reflected the resentment of his constituents at his accepting a non-voting, non-speaking office in order, it was said, to keep the Labour Government in office. However, this could not have been so because the swing to Labour in his Cardiganshire constituency was almost identical with the national swing.

About this time there was a minor upheaval in No. 10. Marcia, after a disagreement with Derek Mitchell, the Prime Minister's Principal Private Secretary, downed tools and walked out. Tommy Balogh, Harold's adviser on economic affairs and a member of the kitchen cabinet, was sent to persuade her to come back, which she did in her own good time.

On 12 September we had a pleasant day-long Cabinet meeting at Chequers, the Prime Minister's idyllic residence deep in the Buckinghamshire countryside. It lasted from 10 a.m. to 5.20 p.m. Harold had become absorbed in the history of this ancient house and its beauty and had developed his own theories about its association with William Shakespeare, particularly with *Cymbeline*, which he was always willing to expound to anyone who would listen. Meetings at Chequers, away from the overcharged atmosphere of Whitehall, were always welcomed by ministers, and Harold was an excellent host; but he was so concerned about accusations of extravagance that he insisted we share cars for the journey from London.

This meeting was mainly without Civil Servants so that it could be a general political stocktaking of the Government's progress in our first session and of our strategy in the new session, which was to begin early in November.

Predictably, Frank Cousins quickly steered the discussion to the prices and incomes policy which his fellow Transport and General Workers' Union member George Brown was labouring to develop with both sides of industry. To Frank, any restriction of free collective bargaining was anathema – particularly one imposed by legislation. George had been greatly encouraged by a TUC decision taken at their conference in Brighton four days previously to approve the TUC's own wages review plan. 'We must have a good substitute if you want to avoid legislation,' said George Woodcock in commending the plan. Whilst George Brown did not think this went far enough, he regarded the TUC plan as a major move towards an incomes policy. It is interesting to recall that the TUC decision at Brighton was opposed by Sir Harry Nicholas, Acting General Secretary of the Transport and General Workers Union during Frank's secondment to serve in the Government. Sir Harry later became the General Secretary of the Labour Party.

But at Chequers Frank was in a minority. On the whole there was a good deal of satisfaction, not merely at our survival, but because at long last there was an improvement in the economy. The more hopeful mood was helped by a new agreement which had been negotiated with other central banks to buttress sterling. The pound was stronger than at any time in the past two years, and gold began to flow back to London.

In considering our legislative programme for the coming session, an informal decision was made not to include the Bill to renationalise steel. A General Election could not be long delayed, particularly as the public opinion polls were moving in our favour. I believe Harold had already made up

174

his mind when he intended to go to the country though he did not tell any of his ministers. In *Inside Number 10* Marcia says that he was 'working towards March'. Herbert Bowden and I pointed out that the last thing we wanted was to have the weeks preceding an election occupied with parliamentary brawling about steel. We painted a picture of interminable late-night and all-night struggles, with the Liberals against us on every division, besides which even our 1965 Finance Bill battles would appear tame. And what an issue on which to fight an election!

As this decision was made in the informal part of our meeting it was not recorded in any minutes. But I was intrigued on 21 October when we were discussing the final draft of the Queen's Speech that Jim Callaghan, Fred Lee, Frank Cousins and Barbara Castle questioned whether we had in fact made such a decision. Fred, Frank and Barbara wanted the Bill to be included, but why Jim allied himself with them was far from clear. However, the Cabinet decided by a majority of 2 to 1 not to include steel in the Queen's Speech.

The major event for the Government in September was the publication of the National Plan a few days after the Chequers meeting. It was launched at Lancaster House with massive coverage by press, radio and TV. It was a remarkably comprehensive statement of the economic strategy the Government planned to follow for the next five years, with all its implications, industry by industry, for resources, manpower, prices and incomes, exports etc. At the General Election, the Department of Economic Affairs had not existed; yet, in ten months, George Brown with phenomenal energy, remarkable ability and a good deal of ruthlessness had assembled a ministry of exceptionally able Civil Servants and produced this first real attempt at national economic planning. *The Times* said: 'It deserves a warm welcome . . . it contains a first class analysis of the British economy . . . it involves a greater commitment to long-term planning than has ever been accepted before except in time of war.' It owed much to Sir Donald MacDougall, Director General of the DEA, but the inspiration and driving force behind it

175

was George Brown's. The major credit rightly went to him.

Economic planning had for long been the theoretical quintessence of socialism. To our faithful throughout the country, the publication of the National Plan was incontrovertible evidence that their Government was moving along socialist lines. I was quite certain that it would delight our Members of Parliament. And I was right. Congratulatory letters to the Government began to flow into No. 12, and our Annual Conference was only two weeks away where, it could safely be assumed, the National Plan would glow over the platform like a bright star pointing the way to the promised land.

Ted Heath condemned it before he had read it and Iain Macleod said it was not a plan but a party political document.

It was neither George Brown's fault nor the Government's that, after six months in which we actually improved on the strategy of the plan, particularly in export targets, the highly damaging seamen's strike disrupted our progress. It was not the first time, nor the last, that the progress of a Labour Government has been brought to a shuddering halt by irresponsible trade union militancy.

A week later another major goody was put on display in our shop window when we published a White Paper setting out our proposals for a Land Commission on which the legislation would be based. But it was a mere shadow of our original manifesto commitment – thanks to Dick Crossman. *The Times*, giving it a guarded welcome, called it 'a far cry from the plan Labour was flourishing before the election.'

This was one of a series of White Papers which we had decided to publish before the coming General Election. If the parliamentary situation made the passing of controversial legislation difficult, we could, by means of these promissory notes, set out in detail what we intended to do when we had a working majority.

Our Annual Conference opened at Blackpool on 27 September and, as party conferences go, was a considerable success. It was our first full-scale conference since the General Election, and some of the excitement of victory still lingered among the delegates. But there was also genuine pleasure and pride at our sheer survival against all the odds and at the forthright way in which the Government was facing its problems. Above all, the very recent publication of the National Plan was well received by the entire conference. Even our Land Commission White Paper was applauded. Of course, the atmosphere owed something to a recent NOP poll which had shown Labour leading the Conservatives by 11 points. There was an unwillingness to rock the boat when, as everybody knew, we had to face the electors again before long. The Prime Minister was at his best and, in giving his parliamentary report, made a scintillating speech which gained for him one of the biggest ovations of his career and crowned a successful conference.

One difficulty we had at Blackpool was the not unusual one of trouble with the BBC, which seemed to be quite incapable of dealing in a balanced way with anything involving the Labour Government. The early-warning system for prices and incomes was to be debated on the Thursday, but the BBC chose to run a programme on it on the Monday, no doubt because they expected it to be the flashpoint of the conference. One third of the programme time was devoted to an interview with Clive Jenkins, who had not spoken that day but was known to be critical of the policy. When we saw the programme [late on the Monday night] the Prime Minister sent for the official BBC representative at the conference, and protested in quite vehement terms, to say the least, and kept him discussing the matter until 12.30 a.m. Two days later the incident and Harold's intervention were reported in some detail in the *Daily Mail* by Walter Terry, who had his own links with the inner circles of the Labour Government. But the content of this piece made it certain that it could only have come from the BBC.

Early in October we published a White Paper on our proposals for an Ombudsman, which, like most of the Labour Government's attractive ideas, had been suggested by Harold in a speech during the run-up to the General Election. Unfortunately, we proposed to call him a Parliamentary Commissioner and decided he could only investigate complaints sent to him by Members of Parliament.

This restriction of access to the Ombudsman was popular with our Members, who saw it as a new means of gaining kudos for themselves, but, in my view, it detracted from an excellent and electorally popular idea.

By this time Rhodesia had almost replaced the economy as the Government's most worrying preoccupation. Throughout the summer there had been many rumours that a unilateral declaration of independence was to be declared. It now appeared to be imminent. Cledwyn Hughes, Minister of State at the Colonial Office, had visited Salisbury in July, but no progress had been made. We were most careful to do nothing which might upset the nonpartisan approach, based upon the five principles, which had obtained at Westminster since Sir Alec Douglas-Home's premiership. There had been a split in the Conservative ranks at their annual conference, led by Lord Salisbury, but Edward Heath, apart from a few wriggles, did not at this stage move far from the tacitly agreed inter-party line.

On 4 October Ian Smith visited London, but after interminable discussions, no progress towards a solution was made. He was quite determined that any agreement with the British Government should give independence on his terms. Failing this, he left us in no doubt that he would seize independence without agreement, although he was well aware that in divesting ourselves of our colonies we had never granted independence until the principle of universal suffrage had been established. The complete Cabinet record of the talks, which I saw, made it only too obvious that Harold had to make full use of his skills as a negotiator to prevent the talks breaking down. But the Leader of the Opposition accused him of ending the talks prematurely.

We even tried to enlist the support of the churches for our stand on the five principles at a dinner at No. 10 on 12 October, at which the Archbishop of York, the Bishop of Norwich and other church leaders were present. So far they had been remarkably quiet in Britain, though the Christian Council in Rhodesia had shown great courage.

On 21 October the Cabinet met at 10 a.m. and again at 5 p.m. Both meetings were overshadowed by Rhodesia.

178

Smith had sent a letter putting all the blame for the impasse on the British Government. At this point Harold decided to take one of those dramatic and imaginative initiatives which marked his premiership. He told me that he proposed to fly to Rhodesia at once with the Colonial Secretary and the Attorney General. The Cabinet agreed, but with the important proviso that he was allowed by the Rhodesian authorities to see anyone he wished.

On the Friday I was fogbound at home. The Prime Minister rang me up about his visit to Rhodesia and also about the election of the new Speaker, which was to take place when he was away. He wanted the election to be carried out in the traditional way and was anxious that there should be no hitch of any kind. I was able to reassure him.

He and his two colleagues arrived in Salisbury on Monday 25 October and spent the following five days in long discussions with Ian Smith and his cabinet, and with representatives of almost every aspect of Rhodesian society – including the African leaders.

His efforts resulted in a somewhat strange proposal for a Royal Commission to recommend Amendments to the 1961 Rhodesian Constitution to satisfy the first four of the five principles – the fifth principle stated that the British Government would need to be satisfied that any basis for independence was acceptable to the Rhodesian people as a whole.

On the Prime Minister's return, both the press and the House of Commons gave him an excellent reception. The Cabinet met on the Monday morning and rather reluctantly agreed the Royal Commission proposal, though many of us felt it would be widely misunderstood, particularly among our backbenchers. However, no sooner had we agreed than depressing telegrams began to arrive from Salisbury from the Colonial Secretary and the Attorney General, who had been left behind, saying that no progress whatever was being made with the Rhodesian Government on the details of the Royal Commission.

Only one discordant note marred Harold's return. After his statement to the House on the Wednesday, David Ennals moved the adjournment of the House under Standing Order

No. 9, a device for securing an immediate debate on a matter of urgent public importance. In refusing his request, the Speaker, being new to the Chair, revealed that David had approached him before the sitting – that is, before he had heard the Prime Minister's statement. But David Ennals was Parliamentary Private Secretary to Barbara Castle, who was strongly opposed to the proposal for a Royal Commission. The Whips later reported to me that Ennals was going to hold a meeting about the proposal with a number of other PPSs, including Shirley Williams, Brian Walden and Ivor Richards, to draw up a motion which he hoped to table on the Order Paper. I then heard that he was giving a statement to the press in the Members' lobby. I sent for him and we went together to see the Prime Minister, whose own private intelligence network had now heard of the campaign against his Royal Commission proposals. Harold read the riot act to him – but, in my view much too gently. After David left, I told Harold that if this quite shocking use of their PPSs by senior ministers was to continue, and this was not by any means the first occasion, he knew what he could do with the job of Chief Whip. He promised to mention it at the Cabinet, which he did the following day – to utter silence.

Parliament had reassembled on Tuesday 26 October for a brief 'spillover' before the new session. The first business had been to elect a Speaker and his two deputies. At the best of times it is a comical sight to see an Honourable Member resisting his Sponsors as they drag him to the one-time dangerous but now most sought after chair in the British realm. On this occasion I watched the struggling Horace King with wry amusement as he became the first Labour Speaker. Sir Sam Storey, the Conservative who had been Deputy Chairman since the General Election, was elected Chairman of Ways and Means to replace Horace, and the Liberal Roderic Bowen, QC, became Deputy Chairman. All was accomplished with good humour and courtesy which revealed nothing of the frantic manoeuvrings over the distribution of these three non-voting offices.

The week after the election of the Speaker was devoted to clearing the parliamentary decks of the last remnants of

180

our first session's legislation. Sixty-five Bills in all – not bad for a Government which was given but a few weeks to live after our election twelve months previously. The ruthless Opposition attack which we had been told by the press to expect now that their new leader was firmly in the saddle did not materialise. On the Lords' amendments to the Rent Bill, for instance, all our majorities were in the thirties.

One particularly pleasing moment came on Monday 8 November when, immediately before Prorogation, the Speaker announced that the royal assent had been given to the Murder (Abolition of the Death Penalty) Bill, 1965. It was a moment of triumph for the veteran parliamentarian Sydney Silverman, who had fought an untiring battle against hanging for very many years.

The slack period in Parliament before the opening of the new session gave me a chance to discuss a number of minor problems – and some rather more than minor ones – with the Members concerned.

Prominent among these was the growing antagonism between Tom Fraser, Minister of Transport, and the Transport Group in the Parliamentary Labour Party. The leader of the rebellion was a tough and able National Union of Railwaymen Member, Ernest Popplewell, from my neighbouring constituency of Newcastle West. The Minister himself had undertaken to prepare in his Ministry a plan for an integrated transport system. But, meanwhile, line and workshop closures were continuing, to the consternation of our Members, who believed that they should be halted until the details of the long-awaited plan were worked out. Tom Fraser was much too quiet and considerate a man to deal with the notoriously egocentric interests in the transport world. They needed a Dr Beeching who would bang their heads together and impose integration on them. After two hours of intense discussion I was quite unable to make the slightest dent on my railwaymen colleagues. They were completely immovable in their determination to see an integrated transport system – but one which was dominated by an expanded railway network.

The last adjournment debate of the session, on 4 November, was concerned with transport. When Ted

181

Fletcher (Darlington) raised the problem of the closure of the Darlington Locomotive Works. These daily debates last exactly thirty minutes, normally divided equally between the Member raising an issue and the Minister replying. However, on this occasion, with uncharacteristic discourtesy, Ted took twenty-five minutes – leaving Tom Fraser only five minutes in which to defend himself. This incident was an indication of the tension which had arisen between back-benchers and our over-conciliatory Minister of Transport. And transport was to dominate one day of the debate on the Queen's Speech, for the Tories were well aware of this chink in our armour.

The Leader of the House and I had to select two of our Members to move and second the Loyal Address of thanks to the Queen for her Gracious Speech. We chose Shirley Williams (Hitchin), who had been elected in 1964 and had charmed everyone with her intelligence, good sense and hard work. As seconder we selected Will Hamling (Woolwich West), also a 1964 entrant, who had displayed phenomenal energy and unflagging good humour, and had, on more than one occasion, provided the Whips with vital intelligence about the party. But when I showed these names to Harold, he said he wanted Shirley Williams for a ministerial appointment and strongly recommended Harold Lever (Manchester Cheetham).

Harold Lever himself merited a place in the Government, but his division record before the 1964 General Election was the worst in the Parliamentary Labour Party, and to promote him over the heads of Members who had always been in the division lobbies to support their Party in the long and tedious thirteen years in Opposition would have caused a rebellion among our backbenchers.

He was, of course, extremely anxious to become a minister – indeed, rather over-anxious – but I had told him after we came into office that he would have to earn an appointment by diligence in the House, which must not take second place to his own private affairs. He understood this and was making a considerable effort to do so. The Prime Minister was keen to have him in the Government because of his financial expertise, which

182

was not too plentiful in the Parliamentary Labour Party. His selection as mover of the Loyal Address in November 1965 was the first signal to the Party that he was on his way. There were one or two complaints from the usual grumblers, but most of our backbenchers felt he should have a place on the Front Bench. But, cautious as always about Party reactions, the Prime Minister waited until January 1967 before appointing him to the Department of Economic Affairs.

In the period before the opening of the new session I also spent a good deal of time reassuring Members who were anxious that they should not be overlooked in the major Government reshuffle which the press were forecasting. They were all the more concerned because there had been some ministerial changes on 9 October. This alarmed the hopefuls on two grounds – first, because they had been passed over and feared this might be the last reshuffle before the next General Election, and second, because an 'outsider' – Lord Brown, a prominent industrialist – had been recruited to be Minister for Exports at the Board of Trade. This was always an unpopular kind of appointment among Members of Parliament.

I assured them all that there would be another major reshuffle before the end of the year.

One eminent QC, pathetically anxious to become a law officer, had almost lived on my doorstep for the past year; and there were others who felt that their special gifts, or their loyalty, entitled them to a place in the Government. I had a good deal of sympathy with some of them. Some came in sorrow and disappointment, others came in anger at the inclusion of obviously less able colleagues and those who had not been notable for their loyalty to the Party. All I could do was to promise to talk to the Prime Minister, which I always did – though, after a year in office, he was beginning to be less communicative about his appointments than he had been in the early days.

The Cabinet used the lull between sessions to try, among other things, to settle the details of the by now highly contentious 'early-warning' legislation on prices and incomes, a topic which could be guaranteed to raise the temperature almost immediately. The crux was the penalties for non-compliance. Should they be fines or imprisonment – or both? Frank Cousins was so incensed at the proposal to bring penal law into the field of industrial relations that he announced to the Cabinet he would not support legislation which introduced penalties of any kind. George Brown was given the task of finding a more acceptable proposal, but we all knew (though no one said so) that sooner or later the problem of penalties would have to be faced if we were to legislate. It was not easy to see how we could continue to claim that we were planning the economy if prices and incomes were to be left entirely to the pressures of the marketplace. This is and has always been the great divide between democratic socialism and the Conservative Party. Mrs Thatcher's policies in the eighties have made this abundantly clear.

But there were other worries. Early in the morning on Sunday 7 November I had a phone call to tell me that a good friend, Harry Solomons, the Labour Member for Hull North, had died during the night – thus creating the first vacancy of this Parliament in a marginal seat. Our majority at the General Election was 1,181. Before that it had been held by the Conservatives since 1955. Erith had not yet polled and so Harry's death reduced our majority to one. We were now faced with two by-elections. If we lost both, and the press predictions about Erith were not too hopeful, we should be in a minority. I immediately rang the Prime Minister, and he agreed to call a meeting of the Officers' Committee the following day, on which Parliament was to be prorogued, to discuss the date for a by-election. Obviously, in view of our rapidly disappearing majority, we could not afford any delay in filling, or trying to fill, the vacancy. On the other hand, there might possibly be an advantage in delaying the by-election until the new Electoral Register was published in the New Year.

The meeting was held on the Monday afternoon in the Prime Minister's room behind the Speaker's chair in the House of Commons, with Ray Gunter in the chair. We decided that 16 December was the most suitable date – or rather the least unsuitable date, for there is no suitable date

184

for a by-election in midwinter. (We later changed our minds twice on this date.)

But once the date had been decided the meeting developed into the most unpleasant I attended in my years in the Wilson Government. George Brown, who had obviously had a drink or two, or three, was in his most truculent mood and became extremely rude and abrasive to Sara Barker, the soft-spoken but very able National Agent of the Labour Party. In a few seconds a flaming row blew up – and no one saw it coming. It was instantaneous combustion! Harold, uncharacteristically, was white with anger. When Sara's eyes began to fill with tears, he moved that the meeting be adjourned – which only had the effect of diverting George's insults from Transport House and all its minions to Harold, before he stalked out of the room, banging the door behind him. I returned to No. 12 but very soon afterwards I received a message to say the Prime Minister wanted to see me at once. Herbert Bowden had also been summoned, so back to Westminster we went, wondering what retribution Harold was planning against George. We found him pacing up and down the room like a tiger in a cage – one of his most disconcerting habits – looking very angry and holding in his hand a resignation letter from George. He told us he was not going to accept it, and said this in terms which indicated that he saw non-acceptance as a punishment. But we took a different view and told him that the time was coming when he would have to say yes – to one of George's frequent letters of resignation.

George was sent for and refused to withdraw his letter; Harold was equally firm in refusing to accept it. George complained that he was being kept in the dark about Rhodesia and a great many other aspects of Government policy. Harold, he fumed, was constantly trying to cut him down to size – and he may have had a point there.

The incident, one of many which were to follow, fizzled out inconclusively. George carried on, his anger subsiding as quickly as it had flared up. Harold quickly regained his equanimity and appeared to put the incident out of his mind.

George rang me up early next morning to tell me I need not worry about him and that he would be present at the Opening of Parliament.

Earlier on the Monday, Frank Cousins had been to see the Prime Minister to say he also wanted to resign because George Brown had been abusive to him in, of all places, the Strangers' Bar in the House of Commons, in the hearing of a lobby correspondent and a Tory MP. Frank, in spite of his strongly held views, was an eminently reasonable and courteous man, and Harold had no great difficulty in dissuading him. But the growing rift between Frank and George, arising in the main from their differing views about prices and incomes policy, was developing into a major weakness in the Government. However, Harold felt he needed them both – for different reasons; George for his rare ability and energy and Frank for his influence in the trade unions. He was determined to bridge the gap between them, but it was an objective which he never wholly achieved.

This otherwise miserable Monday was not all gloom and disagreement, for it was the day on which our first parliamentary session ended with the Prorogation of Parliament. Normally there is about a week between Prorogation and the State Opening of the new session, but, in view of the serious situation in Rhodesia, the Queen was to open the new session the following day. A unilateral declaration of independence would require immediate parliamentary action – which had, of course, been planned for some time.

Prorogation serves two useful purposes – at least for the Government. First, the whole parliamentary slate is wiped clean. Any unfinished business, whether initiated by the Government or by Private Members, falls from the Order Paper. Secondly, there is a Prorogation speech, which sets out the Government's achievements in the past session and, on this occasion, we proudly listed our 65 successful Bills, including the mammoth Finance Bill as well as the important Silverman Bill abolishing capital punishment – all achieved with a majority of three.

The evening also was much more pleasant than much of the day had been. The pre-sessional party was held as usual in one of the state rooms at No. 10 to hear

186

the Queen's Speech read behind locked doors. It was well received by those present: ministers, Manny Shinwell (the party chairman) and the proposers and seconders of the Loyal Address of thanks to Her Majesty – Harold Lever and Will Hamling.

Whilst we fully intended to push ahead vigorously with all the legislation listed and to publish White Papers where the Bills were not ready, it was not really a programme of work for a new session but a manifesto for the coming General Election. It promised legislation on a great many topics, including prices and incomes, dock and dock labour modernisation, agriculture, consumer protection, the Land Commission, the coal industry finances, leasehold enfranchisement, Exchequer assistance for local authority housing at a fixed interest rate of 4 per cent, building licences, reducing the burden of rates, earnings-related social security benefits, improved workers' compensation, improved sick pay for agricultural workers, the Ombudsman, road safety legislation, the co-ordination of public transport, company reports to shareholders showing political contributions, etc. In addition it pledged unremitting efforts to find a peaceful solution in Rhodesia, restoration of a balance in our external payments in 1966, the implementing of our National Plan and the setting up of a Public Schools Commission.

There was something for everyone, and it was equally relevant both to the needs of the country and to the winning of votes in the coming election.

Immediately after the formal Opening ceremony the following day, the Parliamentary Labour Party met in a committee room upstairs. Most MPs are sensible, experienced men and women who know a good election manifesto when they see one, and there was obviously quiet satisfaction with the programme. If any Queen's Speech could ensure their re-election, this was it – and in any democratically elected Parliament re-election must always be a major preoccupation of its Members. Nevertheless, there were rumblings from Michael Foot, John Mendelson and others about the omission of steel renationalisation, and Manny Shinwell agreed to a further meeting the following day.

Later on the same day Michael sent me an amendment to the Loyal Address, regretting the omission of steel, which he proposed to table. I heard also that an attempt was being made by the left to persuade Members to add their signatures to it, and so all the Whips were sent into action to try to prevent this. We also took the precaution of ensuring that another motion was tabled welcoming the Government's determination to renationalise the steel industry.

When the recalled Party meeting took place the following day, it was devoted almost entirely to steel. It was dominated by a speech from Michael Foot and an excellent but short winding-up speech by Harold, who was at his skilful best and took the steam out of the controversy. In particular, he dealt with the niggling fear which still lingered in the Party that we were angling for some kind of a deal with the steel owners which would amount to less than full public ownership. He successfully allayed the fears of most of our backbenchers. But the fear in Michael Foot's mind was that the omission of steel implied an agreement with the Liberals. *The Times* political correspondent had developed this theme two days earlier: '. . . those nine votes [the Liberals] producing an effective majority over the Conservatives of 20 or so – will be at Mr. Wilson's disposal in his days of need.'

No one can know what the Cabinet's real motives were when they decided to leave out steel. The knowledge that it was the sticking point for any help the Liberals might give us in difficult situations was no doubt in some members' minds; but the major consideration was the parliamentary battle which would be involved, and of having to fight a General Election dominated by it. What is quite certain is that there were neither formal nor informal talks of any kind with the Liberals about collaboration with the Government. Except, perhaps, for one strange incident.

On 10 September I had seen a copy of a minute sent by John Silkin to the Prime Minister, describing in detail a conversation at a lunch he had had with the Liberal Chief Whip. John had been Pairing Whip since the General Election and had made a name for himself by the never failing accuracy of his daily arithmetic. But I was surprised that one of my most junior Whips should send a minute to the Prime Minister – and all the more so when I read its opening words: 'As suggested, I had lunch with ...' Presumably this meant that the lunch had been suggested to him by the Prime Minister, unknown to his two business managers, Herbert Bowden and myself. The minute set out Eric Lubbock's views on Liberal support for our legislation, the selection of a new Speaker, proxy voting and a number of other issues. To know the attitude of the Liberals on these matters was, of course, helpful. But was it a feeler put out by Harold about Liberal support if we found ourselves *in extremis*?

At the annual conference of the Liberal Party in late September, Jo Grimond's message was that his Party would continue to behave towards the Government as they had done in the previous session but, if we lost our majority, they would have to turn us out unless an agreement on policy had been arrived at. As far as we were concerned this meant exactly nothing. Up to the Whitsun recess they had voted with the Government 41 times but against us 95 times. But from May onwards they showed outright hostility to us by bringing us to within three votes of defeat on the Finance Bill.

In the debate on the Queen's Speech, Michael Foot said that if the Government was trying to placate the Liberals – 'that bunch of milk-fed carnivores' – it was making a foolish mistake. Indeed, it might destroy the long-term prospect of Labour Government in Britain if the Government were to forsake principles for manoeuvres. 'I would not advise them to place much trust in a reed shaken by every wind,' he thundered.

I have often wondered how Michael reconciled the Liberal-Labour pact which he, as Leader of the House of Commons, operated during the last years of the Callaghan Government with these uncompromising views expressed thirteen years earlier.

Two days after the opening of the new session, our candidate, James Wellbeloved, won the Erith by-election with a majority of 7,032. Obviously, in this first test of public opinion since the Queen's Speech, the electors liked our programme. It was a wet day, always bad for the Labour

189

vote, but the result was better than we dared to hope. Our share of the vote had risen from 53.1 per cent to 55.4 per cent. While this was probably not much encouragement for the Prime Minister to go to the country, there was even less encouragement for the Liberals to turn us out of office, for their share of the vote had halved from 14.4 per cent to 7.2 per cent. Because of the poor Liberal showing, the Erith result made us all feel rather more secure; but for a pointer to the timing of the next General Election we would have to await the result in the marginal constituency of Hull North, which was still two months away.

On the evening of the Erith by-election, the Ambassador of Israel came to see me about an exchange of prisoners between Israel and Egypt – a tricky matter to organise in those pre-Camp David days when the only contact between the two countries was armed conflict. He felt that an unofficial approach might be successful. He knew that my *enfant terrible*, Woodrow Wyatt, had established a friendly personal relationship with President Nasser, and I agreed to sound him about making a quiet visit to Egypt. Without a moment's hesitation Woodrow consented.

Later in the evening I had dinner and a long discussion with Dick Crossman at his house in Vincent Square. He agreed to reject a Local Government Boundary Commission recommendation for Tyneside and establish instead a large Tyneside Borough from Newcastle along both sides of the Tyne to the coast, with all the powers of a county borough, including education. It was a promise which he never kept, but which made much more sense than the Tyne-Wear Metropolitan County eventually created by the Heath Government.

The situation in Rhodesia had deteriorated rapidly over the past two weeks until at 11.20 a.m. on 11 November, the fateful message arrived in Downing Street that the Smith Government had unilaterally declared independence. This rebellion against the Crown by ministers who had each taken a solemn oath to 'be faithful and bear true allegiance to Her Majesty Queen Elizabeth her heirs and successors' was doubly squalid when made on Armistice Day – and at 11

190

a.m. The Prime Minister called a meeting of the other party leaders in the White Drawing Room at No. 10 twenty-five minutes later. As well as the party leaders, the Lord President, the Attorney-General, Willie Whitelaw and I were present. The Prime Minister gave us all the information he had about events in Salisbury and the parliamentary action which would be required at Westminster. Ted Heath was obviously shocked and worried. Herbert Bowden and I knew all about the growing problem in his party on Rhodesia and felt sympathy for him. In contrast, Jo Grimond was extremely helpful. He was the type of party leader who needed an atmosphere of crisis to bring out the best in him.

Later in the day, when the Prime Minister made a statement to the House, Ted Heath had to tread very warily indeed because of the many hostile noises from his Party behind him, particularly at any mention of United Nations involvement, which always provoked sections of the Conservative Party. Willie Hamilton said of him later that he was 'straining at every nerve to find differences rather than to find an area of agreement.'

We heard, in the evening, that there had been considerable opposition in the 1922 Committee to imposing sanctions on the illegal regime. Some Conservatives would have liked Ian Smith to get away with his independence, and it looked as though their Leader was trying to find a point of departure from the bipartisan policy which he had inherited from Sir Alec Douglas-Home. But this was not the case with his Chief Whip, who was only too anxious to preserve a united front in Parliament in the face of rebellion.

It had been agreed at the Downing Street meeting that the House of Commons should have a day's debate on Rhodesia the following day (Friday), and Willie Whitelaw proposed that it should be part of the long debate on the Queen's Speech so that his wild men would not have a chance to vote at the end of the day.

When the debate took place Ted Heath was obviously wilting a little under the pressure from behind him. There were unmistakable signs of the coming great divide in the Tory Party – particularly in his utterly illogical demand that any sanctions imposed should not be punitive. What he surely meant was that they should not be effective, commented Jo Grimond.

The Conservative Leader did not have a good press. The *Economist* said that Mr Smith must not be allowed to get away with his rebellion: '. . . the test is as much Mr Heath's as Mr Wilson's. If the Tory Leader is as firm with his right wing over Rhodesia as Mr Wilson has been with his left wing (including Frank Cousins) over Vietnam, the bomb and the unions he will be doing what he knows to be right by his country.' 'Lord Salisbury's lieutenants are intensifying their activity,' said *The Times*. And there were more critical remarks in the weekend press. Maybe because of this, he was rather more helpful the following Monday when the Enabling Bill, under which sanctions could be imposed, was debated and passed through all its stages.

By the Friday of that week the facade of unity had been restored to the extent that, at the instigation of the Prime Minister, all three party leaders tabled a unique motion on the Order Paper, congratulating the Governor of Rhodesia on his courageous stand against the illegal declaration of independence. I left London after the motion appeared, but when I reached my house in the North I had a call from No. 12 to tell me that No. 10 had asked the Whips to try to ensure that all their Members, including ministers, signed the Leaders' motion – but that nothing was to be said to the other parties about this. Not unnaturally, a leading Tory, Peter Walker, referred to this manoeuvre in a weekend speech as a trick. It was a silly initiative by someone in Downing Street, undertaken without a word to Herbert Bowden or myself, the sole purpose of which must have been to embarrass the Tory Leader. I could not believe that Marcia was behind it – she was much too perceptive a politician for that. It was probably one of George Wigg's ideas. But it caused a major hiccough in the inter-party mechanism for regulating parliamentary business. Willie Whitelaw was furious as only Willie can be, and felt that we had undermined his efforts to preserve the bipartisan approach.

By the second week of the new session, the euphoria generated by our attractive programme and the chips-down

192

situation in Rhodesia was already wearing thin in the Parliamentary Labour Party. A series of four events created a niggling, critical atmosphere. First, the trouble over our transport policy erupted once again, in spite of all my efforts to sit on it, on 16 November when an Opposition amendment to the Loyal Address was debated which was designed both to lay bare our differences on transport and to embarrass Frank Cousins, the Minister of Technology. It read: 'But humbly regrets that the Gracious Speech contains little promise of progress in the modernisation of industry, notably in the fields of transport and technology.'

Once more the opposition on our own benches was led by Ernest Popplewell, who came to see me before the debate to warn me that he was going to be extremely critical – which he was. 'Sometimes I have subjected him to tremendous criticism ... we pledged ourselves to a coordinated, integrated transport system and we must honour that pledge,' he said. He was supported by Ron Lewis (Carlisle), another railwayman, and many others. They were much more vehement than the official Opposition. It was not a happy day for the Government.

Second, the Government itself was having considerable trouble in reaching agreement on legislation to deal with drunken driving. Our agonised discussions on whether or not there should be random tests of motorists were, as always, leaked to the press. We encountered severe criticism from such bodies as the AA, and the arguments spilled over into the Parliamentary Labour Party, where Members lined up rigidly on one side or other of the argument. Almost anything connected with the by now highly evocative word 'transport' aroused quite inexplicable passion among Labour Members of Parliament.

Third, towards the end of November the Coal Board added to our domestic problems when its regional boards announced an extensive five-year programme of pit closures and large-scale redundancies. In my own region, the Northeast coalfield, forty-eight pits were to close. Predictably I had two delegations of miner MPs (of whom there were a large number in Parliament at that time) waiting to see me as soon as I arrived in London. They demanded an immediate

193

debate on the closures but, to their chagrin, I could offer no hope of finding time in the near future – for which I was not sorry. I did not relish a repetition of the punishment the Government had received from its own followers in the recent transport debate.

The following week three earnest young miners came down from Northumberland to see me and assure me that they intended to put up their own candidate at the Hull North by-election unless the Government intervened to halt the closures. I spent an hour with them and, as I saw them off at the front door of No. 12, one of them turned back and said, 'Tell Fred Lee and Harold Wilson we're not kidding.' On 1 December Fred came to No. 12 for a meeting with the Whips, who left him in no doubt about the anger and resentment among their Members from the mining areas.

On 9 December he came to see me again, this time to complain bitterly about a vitriolic attack alleged to have been made upon him and the Government by Lord Robens, Chairman of the National Coal Board, when a group of MPs visited his headquarters in London, I knew Fred was to see the chairman in Blackpool a few days later, and I advised him to seek the Prime Minister's approval to tell the chairman that he would be happy to release him from his five-year contract. The following week I had a visit from John Morris (Aberavon), Parliamentary Secretary at the Ministry of Power, also to complain about remarks made by Lord Robens. It was clear to us all that this ex-Labour minister, appointed to the chairmanship of the Coal Board by a Conservative Government, was rapidly distancing himself from 'the base degrees by which he did ascend' as many others have done before him – and since.

Fourth, the normally fairly innocuous debate on the Expiring Laws Continuation Bill on 23 November developed into a heated eleven-hour debate on the Government's immigration policy – a topic which can always be relied upon to raise the temperature on the left of the Party. We were savaged from our own benches as never before. Frank Soskice, the Home Secretary, was under constant pressure throughout the debate – as was his Under-Secretary, George Thomas. They were attacked for going too far by Reggie

194

Paget on the right, and for not going nearly far enough to admit Commonwealth immigrants by Michael Foot and others on the left. It was a trying evening for Frank because he was labouring under the difficulty of deteriorating health. But it was equally galling for George Thomas to be attacked from the left, for he had supported most left-wing causes since entering Parliament in 1945.

But there was one considerable ray of light in the pre-Christmas gloom which these embarrassing debates and the pit closures had cast over us. On 19 November the NOP poll in the *Daily Mail* gave us an almost incredible lead over the Conservatives of 18.5 per cent and an equally satisfactory 73 per cent who said they were satisfied with Harold Wilson as Prime Minister. This could probably be attributed to Harold's superb handling of the Rhodesian rebellion, and we know that his TV broadcast on the day of the UDI was watched in 250,000 homes. Rhodesia was his 'Falklands factor'.

Excellent news, which, one would have thought, would have improved the climate in the Parliamentary Labour Party and made life easier for the Whips. But not a bit of it! The added feeling of security which the polls created encouraged some of our Members to begin rocking the boat – ever so slightly, but rocking (or knocking) it nonetheless. The first sign came over the second annual election of the Party Chairman and his two vice-chairmen. In view of his quite outstanding success since the General Election, I had hoped and assumed that Manny Shinwell would be re-elected unopposed. But the left nominated John Hynd (Sheffield Attercliffe) as chairman, and a Member from the far left, Will Griffiths (Manchester Exchange) as vice-chairman. Fortunately Manny Shinwell trounced John Hynd, and Will Griffiths also failed miserably.

If my term as Chief Whip to a Labour Government taught me anything about Members of Parliament, it was that there is a correlation between the way in which they see their own security of tenure and their degree of rebelliousness. Francis Pym, an experienced ex-Chief Whip, was simply making this point in the 1983 General Election campaign when he made his remarks about the most desirable size of a Government majority which were said to have cost him his place in Margaret Thatcher's second administration.

In mid-November widespread snow and frost marked the beginning of one of the worst spells of early winter weather since records were kept. This added enormously to my anxieties about getting our Members to London. The British constituency system demands the presence of a Member in his constituency at very regular intervals – usually weekly. Indeed, at that time the majority of Labour MPs lived among their electors, particularly in such areas as Scotland, Wales and the North of England. Paradoxically, in recent years, despite improvements in travel conditions and Members' pay, the practice of an MP living in his constituency has become much less prevalent.

On Friday 26 November I went to Heathrow, only to find that my plane to Newcastle had been cancelled. I then had to return to London and catch a train from Kings Cross, reaching my home in the early hours. The snow continued throughout the weekend and on Monday, when we were debating a Temporary Import Charges Order in the House of Commons, a blizzard swept the country and raged throughout the day. I heard that the Liberals had decided to vote against us – no doubt calculating that they could safely exploit the problems the weather caused us; a defeat would not bring the Government down, but would be a considerable embarrassment to us.

The Whips as usual spent the day at their telephones in touch with their Members, the airlines and British Rail, and such was their success that when the division took place at 10 p.m. the Government had a majority of three – despite both the weather and the Liberals.

The most bizarre of all the strange incidents and crises with which I had to deal as Chief Whip came to my notice at this time. I heard that one of our Members who had become obsessively involved with Arab affairs (and the Middle East has often had that effect on British parliamentarians) had inadvertently become caught up in an international plot to assassinate the Shah of Iran. I had got to know and like the

Shah during a visit to Iran in 1956, and I had dealt, I hope reasonably successfully, with a great variety of domestic problems during the past year, but a plot to assassinate a powerful and friendly head of state was out of my league. I decided it was made to measure for the Paymaster General. George Wigg and I met the Member concerned, with Sara Barker, our National Agent. After that it was dealt with solely by George Wigg with great skill and discretion.

In November I was approached by Eddie Milne, who had been elected at Blyth in the by-election caused by Alf Robens' appointment to the Coal Board. We had quickly discovered that he was quite unable to control his comments about his fellow men, and he was given to the most outrageous accusations about anyone with whom he disagreed. I had had to warn him, on more than one occasion, that sooner or later someone would sue him for defamation. My warnings were not heeded and he was sued for libel by Ernest Marples, who was awarded substantial damages and costs against him. He told me he could not pay the large amount involved and looked to me to raise the money for him. One of the marvellous things about the Labour Party at that time was the readiness of Members to help each other. Such generous Members as Robert Maxwell, Harold Lever and George Strauss were always willing to give me £50 or £100 whenever a fellow Member was in trouble and, on this occasion I raised the whole amount of both damages and costs within a few days. But there are people who can never forgive a kindness, and Eddie Milne was one of them. Some years later, when he had left the Labour Party, he repaid me for my efforts by libelling me, as well as John Silkin and a number of others, and we were awarded damages against him – which he had to pay without any assistance from a Chief Whip.

Meanwhile, my rather troublesome contacts with the two broadcasting authorities continued. On 24 November Sir Robert Fraser, Director-General of the Independent Television Authority, came to see me about my request for a list of MPs who had appeared on independent television programmes. We suspected, from our own monitoring of

197

their programmes, that there was not only an imbalance between the two sides of the House but an equally significant imbalance between left and right among Labour Members who had appeared. He courteously refused my request, and when a letter arrived from Sir Hugh Carleton Greene, Director General of the BBC, refusing a similar request which we had made to them, it seemed obvious that there had been an agreement between them not to supply this information to the Government.

A fortnight later I had lunch with a very senior official in the BBC, and it was clear from our conversation that the upper hierarchy of the BBC took a cynical, indeed almost contemptuous, view of Government representations to them – not only from the Labour Government, but from any government – and did not take our many protests at all seriously. However, these protests did not affect my personal relations with Fraser, Greene or Lord Normanbrook (Chairman of the BBC before Lord Hill), which remained extremely friendly.

By the weekend of 5-6 December the date of the Hull North by-election had leaked to the press. The date of a by-election is chosen by the party holding the seat when the vacancy arises. It is, of course, part of the tactics to keep the opposing party in the dark about the date as long as possible, and so a furious Sara Barker rushed over from Smith Square to demand that we should change the date. Accordingly, the Prime Minister reluctantly called another meeting of the Officers' Committee – with some trepidation – and we agreed to move it to 27 January. At the same time we decided to book a party political broadcast on 23 February – just to confuse our opponents, who knew we were torn between an early election, as the polls were in our favour, and waiting for the new Electoral Register. Kevin McNamara, an impressive young law graduate, had been selected as our candidate and we were confident he could hold the seat.

Rhodesia continued to be the Government's major preoccupation – time consuming, frustrating and increasingly intractable. A plan to station British forces in Zambia, at

Zambia's request, came to grief when President Kaunda would not concede our right to veto forces coming from other countries. The planes carrying our forces were actually en route and were held up at El Adam in Libya when the disagreement arose. We then decided on a new and tougher range of sanctions. But, unfortunately, we were encountering some reluctance on the part of the United States to support the most important sanction of all – on oil imports – and without their support there would be little point in going ahead with it.

There was a good deal of disquiet in the Party on this issue. It surfaced on 7 December, when the business of the Commons unexpectedly ended at 6.23 p.m. When this happens, the daily adjournment debate, which normally lasts from 10 p.m. to 10.30 p.m. can start early and any topic may be raised. Members ballot for these debates and use them almost invariably to raise constituency problems. On this occasion David Weitzman (Stoke Newington and Hackney North) aired the difficulties a constituent was having about his war pension. This had been fully discussed by 7 p.m., and the House found itself with three and a half hours of prime debating time, which was used by the left, led by Eric Heffer and Michael Foot, to debate the Government's refusal to prevent a British tanker which was approaching the east African coast carrying 12,000 tons of crude oil for Rhodesia from going into port in Mozambique. Michael Foot, who was always meticulous in observing the parliamentary courtesies in these matters, told me of their intentions as soon as it became obvious that a debate could take place, and I had ensured that Arthur Bottomley, Secretary of State for Commonwealth Relations, was present to reply. The Cabinet had taken the decision not to stop the tanker, largely because it would have been a worthless gesture as Rhodesia was getting all the oil it needed. It might also have impeded a wider solution to the problem. Because of the American attitude there was no very great hope that an oil embargo could be organised, but the belligerent left wing of the Party were demanding it with increasing vehemence. Heffer brushed aside the effect it might have on the economy of Zambia – another Commonwealth country. If we could organise an airlift to Berlin, he asked, why not one for Zambia?

Arthur Bottomley's task in replying to the many excellent speeches by Michael Foot, Jeremy Thorpe, David Steel and others was all the more difficult because the Government had supported a United Nations resolution a fortnight previously which, among other sanctions, called for an oil embargo. It required some considerable skill to reconcile our refusal to stop the tanker with our support for the resolution, but Arthur rose to the occasion admirably.

Unwelcome though this unexpected debate was, at least it did not cost us any parliamentary time, and it served as a safety valve for the pent-up feelings of our Members. Unfortunately, Rhodesia was beginning to absorb most of the time we had set aside for contingencies in our plans for the session. Every day, every hour of sitting time, was cherished and ferociously guarded by Herbert Bowden and me against marauding ministers, keen backbenchers and Opposition stratagems, and used to implement our Queen's Speech programme. We were getting apprehensive about the time Ian Smith and his misdeeds were costing us.

The African states, at a meeting in Addis Ababa, had decided that they would break off relations with Britain if we did not solve the Rhodesian problem by 15 December! As the deadline approached, a number of heads of state began privately sending personal messages to the Prime Minister, begging him to find a formula which would get them off the Addis Ababa hook. But he took the view that they had got themselves into this foolish situation and they must get out of it themselves. In the event, only Ghana and Tanzania severed relations with us over Rhodesia.

To add to our problems with the weather and Rhodesia, a troublesome industrial dispute blew up quite suddenly. Negotiations on a pay increase between the Bakers' Union and their employers broke down, and we found ourselves with a bakers' strike on our hands in the worst winter for many years. The bakers were demanding an interim payment of £1 a week as their minimum terms for calling off the strike. The Cabinet instructed Ray Gunter to meet the union and suggest that they accept an immediate increase of 3.5 per cent, which was the upper limit of the norm we had laid down in the White Paper *Machinery of Prices and Incomes Policy*. If they accepted this, the Government would then refer the rest of their claim to the National Board for Prices and Incomes, which had been established in February under the chairmanship of Aubrey Jones, ex-Conservative Minister, and much to the consternation of many of our Members of Parliament and Party members in the country.

There were real fears in the Government that the prices and incomes policy, which was central to our economic strategy, would lose credibility and degenerate into chaos if we tried to use the Board as an arbitral body – which was the intention in the case of the bakers. Some of us saw this as a quite fundamental departure from the purpose we had intended the Board to serve. The award of an arbitration body is almost always a compromise between employer and union. The national interest does not affect its decision. The expedient may have been justified at the time, and it would not have been easy to sit out a bakers' strike when the entire country was frost and snow bound, but it marked a point in the fortunes of the Labour Government where it became essential to decide how our prices and incomes policy was to be developed if the strategy of the National Plan was to have any chance of success.

On 1 December we had a special meeting of the Parliamentary Labour Party on housing. Many of our Members were, like myself, representing areas suffering from the most acute urban decay, so housing was, perhaps the major domestic topic, after prices and incomes. Dick Crossman made one of his mesmeric speeches which greatly enthused everybody and encouraged them to demand a bigger housing programme from the Government. This meeting was a blatant mobilising of opinion within the Party. But Jim Callaghan knew what Dick was up to! A week later, when Dick made a formal request to the Cabinet for 'a few thousand' additional houses, citing in support the feelings expressed at the meeting, his plea was rejected by the combined opposition of the Chancellor and other spending ministers, who were unwilling to see clever Dick get more than his fair share of the carefully apportioned national cake.

This was another example of the power of the Treasury in the British Cabinet. But the Treasury was less successful a week before the Christmas recess when Tony Crosland, with the full support of the Chancellor, requested an increase in the price of school meals from 1s. to 1s.6d. Every member of the Cabinet opposed the increase and the proposal was ignominiously thrown out, to the obvious annoyance of the Treasury ministers, who saw this kind of increase as an alternative to taxation.

Fortunately, on 9 December, when I opened a block of flats in my constituency, I was able to announce that the Government had approved Newcastle's housing programme of 6,400 houses for the next four years.

While Crossman used all his considerable skills of manoeuvre to get his way, he was equally energetic in trying to impede other ministers' plans with which he disagreed.

In mid-December a ministerial meeting was held to consider the imaginative proposal made by Harold Wilson in 1963 for the establishment of the University of the Air, which would be open to all, with tuition by radio and television. In addition to Tony Crosland and Jennie Lee (Cannock), Minister for the Arts – still illogically sited in the Ministry of Public Buildings and Works – Lord Snow from the Ministry of Technology and Dick Crossman were also present. Dick was utterly opposed to the use of the word 'university' for the proposed new institution and argued strongly against it. But the rest of us were quite firm in our view that it must have a royal charter, the legal basis of most other universities. By this time Dick was engaged in a vendetta against another of Tony Crosland's proposals in the field of higher education: the creation of a binary system, with large public-sector bodies called polytechnics having the authority to award degrees side by side with the autonomous universities. Dick saw this proposal, like the University of the Air (later to be called the Open University), as diluting his elitist view of a university, and he did not hesitate to use his Parliamentary Private Secretary to propagate his views among our backbenchers. His influence was clearly visible in an article opposing the binary proposal in the NUT's journal *The Teacher*.

202

This was a constant problem in the Wilson Government. Ministers were ostensibly loyal to the Government and to each other, but one could never be quite certain whether or not they were involved in underground campaigns against policies with which they disagreed.

During the second weekend in December, Jo Grimond made a rather savage attack on the Government – particularly on the Prime Minister. The press overreacting as usual, saw this as the start of a new phase in the Liberals' relations with the Government and, with the *Spectator* in the lead, began to forecast a March General Election, in sharp contrast to what they had been saying after the agreement between Whitelaw and myself on the pairing of the sick. In a weekend speech, Edward du Cann (Taunton), Chairman of the Conservative Party and probably the most influential Conservative back-bencher, also forecast an early spring election. But we saw Jo Grimond's speech quite differently. The Liberals had been giving us a good deal of covert support in both Houses, and we were quite certain that their leader's apparent hostility was a smoke screen behind which this could continue without upsetting the Liberal faithful in the country.

Not only were the media now speculating about an early election, but they were singling out individual ministers for special attack in a way which was complicating the reshuffle the Prime Minister was planning. Nora Beloff's column in *The Observer* was headed 'HOW LONG CAN POOR SOSKICE LAST?' And the BBC lampooned Tom Fraser. It offended against Harold's deep sense of loyalty to appear to be moving or sacking a minister because of pressure from the press. Nevertheless, he had promised a reshuffle before Christmas, and there were some changes he felt he had to make.

On 6 December he showed me the list. He had it in mind to move Frank Soskice from the Home Office to become Lord Privy Seal, whose duties are minimal. He would be replaced as Home Secretary by Roy Jenkins, who had refused the offer of the Department of Education and Science when it was vacated by Michael Stewart. (Roy, like Jim, had his eye on the top job.) Barbara Castle was to become Minister of Transport in place of Tom Fraser, who would become Minister of Aviation. I asked him why on earth he was moving Barbara Castle to the Ministry of Transport, for which she appeared to me to be totally unfitted. He replied that she always got her own way and would be able to control those so-and-so Civil Servants who had controlled Tom. In addition, he saw great electoral advantage in legislating on drunken driving, and he felt that Barbara would be able to resolve the disagreement on random testing.

Eventually Tom Fraser told the Prime Minister that he and his wife had had enough and he wished to leave the Government. There was a good deal of regret in the Government and the Parliamentary Labour Party about the loss of this congenial and able colleague. Harold has since said, 'He and I had entirely miscalculated the glare of publicity which beats down on the Minister, mainly because many newspapers readers are motorists.' The glare of publicity would not inhibit Barbara; indeed, she would revel in it. She is at her best in such conditions. But the real mistake had been Harold's choice of office for Tom Fraser. A minister must be temperamentally fitted to his office, and this was the last department for a man of his sensitivity. Fortunately, he went on to distinguish himself in a number of important public offices outside Parliament.

About this time we had a sad personal problem involving one of our most able ministers. Simple adultery was one thing, but if the lady concerned was Russian and the adultery was alleged to have taken place on the continent, that was quite another matter. And, of course, if he was sued for divorce, the adultery would become public knowledge. Herbert Bowden and I were of the opinion that the risk to a Labour Government was such that at the first indication of divorce proceedings, our unfortunate colleague must be asked to resign. But Harold, as magnanimous and loyal to his friends as ever, was quite unwilling to make up his mind.

On 4 December an Anglo–Irish Trade Treaty was negotiated with considerable skill by Arthur Bottomley and the Prime Minister on our side and the Taoiseach, Sean Lemass, from the Republic. As with any development which improved Anglo–Irish relations, it was warmly welcomed by our backbenchers.

The day after the signing of this treaty, the Prime Minister, accompanied by Mrs Wilson, left for Washington. On his arrival he found a telegram waiting for him signed by sixty-eight Labour MPs, from the left and centre of the Party, demanding an end to the bombing of North Vietnam. There was a real fear at that time that the persistent bombing of the North could escalate the conflict into war with China. This telegram had been organised and despatched in complete secrecy to coincide with the Prime Minister's arrival, and I had to tear strips off my Whips for not having detected it. I had my suspicions. A very skilful operator had organised it, and the daddy of them all lived in No. 10 Downing Street.

In addition to this initiative, immediately it was known that the Prime Minister's plane had left Heathrow, the mice started to play in other ways. Stanley Orme (Salford West) and Eric Heffer came to me and handed me a petition signed by twenty-eight Members asking for a special Party meeting on Rhodesia. I told them it would be grossly unfair to hold such a meeting during the absence of the Prime Minister, who had dealt with the Rhodesian problem personally – particularly as it was common knowledge that a major purpose of his visit was to persuade the United States Government to agree an oil embargo. As always, I had an ally in Manny Shinwell, the chairman of the Party, who agreed with me and refused to call such a meeting.

About the same time Manny was getting rather rattled by the antics of a number of our Members and belaboured me for not taking 'strong action' (as he put it) for example against Reggie Paget, whose views were diverging from those of the Government on Rhodesia, immigration and a number of other issues. I had to point out to Manny that with a majority of two, as it was at that time, there was really no action I could take to discipline anyone and, anyhow, no amount of stern words would alter our foxhunting man in the slightest degree. Although I often cursed Reggie, I also liked him enormously. He was one of those MPs who, with a few deft sentences, could throw a shaft of light on an otherwise mediocre debate – which he still does, but now in the House of Lords.

On the evening of the Orme–Heffer approach, I encountered another and potentially dangerous problem. Richard Crawshaw (Liverpool Toxteth) a barrister and TA lieutenant colonel, informed me that he intended to abstain the following day in a division on a White Paper outlining certain changes in, of all things, the Territorial Army. This was the very last issue on which I had anticipated a rebellion. In vain I pointed out that we, the party under whose banner he had been elected, could be left with a majority of one.

Because of Crawshaw's obduracy, the following day was something of a nightmare for the Whips. As the fateful hour of 10 p.m. approached we thought we were likely to win, but we could not be sure. I had spoken to Harold in Washington earlier in the day and he told President Johnson that, even as they talked, the Labour Government might be defeated. However, to the relief of us all – including, I suspect, Crawshaw – we survived with our majority of one.

Thanks to the goodwill of President Johnson, by the Friday of that week an oil embargo on Rhodesia, fully supported by the United States, was announced. The Order to give effect to the embargo had, of course, already been drafted and was immediately approved by the Queen in Council, but it still required the approval of both Houses of Parliament. The following Monday was the first day of a two-day debate on foreign affairs, which was to be debated on the procedural device of a motion to adjourn the House. (Debates in Parliament can only take place on a motion of some kind.) The Prime Minister made a statement on the embargo, to the delight of our own Members, and got a better reception from the other side of the House than we had expected. Then Ted Heath tabled an amendment regarding the use of force in Rhodesia for the following day, but we refused to give it a place on the Order Paper, because it did no more than state the lowest common denominator of agreement on Rhodesia within his Party, and this gave them the narrowest base on which to demonstrate their rapidly diminishing unity. And Harold would have none of this. If they were, in fact, moving away

206

from the bipartisan approach which had existed since Sir Alec's time, he was determined to expose their disunity. Of course, had the amendment been a motion of censure on the Government, we should have been obliged to table it and have it debated on the earliest possible occasion. But the Leader of the Opposition had not taken up the challenge to table such a motion. Instead we put down an amendment of our own, which Harold drafted at the Whips' annual Christmas party in No. 12 that evening. At 10 p.m. we had a majority of 27 against the adjournment motion, but then there followed one of the most fascinating short debates of the whole Parliament on a Government motion. Immediately the Attorney-General sat down after moving the motion, to approve the Order giving effect to the oil embargo, the Tory Rhodesian lobby moved boldly out into the open glare of parliamentary debate for the first time for all the world to see – including the African Commonwealth nations. Robin Turton (Thirsk & Malton) gave the signal. The Prime Minister had, he said, 'passed beyond the boundary where he can get the support of the House.' Tory after Tory declared that they would vote against the Order – or abstain from voting. Apart from four brief speeches and a knockabout from Manny Shinwell, our Members were content to sit back and watch the Opposition in turmoil. Eric Lubbock spoke for the Liberals and, while supporting the oil embargo, complained that the Prime Minister had 'tried to drive a wedge in the Conservative Party and to widen and exacerbate the divisions which have already appeared.' And, of course, he was right.

During the debate I had a sherry with the Speaker in his apartment and he agreed he would accept a motion from me at midnight to close the debate. When the question to approve the Order was put, we had a majority of 228. The division lists revealed that while the official Opposition, including the Leader, abstained, 50 Conservatives voted against it and 30 voted with the Government. Reggie Paget also abstained.

When I left the Commons at 12.30 a.m. I went to the tail end of a Christmas party for Labour Party staff at No. 10. Giles Wilson, the Prime Minister's younger son, was

207

trying out a new Polaroid camera which he had received for Christmas. He took a snap of Harold and me on the back of which Harold, with characteristic generosity, wrote:

'To a great Chief Whip on the occasion of the three-way split.
Harold Wilson 20.XII.65.'

This division, unfortunately, marked the end of the bipartisan approach to Rhodesia.

In the early hours I wrote in my diary, 'What a way to end 1965', but I soon discovered that our difficult parliamentary year had not yet ended. The following morning a group of trade-union-sponsored MPs, led by Stan Orme, came to see me to protest about the prices and incomes legislation we were planning. George Brown had met the TUC the previous day and encountered a good deal of hostility towards the legislation; in fact, the General Council was up in arms against it. As always, this rebellion of our union allies was leaked to the press and to our Members. Stan Orme's group were, on the whole, moderate Members who had no wish to embarrass their Government. They did not actually threaten to oppose the legislation, but they left me in no doubt that some of our Members would do so, and without Liberal support there would be little chance of getting it through Parliament. As the prices and incomes policy was a cornerstone of the Government's economic policy and a major commitment in the recent Queen's Speech, this would be a quite untenable position for the Government. The motion to give the Bill a Second Reading would be a motion of confidence, and its defeat would mean the resignation of the Government. I did not, of course, tell them I had a good deal of sympathy with this point of view. I simply exuded my usual confidence that the Government would succeed in implementing its plans.

I discussed the problem with the Lord President and the two of us then had a long talk with the Prime Minister, who was as aware of this dangerous rock looming out of the water ahead as we were. When we left him, both of us were convinced that he was too good a politician to destroy his Government by attempting the impossible. The dilemma over this legislation was undoubtedly to be an important factor in his choice of a date for the General Election.

The Government changes were announced on 22 December. The senior ministerial changes were the ones I had seen a fortnight earlier, except that Fred Mulley became Minister for Aviation and Merlyn Rees replaced him in the Ministry of Defence. Anthony Greenwood replaced Barbara Castle as Minister for Overseas Development, and Lord Longford became Colonial Secretary in addition to his not too onerous duties as Leader of the House of Lords. And I had a mini-shuffle in No. 12. George Rogers, our artist Whip, resigned his mouth-filling title of Lord Commissioner of the Treasury, and John Silkin replaced him. Charles Morris (Manchester Openshaw) became an Assistant Whip and was to play a notable part in our efforts to track down the sources of the leaks in the months ahead.

Earlier in the day I had attended a Privy Council meeting at Buckingham Palace. When Her Majesty was told that we needed another meeting the following day to swear in the newly appointed ministers, she was somewhat displeased as she had to leave early for Windsor because her housekeeper had the 'flu. We were sorry about this inconvenience, but how comforting to know that even our beloved monarch had her troublesome domestic problems, like all the rest of us.

The House of Commons adjourned that day until 25 January. Harold once more went off to his island, after he had dealt with the mass of paper which his thoughtless ministers had piled into No. 10 – in clearing their own desks they had almost submerged his. This practice infuriated him and he complained about it with some feeling. He was a great believer in everyone taking a complete holiday of at least three weeks – a week to wind down and two to relax – though no minister can ever escape the red boxes which pursue him wherever he is, demanding the reading of documents, decision making and endlessly letter signing. But Harold rarely got the kind of break he insisted on for everyone else, and the 1965 Christmas recess was no exception. In fact, his recess only lasted a few days during

209

which he had to deal with such matters as a shipment of infected corned beef from South America. He was back in London on 1 January to meet Arthur Goldberg, President Johnson's special envoy, who was visiting a number of countries to try and mobilise support for a negotiated settlement in Vietnam. On 10 January he left for Nigeria, having opened a new library for the AEU earlier in the day. Sir Abubuker Tafawa, the President of Nigeria, had called a Commonwealth Conference on Rhodesia which was notable only for the personal success of Harold in restraining the African states.

I give these details of Harold's Christmas recess to illustrate the appalling burdens he imposed upon himself. An appreciation of this fact is essential to an understanding of Harold Wilson's premiership.

But I and all his other ministers and MPs went home to enjoy our second Christmas in office and left Whitehall to the Civil Servants.

IV

To the breach once more

I returned to London for two Cabinet meetings in the third week in January. At the first of these we made a firm decision to go ahead with the dreaded legislation on prices and incomes, which was not yet drafted. The alacrity with which Harold agreed to this convinced me that he had already made up his mind about the date of the General Election and that he knew that the Cabinet's decision would not be implemented in the present Parliament. If we were returned with a working majority, we could ignore the opposition both in the Party and in the unions; if we were again returned with a bare majority, we could always reconsider our decision; if we were not returned there would be no problem.

This view was confirmed a few days later when he sent for Herbert Bowden and me to tell us that he had now firmly decided on an election in March or April and asked us to work out timetables for 31 March and 27 April – but, he said, 31 March was virtually certain to be the date. Of course, a complete recasting of the parliamentary timetable would be involved so that essential supply (money needed by Government departments) could be voted and other urgent business transacted before the dissolution of Parliament.

When the date was made public at the end of February it was the unanimous view of the press that his choice of March was a direct result of the Hull North by-election on 17 January. In *The Labour Government 1964-1970*, Harold says that his mind 'hardened' on March as he read a report of the Prices and Incomes Board, published on 14 January, on a railway pay dispute which, he feared, would lead to industrial action on the railways. But whenever he made his decision, he told Herbert Bowden and me five days before our Hull victory.

A few weeks later he showed me how he had convinced himself that the surprising date, 31 March, was the right choice – no General Election had been held in March for 85 years. He had divided a large sheet of paper into two columns. Down the left side he wrote all the factors favourable to March, and all the adverse factors on the right. He then made a numerical evaluation of each factor

213

– for example, the probable weather in March scored more than the certain accusations in the press that he was dodging a harsh Budget. The final totals at the bottom revealed a much higher score for the favourable factors. He has also said that in choosing 31 March he had in mind the timing of the 1970 General Election. Knowing the way his mind worked, I could believe this!

Now that the decision was virtually made, one would have expected Harold's famous adrenalin to be in full spate but, strangely, he appeared to be depressed in the latter part of January. Herbert Bowden and I both noticed this and thought maybe it was fatigue after the Lagos conference and his failure to get a reasonable break at Christmas. I decided to talk to him about it, although it was never easy to discuss personal matters such as his health with him. He told me he was not depressed so much as irritated. When I pursued this, he said that one thing which was getting on his nerves was the constant attempt by Frank Cousins to resign because he could not accept any legislation to regulate incomes. Another was the embarrassment caused by a visit of the Rhodesian Chief Justice, Sir Hugh Beadle, who was in London as a self-appointed messenger for the illegal regime and thus speaking with two voices. He was particularly annoyed by an article Sir Hugh had written for the Beaverbrook papers.

I was not at all convinced by this explanation; he was not the man to be upset by minor irritants of this kind, which are the daily lot of all Prime Ministers. He had borne up under all the problems of the past year and inspired all of us with his never-failing cheerfulness. Indeed, he was at his best when the sky appeared darkest to everyone else.

I was not alone in feeling that his spirits were low. A few days later George Wigg came round to No. 12, by now a rare event, to tell me that he also was worried about the Prime Minister. And George Wigg, still at this time closer to him than either Herbert Bowden or me, was in a position to know his state of mind. He told me he knew Harold was disappointed that his senior ministers were not giving the Government's prices and incomes policy their full support in their weekend speeches – particularly normally such voluble ministers as Barbara Castle. But I felt this was George's own

214

annoyance much more than Harold's. In time the depression seemed to pass but, looking back, I believe it marked the beginning of his disillusion with high office, which eventually led to his otherwise inexplicable resignation in 1976. He was working so prodigiously hard, probably harder and longer into the night than any other Prime Minister, mastering the most minute details of every one of the great stream of papers which flowed constantly across his desk, shouldering the major part of the burden of maintaining the value of sterling, taking over the whole of the Rhodesian problem and all the foreign policy implications of Rhodesia and the Vietnam war. It was a burden which no one, not even someone as adroit and organised as he, could bear for long without the strain showing. Could it be that in January 1965 he half-dreaded winning the election on which he had finally decided and which would almost certainly mean carrying the burden for another four or five years?

Before the end of January Harold and all of us were greatly cheered by the result at the Hull North by-election – the thirteenth since October 1964, but the first in a marginal seat. It had been held by the Conservatives from 1950 to 1955, when Labour won it with a majority of 1,181. Our candidate, Kevin McNamara, increased the majority to 5,351, a swing to Labour of 4.5 per cent over 1961. There were two significant features of the election. First, the abysmal failure of a left-wing candidate, Richard Gott, a former *Guardian* leader writer, who we feared might have fatally split the Labour vote. After campaigning mainly against our policy on Vietnam, he polled a derisory 253 votes, which delighted the Prime Minister as he was particularly sensitive to criticism of his policy on Vietnam. Second, anonymous leaflets printed in Rhodesia, urging voters not to support the Labour candidate, had been circulated during the campaign. The result could, therefore, be seen as an endorsement of the efforts made by the Government to find solutions to both the Rhodesian rebellion and the tragedy of Vietnam.

I rang up the Prime Minister as soon as the result was announced, and he took the view that, rather than being the green light for an appeal to the country, it meant that the electors liked what we were doing and wanted us to carry on and implement the whole of our programme. Many of our most electorally attractive policies, such as the legislation which would give leaseholders the right to purchase the freehold of their houses, were still at the White Paper stage. But when I asked him if he still intended to go ahead with the date he had given Bowden and me a few days earlier, he replied, 'Of course.'

On the day of the Hull by-election a popular Conservative Member, Edith Pitt, died. And so the Great Reaper continued to deal even-handedly with the two sides of the House of Commons. From October 1964 to March 1966 there were 7 deaths – 4 of which were of Labour Members. Thus the death rate among MPs was only slightly lower than the *Spectator*'s actuaries had calculated. Considering that there were 186 Members over the age of 60 and the strain which had been imposed upon them, this said a great deal for their stamina.

In politics as elsewhere, nothing succeeds like success. A week after Hull, the Gallup poll gave Labour an 11 per cent lead over the Conservatives. In a General Election this lead would have produced a landslide of almost 1945 proportions. The bookmakers were offering odds on a Labour victory of 4 to 1 on.

Not unexpectedly, the by-election and the public opinion poll generated a stream of Members to my room imploring me to urge on the Prime Minister that he should go to the country while the going was good and before the railway unions started their threatened disruptive action, which could destroy our prospects overnight.

Looking back over the eighteen months since we came into office, the Government's standing with the electorate had gone through three clear stages. In the autumn of 1964 we had enjoyed a brief honeymoon period when the polls showed a growing Labour lead which actually rose to 13 per cent at one point. Then came a second, less favourable, phase starting with the low of Leyton, continuing through poor by-election results and local authority losses and showing a sizeable swing to the Conservatives. This continued until September and the Rhodesian crisis. Since then there had been a steady rise in our support to the peak of Hull

North and the February opinion poll results. Was this the tide in the affairs of the Government? Most Labour MPs thought so and, I believe, their Leader thought so too, though he had to conceal his real views about the election until he was ready.

The Party's elation was almost dissipated three days later when the United States resumed the bombing of North Vietnam, after Hanoi had made no response to their plea to extend a Christmas bombing truce indefinitely. All the fears of war with China were revived. Two decades later it is not easy to appreciate how real those fears were to our backbenchers. Conflict between the United States and China could have ignited a third world war. Immediately the news of the resumption of bombing was known, the Foreign Office with crass stupidity and almost unbelievable disregard for the feelings of our Members and the public – and without consulting the Prime Minister – issued a statement saying, 'We understand and support the American action.' 'We' presumably meant the British Government.

The Parliamentary Labour Party erupted in anger from the centre to the far left. Ninety-four Labour MPs sent a telegram to Senator William Fulbright warmly supporting his attack on President Johnson. I tried everything I knew to persuade the organisers not to send this message, though had I been a backbencher, I would have signed it myself. But I was quite powerless against the anger of our Members. Some of them tried unsuccessfully to persuade the Speaker to allow an emergency debate under Standing Order No. 9.

At the Parliamentary Labour Party meeting next day, when we should have been considering the by-election and trying to assess its message about public opinion, we were embroiled in a near brawl about the Foreign Office statement. Harold spoke for thirty minutes but, skilful though he was, he had his hands tied behind his back. He could not let his Foreign Secretary down either by revealing that he did not know about the statement or by disassociating himself from it entirely. Manny Shinwell, in the chair, issued a stern warning that a General Election could be just around the corner – though, he added with a faint note of pique, he had no knowledge of the date – and we could not hope to win if

217

we presented an image of disunity on Vietnam or anything else. 'Tell Michael Stewart that,' shouted a Scottish Member. The prospect of electoral disaster is the great unifier in politics. That alone restrained our Members, but a full report of the angry exchanges appeared in the papers next day.

After the meeting, Bill Warbey stormed into my room and shouted once more, 'This is the end.' He said he was leaving the Party. He could stand the Prime Minister's treachery no longer.

At the weekly Cabinet meeting on 3 February, I had an angry exchange with the Foreign Secretary about his statement and told him that he might show a little understanding of the difficulty of holding the Party together with an approaching election. Michael was furious that I should dare to criticise him on this score and defended the statement. But I had the sympathy of the rest of the Cabinet.

On the same day the Opposition devoted the day's debate on the Consolidated Fund Bill, when the choice of topics was theirs, to Foreign Affairs. They did their utmost to lay bare our differences on Vietnam, which was not too difficult, for the feelings on our side of the House were such that they could not be – and should not have been – concealed. The Prime Minister had to tread a careful path between the Scylla of his party's anger and the Charybdis of President Johnson's equally easily inflamed feelings.

When I was on my way to London airport on the Friday of that week, I heard on the car radio that Frank Hayman had died. Frank was one of those MPs who appear to be made to measure for their constituencies. An MP's so-called personal vote is, I believe, often mythical, but if anyone had a following crossing party lines, it was Frank Hayman. He was a local man and one of nature's gentlemen. There had been 13 by-elections since the 1964 General Election, 5 of them due to deaths, 6 to the creation of life peers and 2 as a result of resignations. Of the 5 Labour seats, we had held 4 and lost Leyton. But Falmouth and Camborne looked more difficult than any of them, because of the small Labour majority (2,926) and Frank's personal popularity. I was extremely pessimistic about the chances of any other Labour candidate holding the seat and, if we lost it, our

218

majority would virtually disappear. Then I remembered the date of the General Election; there would be no by-election in Falmouth and Camborne. Thank heaven for that! In the General Election, however, we held the seat with an increased majority, which tended to confirm my doubts about personal votes.

As soon as I reached Newcastle there was a call from Downing Street about a television discussion programme on Vietnam between Roy Hattersley (Birmingham Spark-brook) and Colin Jackson (Brighouse and Spenborough) which was to be screened at the weekend. I then heard of similar discussion programmes in a number of the regional ITV companies, in most cases between Labour MPs who held differing views. All of them were designed to present a spectacle of Labour disunity. The media were making the most of our divisions. I suppose this would have been fair enough, had they not virtually ignored the gulf between the Labour and Conservative parties. I spent most of the evening telephoning all the Members involved, imploring them to show restraint – which, I was relieved to hear, most of them did. But I had an angry call from Tom Driberg, who was furious at being taken off a television programme. He blamed me but, for once, I was entirely innocent.

I had to return to London the following day for a whole-day meeting of the Cabinet and the National Executive of the Labour Party at Chequers on the Sunday. On the train south I met Ian Mikardo, who showed me a fairly hostile motion on Vietnam which he, Michael Foot, Konni Zilliacus, Stan Orme and others in the party's Foreign Affairs Group were proposing to table on the Order Paper if they did not get any satisfaction from a meeting with Michael Stewart. As I expected, they got no satisfaction and tabled their motion. I then got all the Whips to try to dissuade their Members from adding their signatures to the motion. But 35 Members signed off.

Our meeting at Chequers on Saturday 6 February was a considerable success. It was part of the constant effort we made to head off complaints that the Government was losing touch with the Party. In my view these complaints were nonsense, as so many members of the National

Executive were also ministers, but Harold was extremely sensitive to them.

The coming General Election, of course, was very much on everyone's mind. Each departmental minister gave an account of the plans he was pursuing, then executive members were free to criticise the minister and make whatever suggestions they wished. Ministers made full use of the opportunity to criticise the Executive for lack of support on occasions when a demonstration of Party solidarity would have been a help – or, at least, a comfort! But the basis of most of the discussions was a policy document prepared by Transport House under the direction of George Brown, and it was decided to begin work on a new document setting out how we saw the way ahead, to be presented to the Annual Conference in October. Everybody collaborated in the pretence that we were preparing for our autumn conference and not for a spring election.

As it was not an official Cabinet meeting, Harold, as always, decreed that we must all provide our own transport to Chequers – those with cars in London giving lifts to those of us who lived in the provinces. I got a lift with Herbert Bowden. This puritan stinginess about the use of public facilities characterised the whole of Harold's premiership and was completely inexplicable to our official drivers, who had been accustomed to more lavish masters.

Early in February I became embroiled in an issue affecting my native county of Westmorland. Manchester Corporation had sought powers to extract a large amount of water from Ullswater, which involved the erection of a dam and the flooding of some areas around the lake. So strongly was I opposed to this scheme that I wrote a formal letter to the Prime Minister, saying that if it was agreed as submitted, I would oppose it publicly – and if the spectacle of his Chief Whip opposing a Government decision was not tolerable to him I would resign from the Government. Ullswater is probably England's most beautiful and completely unspoilt lake and I was not prepared to remain in a government which would allow it to be turned into a reservoir in the way in which Haweswater and Thirlmere had been

220

impounded and destroyed by Manchester. Both valleys had been defaced by the erection of colossal and unsightly dams and their water levels raised to submerge a whole village at Haweswater and many houses and farmsteads at Thirlmere. Public access to both lakes had been lost and the widespread planting of conifers around them had completely changed their character and turned them into Bavarian lakes. Our remaining lakes were a precious heritage – to me, if not to Dick Crossman – and I was not prepared to be a party to the destruction of any of them.

But the Prime Minister simply did not understand what I was making such a fuss about for, as he saw it, water is one commodity Britain has in abundance. Nevertheless, as he and Mary had done a good deal of their courting in the area, he was sympathetic about Ullswater. I was saddened that I got little support from my colleagues in the Government. Labour, it seemed, was in danger of losing its traditional concern for the environment.

Before I went to the Home Affairs Committee of the Cabinet, I asked the Cabinet Office to see that there was a blackboard in the room. I turned up armed with maps and diagrams provided by my friend Paul Wilson, the Lord Lieutenant of Westmorland. Dick Crossman was visibly furious that I should have gone to this trouble to oppose him. Most ministers at Cabinet committees are content to read out the departmental brief prepared for them by their Civil Servants. I had no department and, therefore, no brief; but my efforts made a dent on the rest of the committee and they decided to set up a group of three ministers to investigate the proposal more thoroughly, and Dick Crossman was asked to visit Ullswater. He knew I lived by the lakeside, but when he came there he drove past my house without calling in or, indeed, letting me know when he was coming. I was always surprised how small and petty a man of his intellectual capacity could be.

Eventually it was decided to allow a limited amount of water to be extracted, provided no dam was erected; all pumping and all other evidence that water was being taken was to be underground, and a device was to be installed in

221

the mechanism to ensure that the amount of water taken could not be increased.

I had won only a partial victory, but at least the beauty of Ullswater was unimpaired.

Although no one in the Government, except the Prime Minister, George Brown, Jim Callaghan, Herbert Bowden and myself knew the date of the General Election, as the month of February progressed parliamentarians, press and public were daily expecting an announcement. There had been rumours of an election almost every week for the past year, but now all the omens seemed to make one imminent. MPs were writing their election addresses; those who had acquired reputations for writing good prose helping the less literate. Constituency party machines were being activated throughout the country. And this preparatory activity was being fuelled by the frenetic speed at which the Government was producing more and more promissory notes – White Papers, draft Bills or other announcements about our plans.

Details of the University of the Air were published and Lord Goodman was asked to negotiate with the broadcasting authorities. Our plans for leasehold enfranchisement were finalised – and, as we always expected, were heavily criticised by the vested interests such as surveyors, land agents, auctioneers and estate agents, but very warmly welcomed by leasehold tenants in South Wales and the north of England.

A White Paper on defence announced the phasing-out of aircraft carriers and our withdrawal from Aden, with considerable savings in Malta, Cyprus and Guyana. We appointed a Law Commission, which has since done much to modernise the more archaic areas of our law. A radical enquiry into the Civil Service under Lord Fulton was announced, and two Royal Commissions were appointed to make recommendations for local government reform in England and Wales and Scotland. (This gave Dick Crossman an excuse not to honour his promise to me to set up an all-purpose Tyneside local authority.) The White Paper on road safety was welcomed by the public, who were increasingly outraged by drunken driving, though random testing, which we at first proposed, was criticised. And the Conservatives, in choosing broadcasting for one of their debates on 3 March, gave Anthony Wedgwood Benn the opportunity to announce the introduction of coloured television.

I do not think that any government in peacetime has ever produced such a succession of policy statements in fulfilment of its election pledges as we did in February 1966. During this month there were ten Cabinet meetings and dozens of Cabinet committee meetings, and at none of them were the words 'General Election' mentioned.

Backbenchers who had harried me constantly for months past about their Government's shortcomings were enthralled at the spectacle. It was like watching Father Christmas decorate the Christmas tree, each new goody pulled out of the bag bringing a gasp of pleasure. In *Inside Number 10*, Marcia said that Harold had always been working to a timetable for the end of March. This now became increasingly obvious, for I believe he had quite deliberately planned that so many of our schemes should see the light of day at about this time. A Government in office enjoys an enormous advantage in preparing for an appeal to the country. In 1964 all our policies had been worked out by small study groups set up by the Labour Party and serviced by the small, overburdened Research Department at Transport House. But in our preparations for the 1966 General Election, the vast Government machine, with all its resources and expertise, assisted us in developing our policies. Of course, the Civil Service is not involved in the preparation of an election manifesto but, for a party in office, the manifesto largely comprises Government policies and their development in the few years ahead.

But February was, literally, not all sunshine. The continuing dreadful weather made great demands on gas and electricity supplies and caused widespread disruption of industry, with stoppages and short-time working in many areas. Of course, the Opposition blamed the Government, but it was not too difficult to demonstrate to the public that we were not responsible for either the weather or the shortage of generating capacity. There had been Conservative governments for the past thirteen years; if the power stations

223

were not equipped to deal with a spell of arctic weather, the deficiency could be laid firmly at their door. There is some evidence that, once this point had been put across to the public, the disruption was electorally advantageous to the Labour Government. And the Whips' Office made quite certain that all our Members were fully briefed about the reasons for the capacity problem.

In the middle of these difficulties we had the threat of a national railway strike – always a matter of the utmost seriousness but, at that time, much more serious than it would be now. The National Union of Railwaymen had been offered and refused a pay increase of 3.5 per cent on their basic pay. The Government decided to refer the matter to the National Board of Prices and Incomes. The Board, in a somewhat harsh report published in mid-January, had recommended no increase on the offer, except for a minimal one for clerical workers. The union responded angrily with an announcement that a strike would begin on 14 February.

This posed a considerable dilemma for the Government. The NUR had always held a rather special place in the affections of the British Labour Movement – indeed, they had persuaded the TUC at the turn of the century to take the initiative which resulted in the creation of the Labour Party. And they represented workers who, we believed, were underpaid. On the other hand, the economic indices pointed to a real improvement in the economy, but so precarious was the improvement that one wrong step now could easily reverse all the more hopeful trends. The world, it appeared, was just beginning to revise its initial unfavourable views about the British Labour Government, and everyone assumed that a General Election was imminent.

Much as we all sympathised with the railwaymen, we could not now endanger all our hard-earned gains by repudiating the first report from the board we ourselves had established.

On 11 February, George Brown called both sides to his office, but failed to find a solution. As they dispersed, a strike three days later seemed quite unavoidable. But one hope remained – the negotiating skill and charisma of the Prime Minister. Harold decided to intervene on the evening of the abortive meeting at the Department of Economic Affairs. The comical tale of how the delegates were fed on beer and sandwiches during these long-drawn-out talks has been told by both Marcia and Harold in their books. Sufficient to say it was the origin of the beer and sandwiches legend, which has been quoted derisorily by our opponents ever since. In fact, in his five and a half years at No. 10, Harold intervened in industrial disputes on only five occasions – and then only as a last resort and never as a court of appeal from his ministers. On this occasion the NUR and British Rail reached agreement in the early hours and the threatened national strike was called off. *The Times* congratulated the Prime Minister for averting a strike 'without the payment of any further ransom money'.

The Downing Street agreement did not add one penny to the offer already made, but the myth of outrageously inflated settlements made in No. 10 over beer and sandwiches lives on to this day.

In addition to the weather, the fuel industry problems and the threatened railway strike, we had trouble with one of our ministers. Denis Healey had skilfully achieved considerable savings in the defence budget.

But he had been unable to carry his Minister for the Navy, Christopher Mayhew with him in his proposal to phase out our aircraft carriers, although the reference to carriers in the White Paper – apart from a firm statement that a new carrier would not be ordered – was deliberately worded in a diffuse way which, with a little imagination, could be understood to leave the question of phasing out open. We . . .'should be able to provide the necessary elements of the carriers' capability more cheaply by other means'. A less rigid minister would have accepted this and remained to fight his battle within the Government. But Christopher Mayhew was determined on martyrdom. Neither my entreaties nor Denis Healey's made the slightest impression on him, and he announced his resignation in the House on 22 February after Denis had made a statement on the White Paper.

The text of personal statements on occasions such as resignations must be approved in advance by the Speaker and must be short, noncontroversial and deal only with the substance of the matter. But Christopher Mayhew's statement fills eleven columns of Hansard and was the longest and most controversial resignation statement any of us had ever heard. And he widened the narrow issue of the carriers to the whole of the Government's defence strategy east of Suez. Any sympathy he may have evoked initially on either side of the Chamber quickly evaporated as he continued his inordinately long speech, abusing – in the opinion of most Members – the privilege of making a resignation statement. A number of Members came to me afterwards to express their resentment both of him and of the Speaker for allowing it.

His contentious diatribe against our defence economies did have one effect which made life a little easier for me. It silenced those of our backbenchers who previously felt the cuts had not gone far enough. If Mayhew thought the White Paper had gone too far, we must have got it about right, they reasoned. The following morning we had a Party meeting. Denis dealt with the debate extremely competently, and the Mayhew episode noticeably muted the criticism we had expected from the left.

Like many resigning ministers before him – and since – Christopher Mayhew imagined the shock waves of his resignation would shake the portals of Downing Street, but not a dog barked anywhere in the kingdom! Indeed, when defence was debated on 7 and 8 March, it was as though he had never existed, let alone resigned.

During the last week in February, the Prime Minister paid a long-planned visit to Moscow. It was an indication both of his stamina and his coolness on the eve of a gruelling election campaign that he should be unwilling to cancel the trip. He was accompanied by Frank Cousins as, we were told, technological exchanges were to figure in the discussions, and by Lord Chalfont, Minister of Disarmament, who spoke Russian fluently. Harold has said, somewhat vaguely, that good progress was made on technological matters. But the real purpose of the Moscow visit was, with the connivance of the White House, to try to secure some improvement in the worsening situation in Vietnam – although he and the Americans had overestimated the influence the Soviet Government could wield in Hanoi. Harold in Moscow was a relay station between President Johnson and Ho Chi Minh. Even the *Daily Express* grudgingly conceded that 'Mr Harold Wilson established one fact of paramount importance ... the Russians want to talk ... they are anxious to keep open the lines to London and through London to Washington.'

And the British electors, whose commonsense grasp of world affairs should never be underestimated, understood this. The visit to Moscow in the middle of all the time-consuming election preparations was a considerable act of statesmanship, but it was not entirely unrelated to the coming appeal to the electors.

Immediately Harold and his party returned from Moscow, Herbert Bowden and I went to bring him up to date on our preparations. The parliamentary timetable had been redrawn so that we could complete essential business between the announcement of the date, which was planned for Monday 28 February and the Dissolution of Parliament. By a remarkable coincidence (or was it?) the twenty-eighth was our 500th day in office. But one essential part of our preparatory work had not yet been completed – election broadcasts. The BBC and the ITA, presenting, as they often did, a united front in dealings with the Government, were being extremely difficult. I believe the BBC were more than usually unco-operative because we had refused them an increase in the licence fee. When we and the other parties met them earlier in the week, they had demanded a considerable reduction in the number of election broadcasts. We had agreed with Willie Whitelaw and Eric Lubbock to accept a slight reduction in the total time given to the broadcasts, but not in their number, and we had dispersed without agreement. Although our refusal to agree to a higher licence fee was quite unconnected with these discussions, it clearly rankled with the BBC, and we all noticed a coolness – indeed almost a frigidity – in our dealings with them. But we knew that when the chips were down and the election announced they could not withstand

227

a united front of Government and Opposition parties. They knew that our stand on the licence fee would be extremely popular with the electorate.

The weekend before the announcement both Harold and I went to Cumberland – he to speak in Carlisle and I to Glenridding. On the Sunday morning my wife and I were about to leave for church when I had a very agitated call from my Private Secretary. Freddie Warren, whom I had believed to be infallible, had made an error in the election timetable. It had come to light quite by chance, twenty-four hours before the dates were to be made public. A Treasury official named Robin Butler – who is now the Cabinet Secretary – had consulted his diary and noticed that St Patrick's day, which falls on 17 March, is a bank holiday in Northern Ireland, part of the United Kingdom. Cautious Treasury man that he was, he immediately began to wonder whether it was necessary to exclude this day from the twenty-one days, excluding bank holidays, which the law requires between a Dissolution and a General Election. He counted the days and found we had not done so. He then rang up the Chancellor's Private Secretary, who rang up Freddie, who rushed to No. 12 by taxi, knowing that a letter signed by the Prime Minister was waiting in No. 10 to be sent to the Leader of the Opposition that day to give him a day's advance notice of the election. Freddie called in his indefatigable secretary, Miss Dodd, who over many years carefully filed the precedents for every possible contingency. But she had nothing about St Patrick's day in Northern Ireland. There had been no March elections in living memory. They then consulted the senior Parliamentary Counsel, one of that small, select group of wise men who know the answers to everything concerning Parliament. He rapped out immediately that the Bank Holidays Act of 1871, which the Representation of the People Act, 1949 uses in computing the time for General Election purposes, had been extended by the Bank Holiday (Ireland) Act of 1903 to include 17 March as a bank holiday, and consequently an extra day was required between dissolution and polling day. We had boobed! We were now faced with the alternative of either putting back the election one day in which case it would fall on a Friday – and on All Fool's Day – or of bringing the dissolution forward a day to Thursday 10 March. Of course we decided on the latter course and had to compress ten days' parliamentary business into nine – including both the Monday of the announcement and the day of dissolution. Once we had made this decision on the phone Edward Heath's letter was sent off.

The Cabinet met on the Monday morning, ostensibly to enable the Prime Minister to report on his Moscow visit, but really to inform his colleagues about the election. He was heard with visible relief all around the table, for in the past week there had been a rumour that he intended to soldier on until the autumn. There was a discussion on the preparation and content of our manifesto – but, of course, high-pressure work on this had been under way for some time. The Party owed much to the vision as well as to the unrelenting drive of George Brown in the preparation of the 1966 manifesto, and to Harold for insisting on graceful, readable prose.

The Chancellor of the Exchequer then regaled us with the details of a 'Budget' speech he was to make in a debate the following day, for Harold was determined to kill stone dead the charge that he had called the election to avoid an unpopular Budget. Jim's speech was to reveal the major contents of the real Budget he intended to introduce after the election. It included a tax on betting and gaming; the option mortgage scheme which would enable people on lower incomes to borrow at 4.5 per cent, compared with the building society rate of 6.75 per cent; relief to ratepayers of £30 million, in 1967-68, £60 million in 1969-70; a promise to hold defence expenditure at the 1964-65 level and a new and attractive Savings Certificate. But, in further pursuit of his ministerial immortality, he also told us he intended to introduce decimal currency. Now when innovations of this kind are contemplated there is no group of people quite so conservative as a Labour Cabinet and, in this case the antipathy of the anti-Europeans was all the greater. After all, someone objected, pounds, shillings and pence had been in use since the twelfth century. But I warmly supported Jim, pointing out the vast amount of time which would be saved in primary school maths teaching. As we had

229

no details at this stage and, for example, did not know that the decimal pound would contain 100 pence no one anticipated the considerable fillip which decimalisation gave to the upward spiral of inflation, otherwise Jim might not have got away with it quite so easily in the Cabinet. On this occasion, because of the pre-election excitement, there were not the usual and well-founded complaints about the Chancellor confronting his colleagues with a *fait accompli*. Unfortunately he did not tell us about another major proposal he had in mind which he introduced in his Budget after the General Election and which caused me, as Chief Whip, and the Labour Party untold trouble.

After Question Time that day, Peggy Herbison, Minister of Pensions and National Insurance, announced the amalgamation of her ministry with the National Assistance Board to form a new Ministry of Social Security and the replacement of National Assistance by noncontributory benefits. Her statement was welcomed by Sir Keith Joseph, who claimed that we were merely implementing policy which he had advocated. But we were doing it; the Opposition had been content merely to talk about it.

At 5.30 p.m. the announcement of the General Election was made from No. 10, together with the date of the first meeting of the new Parliament (18 April) for the election of a Speaker, followed by the swearing-in of Members and the State Opening by the Queen on the twenty-first. *The Times* commented: 'Everybody's secret is now everybody's news.'

Later in the evening, the Prime Minister spoke on a *Panorama* programme on BBC. 'This is a make or break year,' he said, and went on to deny the accusation made by Ted Heath and Jo Grimond that he was taking advantage of a favourable moment before things got worse. 'The economy is getting better' he claimed, but added, 'I think the country wants a Government able to do the job of governing. There is a great deal we have to do, especially to make the country sound economically.'

At 10 p.m. the Whip on duty moved the adjournment of the House to enable Herbert Bowden to announce the revised business for the remaining days, including voting the

230

cash to carry on the government of the country in the hiatus between the two Parliaments. The exchange which followed took less than half an hour. By this time there were few Members left in the chamber, though there were crowds of them in the tea room, smoke room and bar, where noisy discussions went on until the early hours.

After the business statement, I sat alone on the almost deserted Treasury bench in the rapidly emptying house. It was exactly five hundred days since we had come into office. I had achieved what I said was my aim at the Church House meeting sixteen months earlier – and it seemed like sixteen years. The Prime Minister had chosen the date of the election himself and had not been forced to go to the country by a defeat in Parliament. And I tried to analyse my feelings. There was enormous relief; gratitude for the good health and good luck (and there had been a fair amount of that) which had sustained me; gratitude to Sydney Irving, my deputy, and to all the devoted Whips who had worked with me; gratitude to the ministers and backbenchers who had willingly accepted the harsh regime I had imposed on them; gratitude for the privilege I had enjoyed of serving a Prime Minister of the calibre and humanity of Harold Wilson. But with the torrent of relief and gratitude there was also an acute sense of anticlimax. The challenge had been met, but was now trickling away into the minutiae of parliamentary history. Things would never be quite the same again for me.

It is said that when one door closes another opens. But in politics you cannot count on it. I was, I now realised, thoroughly sick of being Chief Whip, and I had tried on a number of recent occasions to raise my own position with Harold, but he could be very obtuse when it suited him. In fairness it must be said that he probably had not had the time to think about his post-election ministerial team and was clearly hoping that everyone would be willing to carry on much the same as before. 'Why change a winning team?' was the usual comment when any of us raised the matter – and there was every indication that we were going to be the winning team by a considerable margin.

231

Of course, there is a point beyond which a minister cannot plead his own cause, otherwise he may find himself out of the Government altogether! A Prime Minister is all-powerful in these appointments. And so I realised that, probably having reached that point, I should let the matter drop, but I did not do so without a firm declaration that I had done the job for which he had appointed me and I now wanted a change.

In the run-up to the election, Harold had also been upset by a disagreement with Sir Laurence Helsby, Joint Permanent Secretary to the Treasury, who had responsibility for the Home Civil Service. The time had come for that paragon of Principal Private Secretaries, Derek Mitchell, to leave No. 10. His relationship with Marcia had never been an easy one and Harold was anxious to have someone at his right hand with whom he and his political office could work in a relaxed atmosphere. The Principal Private Secretary, together with the Secretary to the Cabinet, are the two Civil Servants on whom a Prime Minister relies most heavily as the entire nation now knows from watching *Yes, Prime Minister.* He asked the Civil Service to appoint Michael Halls, who had been his Private Secretary at the Board of Trade in the Attlee Government – another example of his loyalty to those who had served him well. But Sir Laurence was very resistant to this appointment, which he regarded as prime-ministerial patronage. Harold was furious, saying he would rather have prime-ministerial patronage than appointments by a self-perpetuating oligarchy. And, of course, he won. A Prime Minister always wins if he is resolute. Michael Halls took over after the election and all of us who were involved in any way with the Downing Street machine found him extremely friendly and helpful. So far as the efficiency of the Private Office was concerned, he was a worthy successor to Derek Mitchell.

One immediate result of the election announcement was that we quickly reached agreement with the two broadcasting authorities on election broadcasts. And on the same day, the Prime Minister received a letter about their finances from the BBC, capitulating on their demand for a higher licence fee. When all the problems are suddenly handed over to the great British electorate for solution, many of them disappear overnight.

The atmosphere at Westminster was now rather like a school in the days before the summer holidays. I wrote in my diary on 29 February: 'I have never known morale and confidence in the Party higher than at present.' Members were chafing to get away to their constituencies to supervise the preparations for the election. And in the Labour Party, with few full-time agents, the MP's supervisory role is much more important than in the Conservative Party.

But we still had six more days of parliamentary business to live through. There were three Supply Days, which the Opposition had at their disposal after the formal voting of Supply had been completed; the Chancellor's 'Budget' debate; and two days devoted to the Consolidated Fund Bill, when Members can raise any topic they wish. We had decided to appropriate the one remaining Friday – which is usually a Private Members' day – to clear up a number of items of Government business. Normally this would have caused howls of outrage – Private Members' time is jealously guarded against Government by the House – but such was the desire to be away to the hustings that no one objected.

We expected the Opposition to choose subjects for debate which had obvious electoral advantage for them; indeed, we were apprehensive about the use they would make of this parliamentary time on the eve of an election. But, quite remarkably, their choices were utterly innocuous. They included a motion of censure on Dick Crossman for his alleged mishandling of a planning application in Islington – not exactly a vote-winner in Newcastle!; comprehensive education, on which the educational argument had been won long ago and on which they did not vote; and broadcasting policy, when their spokesman did not even mention the central issue of finance, thus giving Anthony Wedgwood Benn a heaven-sent opportunity to publicise the BBC's letter on the licence fee, and again without a vote. This was followed by a completely non-controversial vote on technical education. The view of our Members was that the Opposition had taken leave of its senses.

The general economic debate had been asked for by Iain Macleod – though he had no idea that Jim Callaghan was going to use the opportunity to uncover his post-election Budget. It took place in Government time on a Government motion supporting 'the Government's determination to strengthen the balance of payments; to achieve an effective policy for raising productivity, holding down prices and increasing the real value of incomes; to plan more rapid economic growth and a better balance between the Regions; to secure greater social justice, and congratulates them on the notable progress they have made towards these ends.'

We expected the Opposition to table an amendment to this motion but, significantly, none appeared and they contented themselves with voting against it.

Jim Callaghan, in a confident speech, said that his intention was 'that the election should be fought with the country having before it a true understanding of our situation'. And he set out to explain in the simplest terms the situation he had inherited and the progress we had made in our five hundred days. And Jim was always admirable at these simple, homely chat-type of speeches. Unfortunately, he did not reveal to either the House or the Cabinet a fiscal proposal he had in mind which, when it was introduced after the election, caused untold trouble in the Party and ultimately probably led to my removal from the Whips' Office. But more of that after the election. The Conservatives mobilised both Iain Macleod and Ted Heath – but to no avail. We fended off their attack with one hand – putting up Jack Diamond (Gloucester), Chief Secretary to the Treasury, to reply. The Prime Minister, apart from the occasional interruption of Ted Heath's speech, did not take part and that, of course, annoyed the Opposition a great deal. The Leader of the Opposition felt that he should have been matched by the Prime Minister and not the Chancellor's assistant. At the end of the debate we carried our motion by a majority of four, the Liberals voting with the Conservatives.

The only substantial debate after this 'Budget' day was in the two days devoted to defence the following week, one day from the Opposition's time and one from ours. This debate had been requested by Enoch Powell, the Opposition

234

Defence spokesman. Denis Healey and I decided against putting down an amendment, in order to reduce the possibility of defeat. Christopher Mayhew agreed that he would vote against Powell's motion, but would not necessarily support a Government amendment. And there was always the ever-present problem of how Bill Warbey would vote. In addition, there were now some doubts whether John Cronin (Loughborough) would support us or follow Mayhew's lead. Of course, a defeat at this stage of the Parliament would have hurt nothing but our pride and our record as the unbeatable Government. I told the Liberal Chief Whip that we had decided not to put down a Government amendment. The Liberals then, without telling me, put down an amendment of their own – no doubt hoping to attract Christopher Mayhew and John Cronin into the lobby against us.

The final moments of this debate were marred by the petulant attempts of Ted Heath to interrupt Denis Healey. However often a speaker may allow other Members to interrupt him during a debate, it is known and accepted that a front-bench speaker should not be expected to give way in the closing moments of the final speech before the division; but Ted Heath persisted. 'Chuck him out,' shouted Ted Leadbitter above the din. After this inelegant scene we had a majority of fourteen, some Liberals and Christopher Mayhew supporting us. Later in the evening a group of backbenchers put down a motion criticising the Leader of the Opposition for his unruly behaviour.

During the last day of the defence debate, I met the Duchess of Northumberland at a function and she rashly bet me a bottle of champagne that the Tories would win the election. How ill-informed the aristocracy are! But the bottle duly arrived immediately after the election.

I was still having problems with my old friend Bill Warbey, who had written to the Prime Minister and to me in February saying he could no longer support the Party – although he did so in the final divisions of the Parliament. He sent copies of his letters to the press. I wrote a reasonably friendly reply, which I also sent to the press. But at this stage in the game our exchanges were all rather academic. The Labour bandwaggon was rolling and, maybe sadly, no individual – Warbey, Mayhew or anyone else – could prevail against it. Bill disappeared in the slipstream. He was not a candidate at the General Election and never sat in Parliament again.

The following day, Ted Heath, no doubt feeling he had to cut a dash before the nation, challenged Harold to a confrontation on television. Harold sent an immediate reply by hand agreeing to the proposal, provided Jo Grimond was included and there were other confrontations 'down the line' between ministers and their shadows.

Meanwhile, our Officers' Committee had wisely decided that Harold should do the first and last of our election broadcasts and that the topics and speakers for the rest should be decided as the three weeks of the campaign progressed. To retain this flexibility was not easy, for there were those among us who wanted to plan a comprehensive coverage of the manifesto, featuring, of course, the principal ministers involved.

The final backbench speech of the 1964-66 Parliament was made by Robert Maxwell at 4.48 a.m., at the tail-end of a series of debates on the Consolidated Fund Bill which had started the previous afternoon. Bob had waited twelve and a half hours to speak on behalf of the tenant farmers in his Buckingham constituency, who were being dispossessed without adequate compensation when their land was compulsorily acquired for development. This was a serious problem in the Home Counties because of the need to accommodate the population overspill from London, but it was also a national problem – 60,000 acres each year were being lost to agriculture because of development projects. As I listened, heavy-eyed, to this final debate, I felt it was a perfect example of the value of the British constituency system, in which an MP immersed in his local problems can often give depth and reality to a national problem which might otherwise remain academic.

At 2.30 p.m. the same day we met briefly to hear the Royal Assent to twelve Acts of Parliament – each title read by a bewigged clerk, followed by the ancient Norman French formula 'La Reine le veult.' After this ceremony came the reading of the Queen's Prorogation speech, which

236

set out once more the achievements of her Government in the short session which was ending. Here was yet another example of the enormous advantage which a Government party has over its opponents when, immediately before a General Election, it can put into the mouth of the monarch a catalogue of what it considers to be both its major achievements and its claim to be re-elected, for example such phrases as 'My Government has been carrying out with success policies designed to strengthen sterling and restore the balance of payments', or 'My ministers have constantly sought means of bringing peace to Vietnam' or 'Provision has been made for a pension scheme for teachers' widows'. And, once again, the speech was carefully constructed to select something for everybody from our endeavours of the past few months.

Immediately afterwards the Commission for Proroguing Parliament was read. Nothing remained but to shake hands with the Speaker, wish each other luck and hurry off to the places whence we had come to submit ourselves to the judgment of our electors. The forty-third Parliament of the United Kingdom had ended.

The last two visitors to call at No. 12 to see me before I left to go North were Arthur Henderson and Frank Soskice, who were not standing at the election and were very anxious that I should remind the Prime Minister of his promise to include them among the peerages in his Dissolution Honours List. I was quite sure he needed no reminding but, as always, promised to do so.

A General Election on 31 March was as carefully calculated a risk as that arch-calculator Harold Wilson could make it, but still, in retrospect, an appalling risk. March, more often than not, goes out like a lion. We could have had a campaign and a polling day in the kind of arctic weather which had caused us such problems in the previous few months, and bad weather is invariably inimical to Labour's chances in an election. But the truly great leader knows exactly when to take a risk. He knows partly by exhaustive calculation, in this case including meteorological forecasts from both sides of the Atlantic, but mainly by instinct. And, after observing political leaders at close quarters for the past thirty-five years, I have long ago come to the conclusion that instinct is the great X factor in their make-up. In March 1966 Harold got it exactly right. The weather in Central Newcastle and throughout most of Britain was like the French Riviera: brilliant days of cloudless skies and unbroken sunshine. I always took pride in claiming to canvass every house in my constituency because it was small enough to enable me to do so. It was also one of the worst-housed constituencies in Britain. But in March 1966 even the meanest slum streets were bathed in sparkling, golden sunshine. I believe that the people felt the weather was an omen of the new and better world which we and they hoped to build.

Harold, at the peak of his powers as a party leader, started the caravan rolling with the first election broadcast on 12 March – his fiftieth birthday. He rightly concentrated on the areas of greatest difficulty and virtually ignored safe Labour areas such as my own Northeast and Scotland, where we could not fail to win almost everything in sight. He fought a scintillating campaign, delighting and enthusing great audiences wherever he went.

The old hands said it was 1945 all over again. But it was almost a presidential campaign between him and Ted Heath, masterminded from the political office of No. 10 and largely independent of Transport House. It owed much to the utterly tireless Marcia, who, in spite of an attack of shingles, spent most nights in a sleeper and every waking moment of every day organising Harold's complex programme, which she did with meticulous attention to detail and rare political acumen. It was not only the logistics of his programme with which she was concerned, but the politics as well, and he was fortunate to have someone serving him who was equally good at both.

Of course there were difficult meetings. He suffered mass heckling by young Conservatives, notably at Dunstable, and by Oxford and Birmingham students at a meeting of eleven thousand in the Rag Market in Birmingham. He was hit in the eye with a stink bomb thrown by a boy at Slough, and commented: 'With an aim like that he should be in the England Eleven.'

Each night he returned to No. 10, as he was anxious to demonstrate that although he was a candidate for election he was still very much the tenant in possession, the active Prime Minister of the United Kingdom. He was also very keen to impress the same point on his ministers. The Government does not cease to exist with the dissolution of Parliament. All ministers were still in office, and if they could not find the time to visit their departments in London they should do anything else they could to emphasise that Labour was still in possession in Whitehall.

My result in Central Newcastle was, as always, one of the first to be announced. I had increased my majority from 12,651 in 1964 to 13,817, which represented a swing to Labour of 7.8 per cent compared with the national average of 3 per cent. Oddly, the results of most Cabinet ministers showed a lower-than-average swing, and in the constituencies of George Brown and Frank Cousins there was actually a swing to the Conservatives. When all the results were known the following day, we had gained 49 seats, the Conservatives had lost 51 and the Liberals had gained 2, giving us an overall majority of 97 (excluding the Speaker). The hopes of some of us had been so high that we thought we might gain an overall majority of votes but, because of the Liberal intervention in many more seats than in 1964, this goal eluded us – as it has every government since 1935. We gained 47.5 per cent, the Conservatives 41.9 per cent and the Liberals 8.7 per cent. Of the candidates who had sat in the last Parliament, 48 Conservatives were not re-elected, but only one Labour MP lost his seat. One of the most pleasing results for us in the whole General Election was the return of Patrick Gordon Walker at Leyton, where he turned the Conservative majority of 205 at the humiliating by-election into a Labour majority of 8,646.

The psephologists analysed the results and reanalysed them; the press searched in vain for any statistical evidence that Labour had not done quite as well as we had hoped and expected; but the simple, irrefutable fact remained that this was a glorious victory. Labour had won power with a massive majority. There could now be no excuses about the difficulty of getting our legislation through Parliament. The electors by giving us the opportunity for which we had asked, had put us fairly and squarely to the test.

V

A different problem

I flew to London on the Monday morning after the election and immediately went to No. 10 to see the Prime Minister, who was already engrossed in his work at the Cabinet Room table. I had decided to let him see that I assumed I would be offered another job, though he had given me no promise, and I greeted him with, 'So what about it? Where are you putting me?' He replied that 'from every point of view' he wanted me to remain where I was for the time being, but, if I insisted, he could offer me the Ministry of Works and Public Buildings. Now in government circles, this ministry, when it existed, was regarded as about the lowest form of ministerial life – looking after the lavatories at Buckingham Palace, someone called it. And he knew quite well that I would not accept. When I turned it down, he said the only other possibility was the Chairmanship of Ways and Means (Deputy Speaker), vacant because the previous incumbent had lost his seat in the election. But he made it clear that he really wanted to use it as a niche for Sir Eric Fletcher (Islington East), whose present post as Minister without Portfolio and spokesman for the Lord Chancellor in the Commons he did not wish to fill. I told him it was the last job I would want to do. And that was it.

I felt, with all modesty, that I had served him well and deserved better treatment. He apologised rather shamefacedly and promised to move me to a more appropriate office after we had got through the next few months, which he felt would be difficult both within the Party and in industry – and he was certainly right on both counts! I tried not to show my acute disappointment and agreed, reluctantly, to soldier on until the summer.

He then rubbed salt into my wounds by asking for my views on a list of about twenty-five ministerial changes he was proposing to make. These were possible because three senior ministers were leaving the Government – Frank Soskice, Jim Griffiths and Charles Pannell – and because of the appointment of a number of additional ministers of state (second rank in the ministerial hierarchy) and the promotion to junior posts of a few of our most promising newer Members, such as Shirley Williams, Peter Shaw and Edmund Dell. The list involved a complicated series of

243

changes, and I found it hard to believe he could not also have moved me.

, Before I left, I urged on him (as I had often done before) the need to promote some of our excellent Whips and loyal, long-serving backbenchers, again mentioning Willie Hamilton and Arthur Blenkinsop, who had been passed over when the Government was formed and in each subsequent reshuffle. But Arthur, then Parliamentary Secretary to the Ministry of Health, had not resigned with Harold and Nye Bevan in 1951 on cuts in the Health Service and, I suspect, had never been forgiven. And he regarded Willie Hamilton's anti-royalist views as an embarrassment.

Next day, when the changes were announced, I found that not only had he ignored my advice, but he had included four names which he had not mentioned to me or Herbert Bowden, probably because we would not have agreed to them.

On the Tuesday I had a long talk with him about the Party problem which would now confront us. We knew that it would be a very different one from that of the past eighteen months. In the 1964-66 Parliament, Party management was the strenuous and often vexatious, but relatively uncomplicated, physical and arithmetical task of parliamentary survival; now, with an overall majority of ninety-seven, survival was assured. Our difficulties would be political.

The Parliamentary Labour Party, then as now, contained every variety of socialist known to man, from the mildly radical reformer to the avowed Marxist. They came together to fight elections on a lowest common denominator of policy but, once the election was over and won, the left used every stratagem to pull the Party towards their views, while the right were equally determined to pull it in the opposite direction.

This tug-of-war was containable and often provided a creative tension between the two wings when the parliamentary majority was small. In these circumstances the ultimate sanction of a General Election muted the struggle. It was feared by MPs more than any other weapon in the armoury of the Prime Minister or his Chief Whip. But our huge majority removed this sanction and both left and right could pursue their causes to the point of defying the Government with impunity.

Harold told me that he had been giving a good deal of thought to giving our greatly enlarged Party a greater feeling of involvement in Government, and mentioned an idea which had been discussed in a desultory way for years, but which attracted him considerably. This was the setting up of select committees for departments of government where political controversy was less acute. Their purpose would not merely be to monitor the departments concerned, which is, of course, the traditional role of Parliament, but also to involve Members in decision-making, for example where they felt it appropriate to draft a Bill.

The departmental select committees which have developed since then were not the brainchild of Dick Crossman or Norman St John-Stevas, but arose directly from Harold's determination to keep his troops usefully occupied and out of mischief after the March 1966 General Election victory. Like so much in our parliamentary system, they owe less to constitutional theory than to sheer expediency.

He undertook to set his ideas down on paper and let the Leader of the House and me have them within a few days, but he also said he intended to speak about it in the debate on the Queen's Speech, which was only a fortnight away. I suggested that he really should have it discussed in Cabinet first, so that he could get the reactions of departmental ministers. Both Herbert Bowden and I were apprehensive about uncovering a plan for establishing these committees before we had considered it in some depth, for we knew that once we had taken one step along this road there could be no turning back. Members of all parties in the House of Commons invariably unite against the Government to defend their rights and, once conceded, this would be a most important right. We felt that we could end up with a full range of powerful American-type specialist committees covering highly controversial departments, such as the Treasury and the Foreign Office, as well as the less controversial ones – although Harold was very much opposed to this. We were afraid that this quite fundamental change in the function and practice of the British Parliament would detract from the functioning of the House of Commons chamber itself by transferring the action to the committee rooms upstairs. Twenty years later, this fear is seen to have been only too real.

But his mind was made up, and when a Prime Minister really makes up his mind there is little anyone can do about it. Indeed, not only had he made up his mind, but he was bubbling with enthusiasm for his plan.

His promised paper arrived two days later. In it he suggested making a start with select committees on Home Affairs and Education. He also said he would submit a paper on his proposals to the Cabinet before the Opening of Parliament. When this discussion took place his plan received, to say the least, a cool reception – even from Dick Crossman, who later, when he became Leader of the House, almost appropriated it as his own. Ministers were, of course, apprehensive about having their departments under permanent review by committees of MPs. Herbert Bowden and I repeated our plea against undue haste – but all in vain. What had been thought up to provide something for idle hands to do was now the centrepiece of a crusade for parliamentary reform, which was itself part of an emerging grand design being woven by a Prime Minister who saw himself less and less as a socialist or even a radical Prime Minister and more and more as a reforming one.

After this Cabinet meeting, the Leader of the House and I stayed behind to discuss the vacant Chairmanship of Ways and Means. We needed a nominee by the time the House assembled. The appointment, like that of Speaker, was made by the House itself, but the nomination was made by the Government, and as the Government then used its majority to ensure his election, it was essential that whoever was nominated should command general support on both sides of the House. With our ninety-seven majority, there was now no need to persuade either of the other parties to allow one of their Members to be nominated, although I felt it would be desirable if they occupied one of the three 'chair' offices. The Prime Minister used all his considerable persuasive powers to get us to accept Sir Eric

Fletcher. Much as we liked Eric and admired his gifts as a lawyer, we doubted whether he would command sufficient authority to control the new House, with its large number of new and as yet unpredictable Members. But we also knew that Harold was merely using the Deputy Speakership as a repository for a minister whom he intended to remove from his Government on grounds of age though he was then just turned sixty-three. And this, we felt, was not good enough.

I suggested Sydney Irving, my highly successful deputy – not that I wanted to lose him – in order to get at least one of my Whips promoted. We were certain he would have the support of the whole House. The only Whip so far promoted had been Ifor Davies (Gower) to the Welsh Office and I told Harold recruiting new Whips would be difficult without the prospect of promotion. But the need for efficient and intelligent Whips now seemed to have passed, though the reverse was nearer the truth. And he did not seem to care very much about the political careers of the team who had served him with such loyalty when he clung to office by his fingertips. But in the face of this united front of his Leader of the House and Chief Whip, he agreed reluctantly to our suggestion. As soon as I got back along the corridor to No. 12, I told Sydney that he was to be offered the Chairmanship of Ways and Means. Anyone called into No. 10 always liked to be pre-warned. As the Speaker was then almost sixty-five years of age, there was the prospect of succeeding him in a relatively few years. However, later in the day, when Harold sent for him, he was offered only the deputy chairmanship of Ways and Means, two places removed from the big Chair itself. He was told that Sir Eric Fletcher was to be chairman 'for a few years' and that he could then succeed him – if the House agreed. Sydney, thinking he had misheard me, accepted reluctantly. And so Harold ignored the advice of both his business managers in the House in order to find a place for a minister whom he wished to demote without hurting his feelings. I had lost an excellent Deputy Chief Whip, and the House of Commons had foisted on it a Deputy Speaker who, competent though he had been as a Minister without Portfolio and as the Lord

Chancellor's spokesman in the Commons, was temperamentally unfitted for the job.

It also would mean that all the three non-voting officers were Labour Members. Although our majority was such that this could not affect the results of divisions, I felt it was highly undesirable for the Speaker and both his Deputies to come from the same side of the House.

Sydney Irving did not become Chairman of Ways and Means until 1968, but would almost certainly have succeeded Dr King as Speaker, had he not lost his seat at the 1970 General Election. Such are the vagaries of political life!

John Silkin succeeded him as Deputy Chief Whip. John had a charming smile, a soothing voice, an easy manner, but a will of iron. He was a successful London solicitor, incapable of missing the smallest detail, and he had performed miracles of arithmetic as Pairing Whip during the period of almost non-existent majorities.

I offered to recommend George Lawson (Motherwell), a Scottish Whip, as Vice Chamberlain of the Royal Household. I felt that the Queen, with her love of Scotland, might enjoy his abrasive accounts of the daily happenings in the House, for that is what I knew he would write. Everything about him was prickly and abrasive – but utterly honest. He refused, with barely concealed disgust, as he did the offer of a CBE, for which I also wanted to put his name forward.

Jack McCann (Rochdale) took on the Vice Chamberlain's job. Jack was one of our most popular Members, with a Lancashire joke for every occasion. He might well have been created by J.B. Priestley and, as I expected, took the daily Palace message in his stride.

About this time both Herbert Bowden and I noticed a change in the atmosphere in No. 10 on our daily visits. Marcia was much more in evidence and seemed more relaxed than she had been before the General Election – I believe this was because she was finding the new Principal Private Secretary, Michael Halls, extremely congenial and co-operative. The relations between the Private Office and the Political Office were the closest they had been since

248

October 1964. Marcia's star was clearly in the ascendancy in Downing Street.

But this change had a curious side effect in the kitchen cabinet. It marked the beginning of George Wigg's estrangement from Harold, to whom he had up to now given almost dog-like devotion. He was only too obviously jealous of Marcia's growing influence and later wrote in his autobiography (*George Wigg*) in the most scathing terms about her influence on the Prime Minister, which he felt was far from benign. The cooling of relations between George and Harold had grown into an unbridgeable gulf by the time he left the Government at his own request early in 1968 to become Chairman of the Racecourse Betting Levy Board.

Although I, and all ministers, often found her difficult, I did not share George Wigg's later opinion of Marcia. As I saw it, she served an invaluable purpose in No. 10. She debunked the Prime Minister whenever she felt he needed it. And a Prime Minister, being human and surrounded by yes-men, becomes intolerably pompous and self-opinionated – as we have seen from at least one of Harold's successors – if there is no one at hand to tell him when necessary to stop being such an ass. Marcia never stood in awe of him, but always told him in plain, often rough, language what she believed he should be told – as opposed to what he often wanted to be told.

The Labour Government owed much to her courage and ability. Unlike my successor as Chief Whip, I never had a close personal relationship with her – as she has said in one of her books – but there was, I believe and hope, a mutual respect between us, which is perhaps a better basis for a fruitful relationship in politics. My complaints against her were that she tended to interfere in matters which were not her concern and that she was much too sensitive to the constant, harping complaints from the staff of Transport House. This, I suppose, was natural enough, as she had worked there as the General Secretary's private secretary at one time, but it was the cause of Harold's near-obsession with liaison between the Government and the Party machine. But these are minor complaints when set against the service she gave.

On Tuesday 5 April we started work on the Queen's Speech. Although the State Opening was only sixteen days ahead, there was less pressure than when we embarked on this task after the 1964 General Election. We now had a queue of legislation which could have kept Parliament occupied for the next ten years, including the greater part of our 1965 programme, still to be implemented.

The problem now was one of priorities, as it so often is in politics. But there were also ticklish problems about wording on such matters as entry into the EEC and prices and incomes legislation, on which the left of the Party and the trade unions were becoming daily more sensitive and suspicious. There was also the need to remove all ambiguity from our repeated promise to renationalise steel, for there was still a hankering after compromise in the air, though it was difficult to pinpoint its epicentre.

But if there was one thing at which the Wilson Government excelled, it was in devising clever formulae – words which superficially were clear, but on closer examination contained convenient ambiguities that could always be pleaded if the worst came to the worst. How could it be otherwise in a Cabinet which counted among its members such superb draughtsmen as Harold himself, such Machiavellian ones as Dick Crossman and such masters of English prose as Tony Crosland and Michael Stewart.

Some items were lifted straight out of the November 1965 Queen's Speech – Vietnam, Rhodesia, implementing the National Plan, prices and incomes policy, relief to domestic ratepayers, housing subsidies, the Land Commission, leasehold reform, the reorganisation of secondary education and increasing the supply of teachers. Others were added; the most important being steel re-nationalisation, which could no longer be delayed. There was also a proposal to create an Industrial Reorganisation Corporation to give assistance to those with modest incomes to buy their own houses, to increase grants to voluntary schools, and a promise of legislation on road safety.

It was a massive programme, but all of it was directly relevant to the needs of the economy, the problems which were concerning our people and the creation of a fairer society. Herbert Bowden and I calculated that, with a good deal of luck and more ministerial restraint than we had so far encountered, it could be enacted in about fifty-two or fifty-three sitting weeks – that is, by October 1967. But the more powerful Cabinet ministers were quite unpredictable in their off-the-cuff demands on parliamentary time for new legislation, and every such concession by the Cabinet (which at times did not hesitate to overrule the Leader of the House and me) upset our careful planning of the parliamentary timetable. Nor had we any idea whether Jim's illusions of grandeur would produce new horrors like those of his 1965 Finance Bill when he came to introduce his Budget, which we had programmed for 3 May. But I fervently hoped that I would not be in my job long enough to have to compress this ambitious programme into the period planned.

On the same day as the Queen's Speech Committee, the Leader of the House and I had once more to select two Members to move and second the Loyal Address of thanks to the Queen for her speech. There are two views in the House about being chosen for this coveted honour. One view is that they are thereby earmarked for promotion from the backbenches, as in the case of Harold Lever, who moved the Loyal Address in November 1965; the other is that they are never likely to be promoted and are being given a minor consolation prize. Research over the past fifty years shows that the latter is more often the case. But on this occasion we selected one of each! Maurice Edelman (Coventry North), our elegant novelist Member, who was never likely to become a minister, was to be the mover; and Shirley Summerskill (Halifax), daughter of the formidable Edith and a near certainty for promotion, was to second.

As the contents of the Queen's Speech had been agreed in double-quick time, I was able, in the few days before Good Friday, to spend some time with the Prime Minister discussing his Dissolution Honours List, which, unlike the twice-yearly lists, was entirely a matter for his personal choice. He told me some of the names he had in mind, though not all of them, as I discovered when the list was published. His list included life peerages for six MPs who had retired at the General Election, including Harriet Slater, who had done such valuable work in the last Parliament as the first woman Whip. But Harriet, preferring to stay at home in Anglesey with her husband, turned the honour down.

I discussed with Willie Whitelaw the names the Opposition wished to include. They recommended five impeccable Tory stalwarts in the Commons, including one lady Member, for life peerages. But there was one notable omission from their list – a Conservative who had given long and dedicated service to the House, but had lost his seat at the General Election. When I asked why he had not been included, I was simply told that the Leader of the Opposition did not want him on the list. This seemed to me to be an example of rather petty spite against an ex-Member whose only sin was that he had perhaps served Parliament better than he had served his Party.

When I reported this conversation to Harold, he immediately deleted the lady Member, who, he said, might be an adornment to the Opposition benches but had never held ministerial office nor distinguished herself in any way and, in her place, he included the ex-Member the Opposition had omitted. He called him to Downing Street for the usual pre-enoblement interview the next day.

On more than one occasion, Mrs Thatcher has followed this practice of putting forward for life peerages Opposition Members who do not find favour with their own party.

I had to begin work urgently on a list of political honours to submit to No. 10 for the Birthday Honours List. Among my recommendations was a BEM for an excellent lady called Kitty who had served behind the counter in the Members' canteen for many years and who was beloved by everyone. When the list reached the Prime Minister's office there was an immediate hostile reaction from the Civil Servants, who felt that her inclusion would give offence to others who were more senior, and they used every stratagem known to them (and they know many) to defeat this modest proposal. Greatly incensed that we were apparently to be prevented from giving a minor honour to someone who had served Members of Parliament faithfully and well, I went to the Prime Minister, who, to his credit, supported me and insisted on Kitty's award. I wrote in my diary: 'A good deal of jiggery-pokery goes on in the matter of honours and the role of senior Civil Servants needs investigating.'

Before I left London with my family to attend the NUT Annual Conference at Eastbourne, I had a long discussion with Frank Barlow, the full-time secretary to the Parliamentary Labour Party, about the arrangements for the initial meeting of the Party which traditionally precedes the election of a Speaker in a new Parliament. We were both acutely aware of the need to plan the meeting with meticulous care, because of the very large numbers of new Members who would be attending their first Party meeting. We already had indications from reports on the election campaign throughout the country that they would be a different breed of MPs – younger, more abrasive, more ambitious, more forthright, even more able, but also perhaps possessing less wisdom than the Members we had known in the past. We also knew that there were many more now who would gravitate to the left or far right of the Party.

One of the main purposes of this meeting was to elect a leader and deputy leader, and it was necessary to do so before the House met. On this occasion, these elections would merely confirm the present incumbents, but Labour Members are great sticklers for constitutionality. The Speaker was to be elected in the afternoon of Monday 18 April, but the previous week was Easter week, and it was impossible to call a meeting before the morning of the eighteenth, even though this would create travel problems for many of our Members from distant constituencies.

The most sensitive item we placed on the agenda was the readoption of our existing Standing Orders – the rules for the conduct of the Parliamentary Labour Party. There are always a sizeable number of Labour MPs who believe that there should be no rules, and we suspected many new Members would argue that as we had a safe working majority, dissidents on both flanks should be able to vote as they pleased. The Standing Order to which opponents took greatest exception was the one which said that a Member might abstain from voting on a matter where conscience was involved, but must in no circumstances vote against a decision of the Party meeting. This raised few problems in the 1964-1966 Parliament, since with a majority of three, each Labour MP knew that he held the fate of the Government in his hands. In 1945 and 1950 the Party had suspended its Standing Orders, and I expected this precedent to be quoted at the meeting.

Frank Barlow, with his great experience of Labour Party organisation, Herbert Bowden, Manny Shinwell and I were of the firm opinion that the Standing Orders were essential, the Labour Party being the kind of party it was in 1966. The Prime Minister was less certain about this when I discussed it with him and was apprehensive about a row blowing up in the Church House meeting.

Apart from his desire for a peaceful, chummy first meeting of the Parliamentary Party, Harold appeared to be changing ground on Party discipline. There were some indications that he was being influenced against the firm-but-fair Bowden–Shinwell–Short rule, which had kept him in office, and was increasingly being attracted to the 'looser rein' idea of running the Party – a term he used some months later when he finally relieved me of the Chief Whip's office.

I left Eastbourne on the Wednesday of Easter week and called in at No. 12 on my way home to the North. I found there among the paper which had come in over Easter, four letters from MPs pointing out that, in our changed circumstances, Standing Orders were no longer necessary. It was obvious that a campaign was underway from those Members, not all on the left, who wanted to be free to vote against the Government whenever they felt like it, for example on defence, foreign affairs and, above all, on prices and incomes. The old concept of 'conscience' had previously been well understood in the Labour Party to have the narrow connotation of pacifism and matters concerning religion, temperance and capital punishment. There had been constant pressure to extend this definition in the previous Parliament to justify abstentions, but the aim now was to legitimise voting against the Government.

On the following Monday morning I took the chair at Church House. The greatly enlarged Party looked younger and fresher than previously. The impression was of eager, bright-eyed schoolboys who were excited that they and the Party had made it. There were at least twenty beards among them and, two decades ago, a beard was still somewhat avant garde! The Prime Minister was sitting next to me, and in the euphoric hubbub before the meeting began, he turned to me and said he had noticed a group of left-wingers in a huddle at the side of the hall and advised me not to take the third item on the agenda, the adoption of Standing Orders. As I was in the chair, I could, of course, have refused to agree, but when a Prime Minister 'advises' one of his ministers to do or not to do something, you follow his advice, however much you may disagree with him. I remonstrated, pointing out that it was now or never, but he was quite firm about his 'advice'.

And so the Parliamentary Labour Party started the new Parliament without any rule about the support which Labour MPs were expected to give to their Government. But we had the kind of meeting Harold wanted. Bob Carvel in the *Evening Standard* said we 'wallowed in treacle'.

Eleven months later, on 2 March 1967, when Dick Crossman and John Silkin had taken over from Herbert Bowden and me, party discipline had deteriorated to such an extent that Harold had to intervene with his famous 'dog licence' speech ('Every dog is entitled to one bite'). I often wondered whether he remembered his whispered 'advice' to me in Church House, for it was from that point in time that the Parliamentary Labour Party ceased to be a coherent, disciplined body. And, in my book, only such a party can achieve the objectives that Labour has always pursued for the people of Britain.

It is an example – and there are countless others – of an important change in politics being traceable to a minor event which at the time appeared to be without significance.

The new Parliament met in the afternoon to elect a Speaker, and once more I was intrigued to watch Dr King being dragged reluctantly to his £9,000-a-year job by two veteran Members, Jim Griffiths and Robin Turton. The following day was taken up entirely by the swearing-in of Members, who can neither vote nor receive their salaries

255

until they have taken the oath of allegiance or made an affirmation. And there was a significant increase in the number of Labour Members who expressed their allegiance without invoking the Almighty. Another sign of our changing Party.

The State Opening by the Queen took place on Thursday 21 April and was televised for the first time. We felt that the spectacle of the monarch reading our programme from the throne could, to say the least, do the Government no harm at all. We had prompted the new Services Committee, which now controlled the Palace of Westminster, to agree to the televising, and we pulled a fast one on the House of Commons by arranging for this decision to be made immediately before the Dissolution, so that there was no time for it to be referred to the House for confirmation. Indeed, most Members heard about it from the press, and many vehemently disapproved. Even Manny Shinwell, the Party Chairman, had not been told, but was being blamed by our Members who were against it. He was extremely cross and raised the matter in the House immediately we returned from the Lords' Chamber. In the evening I met my first angry deputation of the new Parliament, led by Willie Hamilton, asking why they had not been consulted about the televising and given the opportunity to vote against it. But, by then, a million TV screens throughout the country were showing the historic occasion – with the Labour Government's programme at the centre.

We followed our usual practice of having a Party meeting, to which members of the Executive Committee of the Party were invited, after the formal sitting and before the main sitting of the day. Judging by the reaction to the Queen's Speech, it was warmly approved. There was some niggling from trade union Members about the promise to introduce legislation agreed with management and unions on productivity, prices and incomes and particularly the highly ambiguous section 'Proposal for legislation to reinforce this policy, while preserving the voluntary principle, will be laid before you.' But even the fears expressed on this sensitive matter were muted by the totally unambiguous promise to renationalise steel.

256

In the week-long debate which followed, the Prime Minister devoted a considerable part of his long speech to his proposal for departmental select committees. He suggested that in some departments, such as the Home Office and the Department of Education and Science, there were considerable areas of administration where it would be arrogant to assume that ministers and Civil Servants had a monopoly of wisdom and in which the experience of Members of Parliament could play an active role in advising, in the monitoring of administration and in the formulation of legislation. Heady stuff to our new Members – a whole new field in which to win their spurs! But older hands heard it with some scepticism, wanting to read the small print of anything Harold said before committing themselves. But the die was cast. It was a speech which eventually led directly to a quite fundamental change in our Parliament. Things would never be quite the same again. Remarkably, a book published in 1984 under the editorship of the Deputy Librarian in the House of Commons on the development of the select committees does not mention this seminal speech. Indeed it says '. . . with the introduction of the so-called Crossman reforms in 1966, a number of new select committees were established.' (*Commons Select Committees – Catalysts for Progress*).

The debate, which ranged over the whole field of government, was finally wound up the following Thursday evening by Herbert Bowden – and it was not his finest hour! It convinced me that the practice of the Leader of the House winding up such a wide debate as that on the Queen's Speech should be abandoned. He is not a departmental minister and cannot do other than read out a composite speech constructed of paragraphs from various departments. If he dares to include a few sentences of his own about, say, Treasury matters, he is in immediate trouble with the Chancellor.

At 10 p.m. we had our first division of the new Parliament on an Opposition motion to add words highly critical of the Government to our motion of thanks to the Queen for her speech. For the first time since October 1964 there was no flap in the Whips' Office over a major division – no frantic telephoning around the country or to airports, no sentries on the exits from the Palace of Westminster, no acrimonious arguments with Members who had other engagements. It was a Chief Whip's dream come true – a little leisurely checking of the figures and nothing more. We won by 331 votes to 249 – 15 fewer than our overall majority. But, marvellous though it was to be relieved of the constant anxiety to avoid defeat, we all felt rather flat after it. The excitement had gone and whipping was going to be a dull business with the kind of majority we now enjoyed.

On the previous day there had been one of those prolonged squalls which blow up without warning in the House of Commons, over our proposals for the allocation of Private Members' time in the new session. The row was initiated by one of our own Members, Dr David Kerr (Wandsworth Central) and immediately had the support of such adroit parliamentarians as Michael Foot and Sydney Silverman, both of whom gloried in this kind of dust-up. Of course, the Leader of the House and I had asked for it. We had been faced with the old problem of doing everything we could to preserve sufficient time for the Government's business from the ambitious demands of Private Members, whose objective was to appropriate as much time as possible for their own debates and Private Members' Bills. In trying to hold a fair balance between the conflicting interests we had proposed that no Private Members' Bills should be dealt with before the autumn – six months away. As the session was to last until the autumn of 1967, we felt that this was reasonable enough. But our Members felt otherwise. After the acrimonious discussion had dragged on until past midnight, Herbert Bowden made a few minor concessions and our Members, feeling that honour had been satisfied, defeated an Opposition amendment to our proposals without difficulty and carried them equally easily.

I mention this heated little row only because it was a foretaste of things to come. It was obvious that many of our backbenchers, now we had a large majority, were going to adopt a very different and highly critical, attitude towards their own Government. All the efforts we had made in the last Parliament to find time for Sydney Silverman's Bill on capital punishment won us little credit from him and his friends in their criticisms of our new, and on the whole generous, proposals for Private Members' time. And their attitude was resented by the majority of our backbenchers who always loyally supported the Government. Almost two hundred of them had to be kept in the Commons until almost 1 a.m. to avoid a humiliating defeat. Not unnaturally they took a jaundiced view of this kind of exercise, particularly as we had to ask them to stay after the deadline for the last trains and buses had passed.

The following week was dominated by Budget Day on Friday 3 May. The previous day, following custom, the Chancellor revealed his proposals to the Cabinet. We had thought that this would almost be unnecessary, because of the dress rehearsal 'Budget' before the election, but most of us were astounded to hear for the first time that he intended to introduce an entirely new kind of tax on employment in the service industries. Its purpose was partly to avoid any increase in either purchase tax or income tax, but principally to encourage the service industries to shed labour and to induce manufacturing industry to take on more.

I say 'most of us' knew nothing about it because Harold has since revealed that the proposal had been under discussion for some time and George Wigg has said in his autobiography (*George Wigg*) that he was 'a member of the committee which reached the decision to impose the tax ... We hammered out the principle thoroughly and left the details of application to a group of able civil servants.' And so the Paymaster General had been consulted, but neither the Leader of the House nor the Chief Whip.

The proposal was to levy a tax of 25s per week for each man employed and 12s.6d. for each woman, on all employees. By 1970 these figures had been considerably increased in subsequent Labour Budgets. Premiums of 32s.6d. and 16s.3d. for men and women respectively were then to be returned to manufacturers for each man and woman employed. Eighteen months later the manufacturers' repayment was abolished, except in the Development Areas and all employers in the rest of the country were left with a poll tax on all their employees.

It was, of course, a period of virtually full employment. In the previous five years, employment in manufacturing industry had increased by 142,000, and in the service industries by over a million. But this was a worldwide trend in all developed countries, reflecting rising living standards, which demanded more and better service industries on the one hand and the growth of technology, which reduced the labour content of manufacturing, on the other. But Jim really believed he could arrest or retard this process in Britain by his fanciful new tax. It was believed in the Government that he got the idea from Niki Kaldor, one of his economics advisers. It was a typically academic concept which looked unbelievably unreal when thought of in terms of real people – which is how most of our backbenchers saw it, i.e. middle-aged John Smith made redundant by the tax from the local co-operative store and Mary Jones from a hair-dressing establishment were to be told they must find their way into a manufacturing industry.

The reaction in the Cabinet ranged from scepticism to outright hostility, but, as always with Budget proposals, it was too late to do anything about it. Once more the Treasury, or the Chancellor, had bounced the Government into doing something which it had neither approved nor wanted.

In the House the following day, Ted Heath made the obvious remark: 'My first reaction is to consider how interesting the effect would have been on the electorate if the Chancellor had announced this in his mini-budget speech ... instead of keeping it until after the election.' And, of course, he was right. It was quite conceivable, indeed probable, that we would not have won the election had he done so.

The initial reaction to the Budget on our benches was, surprisingly, better than in the Cabinet, though I felt that this was partly relief that neither purchase tax nor income tax were to be increased, as had been widely forecast, but mainly because Selective Employment Tax was not at first understood. But as the long Budget debate continued, signs of frantic briefing against the tax began to show in the speeches on both sides of the House. On the first day, Laurie Pavitt (Willesden West) gave global figures based on the total labour force of the co-operative movement and estimated that the new tax would probably wipe out the dividend which was then running at a national average of fourpence in the pound. But on the third day, W.T. Williams (Warrington) could describe in detail the effect the tax would have on a specific London Co-operative Society where the dividend would fall, he said, from sixpence to threepence in the pound. The 'Co-op divi' was still at that time of totemic importance in the Labour Party. Most of the middle-aged and older members, including myself, had come from homes where it was about the only means of saving. To do anything which might endanger it was a high crime against socialism, yet this was precisely what a Labour Chancellor of the Exchequer was proposing. And we were a Government which had been elected with considerable help, financial and otherwise, from the Co-operative Party and the movement generally.

At that time we had on the Labour benches eighteen Members, including four Ministers, who were designated Labour and Co-operative MPs – that is, they were sponsored by the Co-operative Party. Normally they were indistinguishable from Labour MPs, but when the interests of the Co-operative movement were threatened, especially in its commercial activities, we were immediately made aware of their separate identity. This is what I feared would happen when the effects of Jim's proposal, embodied in a White Paper, were assessed in co-operative societies throughout the country and the powerful Co-operative Wholesale Society.

In addition to our Co-operative MPs, we had eight Members who were sponsored by USDAW, which represented shop workers, many of whom could be made redundant by the tax. Also, its effects on familiar and popular charities worried Members. For example, it would cost Dr Barnado's Homes £100,000 a year, the Church Army £40,000 and Imperial Cancer Research £20,000.

The reaction to the White Paper was not long delayed. Over the next few weeks, Selective Employment Tax caused me more trouble among our Members than any other Government proposal in the whole of my period as Chief

Whip, mainly, though not by any means entirely, from our Co-operative and USDAW-sponsored MPs.

The Steering Committee of the Co-operative Parliamentary Group called a meeting on the evening of Monday 9 May, to which I was invited. When I got there I found that the Co-operative ministers had sent their apologies. All conveniently had other engagements. After an angry half-hour when I was left alone to defend the proposal (which I personally thought was a piece of lunacy) the meeting decided on the, for them unprecedented step of issuing a press statement, saying that they had met to consider the tax proposal, but that 'because of the absence of Ministers, the meeting was adjourned to enable them to be present, until tomorrow morning ... so that they could take part in the serious decisions that will require to be made.' The main 'serious decision' they had to make was whether they should vote for the Ways and Means resolution concerning the tax, abstain, or actually vote against it. Their problem was that, with the majority we now had, no threat they could make could divert the Government from the Chancellor's intention to impose the new tax.

When we met the following morning, I was able to persuade these sensible, moderate Members to support the Government later that day – on the understanding that all their points about the effect of the tax on the Co-operative Movement would be carefully considered by the Chancellor, and that they would be free to try to secure changes in the long discussions on the Finance Bill.

That is how it so often is with the Chief Whip. He lives a day at a time – often getting by through pushing the problem forward into the future. In the division, we had a majority of 81, which was 16 less than our overall majority; but every Co-operative-sponsored MP voted with the Government, loyal colleagues that they were. However, in later years some voted against the Government and others abstained on SET Budget resolutions.

Year by year, as successive Labour Budgets increased SET – and by 1970 it had risen by almost one hundred per cent – the Co-operative Congress passed increasingly hostile resolutions. Laurie Pavitt, a Co-operative MP, said

262

in a speech that it would bring the fifty-year relationship between the Co-operative Movement and the Labour Party to an end. Ted Graham, Secretary of the Co-operative Party, wrote that 'the Co-operative Party could disintegrate and collapse' and forecast an end of the agreement with the Labour Party. Deputations saw the Prime Minister and the Chancellor and there was a mass lobby of Parliament on 14 July. But all the protests and fulminations were in vain. The Chancellor continued with his hated tax and the Labour and Co-operative movements drifted further and further apart.

The rebellion on SET was only one of my problems in the fourth week of the new Parliament, but it diverted my attention from what was happening elsewhere. The various study groups of the Parliamentary Labour Party were meeting about this time to elect new officers, and the first to do so were the important Foreign Affairs and Science groups. At both meetings there were carefully planned coups by the far left, who seized all the offices in both groups, and a far left faction, as opposed to the old familiar sensible left, was now appearing. When we heard about this, the Whips went to work immediately to ensure that the other groups did not go the same way. This was (and still is) achieved by packing the meeting with 'safe' Members and by seeing that widely acceptable nominations are made – all done if possible (and it rarely was) without any fingerprints being left by the Whips! How successful we were in this Whips' exercise was seen in the next three group meetings – Finance and Economics, Defence, and Education – at all of which the far left nominees were defeated. Rather below the belt, but at least it gave them a more healthy regard for the ability of the Whips to intervene in these matters. The trouble with these rather innocuous study groups was that they were considered – particularly by the United States Government – more important than they were. But, overshadowing all the manoeuvring was the most menacing cloud the Labour Government had encountered so far.

The National Union of Seamen, an unpopular union which had never quite lived down the fact that it had scabbed in the General Strike and had for many years been believed to be in the pockets of the shipowners, had suddenly become militant in support of a claim for a 17 per cent pay increase and a 40-hour week. Its members had genuine grievances about some of the archaic conditions imposed on them by the Merchant Shipping Act of 1894, which was long overdue for a radical revision.

From the beginning of May it was obvious to the Government that the NUS was determined to force the employers and the Government, who alone could change the Act, to agree to their demands or suffer the consequences of a seamen's strike. We knew that appalling damage, maybe irreparable damage, could be done to the economy if this happened, but we also knew that any attempt by the Government to lean on the employers to accede to the union's demands on pay would have disastrous effects on our efforts to restrain pay increases and, equally dire consequences on our credibility as a government in the eyes of the world.

During the first two weeks in May innumerable attempts were made to dissuade the union's executive council from striking, but they were spoiling for a fight. Ray Gunter had met employers on 9 May and the union on the 6th and again on the 11th, as did George Woodcock, General Secretary of the TUC, but their appeals were rejected after the most cursory consideration. Among the suggestions Gunter had made was the traditional one of setting up a Court of Inquiry, provided there was a return to work in the meantime. But this was rejected.

The Prime Minister felt that the situation was so politically damaging that he should intervene, but the Cabinet was divided on this. After strenuous opposition from the Chancellor of the Exchequer, it was agreed he should do so – only the second time he had become personally involved in an industrial dispute since October 1964.

The meeting took place in Downing Street on 13 May but, once again, in spite of a stark recital of the consequences for the country and the Labour Government of a seamen's strike, they rejected the employers' offer of a 5 per cent increase with further increases of 4 per cent in each of the next two years. And they demanded that all work over 40 hours should attract overtime rates, which would give them their increase of 17 per cent, or £20 a week, on earnings. The die was now cast, and two days later one of Britain's most wounding strikes began.

The Prime Minister spoke on television in the evening. After mentioning the offer of an interim wage increase, a Court of Inquiry and revision of the 1894 Act, he said: To accept the seamen's demands would breach the dykes. . . . If our present advice were not taken it would be the duty of the Government to resist the action taken, for this would be a strike against the State, against the community. . . .' The seamen took this to mean that the Government would not agree to any settlement which exceeded our declared limit of 3.5 per cent. Thus from day one it was as much a strike against the Government as against the shipowners.

As the strike could only take effect as ships came into port, its build-up was gradual. This was fortunate, as the country only had food stocks for a short period.

The Government now had two preoccupations – to end the strike as soon as possible; and, in the meanwhile, to stop it spreading to the docks, where Jack Dash was doing his utmost to bring out the London dockers. Fortunately, the Transport and General Workers Union, which had seconded their General Secretary to serve in the Government, resolutely and successfully opposed all attempts to involve the dockers, and George Woodcock was able to convince the International Transport Workers' Federation that the TUC did not support the strike. As a result, there was no boycott of cargoes for Britain by foreign seamen, which the NUS had been desperately trying to organise.

In the early days of the strike our left-wing Members used every opportunity to support the seamen's claim. It was sheer bad luck, and maybe bad planning on my part, that two days after the strike started we brought a Judicial Officers' (Salaries) Order before the House for approval. And this followed earlier substantial increases for doctors. Certain Labour MPs appear to have an almost permanent hatred of judges, and any attempt to increase their salaries (which can only be done by Parliament) arouses vigorous opposition at any time but, on this occasion, it provided a perfect opportunity to demonstrate support for the seamen. Although Sir Elwyn Jones, the Attorney General, pointed out that the average increase for all the officers covered by the Order was 3.5 per cent, Eric Heffer and others had no problem in comparing the cash increases of £8 a week for the Recorder of Liverpool with the £15 a week total wage of a seaman. As Ian Mikardo put it, '3.5 per cent on £5,000 a year is a different cup of tea from 3.5 per cent on £600 or £700 a year.'

The Government's lack of support on the left of the Party was summed up by Stan Orme who said, 'If a 3.5 per cent increase is justified for Recorders and lawyers, then the Government have no right to stand in the way of other claims and they ought to be saying to the shipowners that they must come forward and take positive steps to bring the other dispute to an end.' This argument completely ignored the fact that the shipowners had already made an offer to the seamen which was in excess of the percentage increases to the judicial officers. But the objective in this debate was to place the onus and responsibility for settling the strike on the Government.

The debate lasted until after midnight and ended without a division. Ian Mikardo had told me earlier in the day that he and his friends would not vote against the Order, but would be highly critical of the Government.

It was only too clear that the major purpose of those on our benches who opposed the Government's handling of the strike was to discredit and destroy the prices and incomes policy.

The House was due to rise on 27 May for the Whitsun recess, which would last until 13 June. On the day before the recess we had a full day's debate on the Proclamation of a State of Emergency which had been made by the Queen in Council three days previously. The Proclamation did not require approval, and the debate, like that on the Queen's Speech, was on a motion thanking Her Majesty for her message to Parliament about the Proclamation. On the whole the debate ran smoothly and ended without a division, though I commented in my diary: 'Criticism from the usual gang. They all got themselves elected a few weeks ago on the Government's record and they have kicked us around ever since.'

At the very moment when he was immersed in the seamen's strike, the Prime Minister suddenly found himself at the centre of a furious row in Parliament which also had repercussions in the Party. It was the kind of trouble that consumes a far greater degree of time and energy than its importance merits.

We were extremely anxious to withdraw from our military commitments in the newly independent South Arabian Federation (Aden) which had been set up by Duncan Sandys, but negotiations had reached a stalemate. There was little doubt that Sandys (later Lord Duncan Sandys) in Opposition was in touch with some of the feudal chiefs in the Federation who were determined to prevent our withdrawal, when he accused the Prime Minister of misleading the House about the attitude of the Federal Government towards our plans for military withdrawal. He tabled a Motion of Censure, which was immediately signed by 140 Conservative MPs – a clear indication of Conservative Central Office organisation behind it. Government backbenchers immediately tabled a contra-motion, drafted, I suspect, somewhere within the precincts of Downing Street, which drew attention to 'the fact that on the eve of the important talks on the future of South Arabia the Rt Hon. Member for Streatham [Duncan Sandys] should have sought to intervene in ways not conducive to a constructive settlement.'

The following day Ted Heath entered the fray with a letter to Harold urging him to make a statement as, he said, 'I feel sure that you would be the first to acknowledge that your personal good faith is at stake.' This letter was given to the press at the same time as it was sent to No. 10, and Harold erupted in fury. He replied to this two-paragraph letter with one of his two-foolscap-page blockbusters, refusing to make a statement, but saying that talks could take place through the usual channels about 'this new and unprecedented situation, i.e. where he [Ted Heath] and another ex-minister were drawn into direct association with a Government, in opposition to the Government of this country.'

The Opposition Chief Whip and I, being the 'usual channels', met the following day. He implored me to get the Prime Minister to say something – anything – even a statement attacking Sandys, provided it ended the matter. But I had to tell him that Harold was in a towering rage at the carefully planned Conservative Central Office plot to discredit him, and I showed him some of the headlines from the Tory press, which had, naturally, joined in with enthusiasm. Why, I asked, should he make a statement in these circumstances? Fair-minded man that he was, I am quite sure that Willie Whitelaw was not a little embarrassed by the whole episode – particularly by his Leader's intervention.

On 24 May Sir Alec Douglas-Home had a question down to the Prime Minister asking if he would make a statement about South Arabia, which, as it was Sir Alec asking, he did. His reply attracted further charges and counter-charges from Opposition Members, but surprisingly and disappointingly, little support was forthcoming from our own benches, apart from brief interventions from Arthur Blenkinsop and Michael Foot.

The reason for the silence became apparent at our weekly Party meeting, when a furious quarrel broke out over withdrawal from East of Suez. The trouble was started by the left, but was joined by Woodrow Wyatt, who made the outrageous charge that we were remaining in Aden because of 'American gold'. Manny Shinwell, in the chair, quelled this fire by the old stratagem of promising a special Party meeting after the recess. Of course, this gave time for tempers to cool and for the Prime Minister to prepare a detailed reply setting out the Government's policy on withdrawal. Later he told me that he spent most of Whit Monday at Chequers preparing this speech. It also meant I could ensure that other selected Members were fully briefed to support him.

Wyatt published a full blow-by-blow account of this Party meeting in a signed article in the *Daily Mirror*, and I received a flood of demands that he should be disciplined by the National Executive Committee of the

Party if the Parliamentary Party was not prepared to do so. I felt that this was making heavy weather of it and referred the complaints to the Liaison Committee. During the weekend, speeches critical of the Government were made by Donnelly, Mikardo, Hugh Jenkins and Foot.

On the same day as our rowdy Party meeting, we had also taken the unprecedented step of setting up a Court of Inquiry into the seamen's strike without a resumption of work. Lord Pearson was its chairman and it included a member of the Prices and Incomes Board, although its report would not be submitted to the Board, but to the Government. The reaction of the General Secretary of the NUS was to announce that the strike would continue for another three weeks and probably six weeks.

In spite of this initiative there were still many angry rumblings among our Members – some overt in the Members' tea room of the House of Commons and elsewhere or in deputations to see me, particularly from trade union Members; others were subterranean. The Whips had great difficulty in keeping track of all the criticism. There was a great temptation among them to say, 'What does it matter? With our huge majority we can ignore the critics.' But I was completely opposed to this attitude. It could, in my view, lead to the disintegration of the Party.

The following day I took a few hours' respite from the Whips' Office to visit the Chelsea Flower Show, which I was now able to do with an easy conscience – and what a joy it was to do so! I have always found that the serenity of gardens, indeed plants and trees anywhere, provided the best possible antidote to the neurotic atmosphere of Westminster.

In the evening I had dinner with Phil Kaiser of the United States Embassy, who, it was all too plain, had invited me to find out all he could about the disaffection which he believed was growing in the Labour Party.

At the last Cabinet meeting before the recess, George Brown and Jim Callaghan once more tried to interest the Cabinet in an agreement with the steel companies, as an alternative to outright renationalisation. To me this was almost unbelievable after the unambiguous undertaking we had given in the Queen's Speech, in our Party meetings and in the House of Commons. Not surprisingly, almost everyone firmly refused to reconsider the matter. 'Surely,' I wrote in my diary, 'this must be the end of the campaign to renege on our electoral commitments.' But it was not quite the end, for representatives of the Iron and Steel Federation came to Downing Street in the week after the Whitsun recess to make a last-ditch appeal to the Prime Minister to abandon renationalisation. Did George Brown, or some other Government source, encourage them to hope that there might still be a chance? We shall never know.

As I travelled North for the recess, I reflected on the past few weeks since our victory in the election, and it reminded me of something in my childhood, which I have described in *I Knew My Place* (Macdonald, 1983). My mother kept ducks, and it was my daily task as a boy to drive the ducks from the river into their shed some distance away. As I drove the flock along the lane in what, with more sensible creatures, would have been a quiet, orderly progression, a sudden noise or other diversion would alarm them and they would fly off towards every point of the compass. Sometimes they fled for no apparent reason, perhaps for the devil of it! The utter exasperation of duck-herding can only be appreciated by someone who has experienced it. And that is how I felt as Chief Whip after five weeks with 'a safe working majority'. John Akass, writing about Chief Whips in the *Sun*, said: 'A miserable, sergeant-major sort of job. Mr Ted Heath once did it for the Tories and so did President Johnson, in the American fashion, in America.' Not only was I exasperated with the willingness of so many of my colleagues to wound their own Government, but I was worried at the image of disunity which we were presenting so soon in the life of the new Parliament. I decided to raise once more with Harold, at the first opportunity, the question of my moving to another job. I even began to consider whether I should resign at the summer recess, if nothing was forthcoming, for I knew that without the disciplinary framework of Standing Orders the deterioration would continue.

Maybe, with the influx of a new generation of MPs it would have continued anyhow. I feared the Labour Party itself was changing. It was daily becoming less and less like the party I had always known.

I returned to London for three days during the second week of the recess, mainly to attend a Cabinet meeting, which, again, was preoccupied with the strike. Because of the gradual effect of the laying-up of ships as they docked in UK ports, there had so far been little effect on the domestic scene – in fact, virtually none on prices – though shortages of food and raw materials, with consequent unemployment, were now appearing on the horizon. But the effect on sterling had been felt from the first day. Our reserves fell by £38 million during the first fortnight, but this figure concealed the total position. In fact, the Prime Minister and the Chancellor were almost back to the early days of the Labour Government, when the situation had demanded hourly vigilance. After the figures were published on 2 June there was a further run on the pound, and it reached its lowest point since the early weeks of 1965. This alarming deterioration caused by the strike continued until the financial crisis in July.

Bill Rogers (Stockton-on-Tees), the Under-Secretary for Economic Affairs asked to see me when I was in London to discuss (as he put it) the 'troublemakers' in the Party. Bill, who was well to the right of centre in the political spectrum, was very concerned about the disunity which had appeared in our ranks since the election – a good deal of it among the seventy new Members, though it was not by any means confined to them. He thought, as I did, that although we were now safe in the division lobbies, we were being weakened in the eyes of the electorate and (always very dangerous for a Labour Government) in the eyes of the world outside Britain. Bill, was a hardliner, who wanted to throw the book at the principal offenders. I had to point out to him that we no longer had a book to throw at anyone, but I sympathised with him. He was expressing what many, probably a majority, of our Members felt, but I was desperately anxious to avoid open warfare between

271

right and left, because of the danger of polarisation always inherent in the Labour Party. Many Members, especially the younger ones, felt they must declare allegiance to left or right but, having done so, they could not retreat without loss of face and forfeiting the respect of one faction or the other – probably both!

But Bill, who some years later was to become one of the founders of the SDP, was far from satisfied. Even then he was acutely unhappy about some of his bedfellows in the Labour Party, though before parting company from us, he was apparently happy enough to serve as Minister of Transport in the Callaghan administration. But he was the type of Member the Labour Party could ill afford to lose.

The few peaceful, Parliament-free days at No. 12 also gave Herbert Bowden, the Lord Chancellor and me the chance to discuss a small, but long overdue reform of a piece of parliamentary flummery which was becoming increasingly irritating to our Members – and the fact that it dated from Plantagenet times did not make it any more acceptable. The Royal Assent to Acts of Parliament was reported to Parliament by a Royal Commission consisting of a number of Lords Commissioners, who sat in front of the throne in the House of Lords, dressed in their scarlet robes. The Commons was summoned by Black Rod. The Speaker, accompanied by any Members who felt inclined to do so, then processed through the lobbies to the other House. They stood behind the Bar of the House – as at the State Opening of Parliament – and heard the titles of the Acts concerned read out by a Clerk of the House. After each Act, the Clerk of the Parliaments, standing at the other side of the table, pronounced the formula 'La Reine le veult.'

The trouble arose because the ceremony took place at unpredictable times, though occasionally I was able to exert sufficient pressure to have the timing changed. But, usually, no matter what was happening in the Commons, nor how illustrious the speaker who was on his feet, when Black Rod knocked on our door, everything had to stop abruptly until the whole ceremony was over, some fifteen or twenty minutes later. For some time past each Royal Assent ceremony had fallen in the middle of a speech by

272

a Member who strenuously objected to being cut off in mid-flight by an emissary from the Lords, and we had undertaken to see whether a change could be agreed with the Palace and the Lords. We decided that all that was necessary was for the Queen to inform the Speaker and the Lord Chancellor of her assent, and that they should then inform their respective Houses. There was no difficulty in getting agreement to this simplification, which has operated ever since then – except when the Royal Assent is notified immediately before a Prorogation Ceremony, when the old formula may still be heard.

Before I returned to the North, I called a meeting of the Whips to discuss the postponed Party meeting on our East-of-Suez policy. We discussed the probable votes of each of our 363 Members and arrived at the alarming figure of 80 Members who could probably be persuaded to vote against the Government, including a hard core who would certainly do so if they got the chance. In addition, there were another 28 about whom we could not be certain. I instructed each Whip to begin work immediately the House returned, first on the 28 and then on any of the 80 who were likely to be amenable to reasonable argument about the damage such a vote would do to the Government's standing at home and abroad.

Lord Pearson's Committee of Inquiry issued its first interim report on the seamen's strike during the recess. It proposed a two-step approach to a forty-hour week, to be achieved by June 1967. This would involve some improvement in earnings. Although the report conceded one of the union's major demands, it was rejected out of hand by the NUS two days after publication. At this point the TUC intervened again and left them in no doubt that they would get no support from other unions. But still they refused to consider compromise of any kind.

The following week Parliament reassembled and there was much concern among our backbenchers about the conse-quences of the strike, which was now in its fifth week. It was known (it always is) that our reserves were under pressure; unemployment in many factories was threatened because the stocks of some raw materials were running out, and supplies to Northern Ireland and the outlying Scottish islands were at last being affected by the laying-up of ships. A number of Members called to see me on the first day back. Most pleaded that the Government's prices and incomes policy was not worth the widespread disruption which now looked inevitable. They were immovably convinced that it was only the Government's insistence on this policy that was preventing a settlement, and they saw the strike as a means of forcing the Government to abandon the policy.

But there were other Members who accepted that the restraining of prices and incomes was the linchpin of our whole economic strategy and urged me to impress on the Government that they must not move one inch outside the Pearson recommendations, or the Government would be doomed. Strange, I thought, that a government so recently elected with a majority of almost a hundred could be doomed!

The Prime Minister had an appalling week, after little or no rest during the break. The Aden row rumbled on, both in the Party and outside, in spite of his statement in the House before the recess. The promised special Party meeting took place on the Wednesday 15 June, when his carefully prepared speech was, by general agreement, a superb effort. A motion that was unacceptable to the Government was moved by Chris Mayhew, but even after all the strenuous efforts of the Whips, 54 Members voted for it. 'The Government has brought in the payroll vote,' said one of the anti-Government group, noticing that all our ministers were present – a charge which was repeated in a number of newspapers.

Meanwhile, the Liaison Committee considered the complaints against Woodrow Wyatt, which I had referred to them. They decided to invite the Party meeting to reprimand him, saying they regarded his conduct as 'deplorable and reprehensible'. However, on a motion moved by Michael Foot and seconded by Stan Orme, the Liaison Committee report was referred back to them on the grounds that Gerald Kaufman, the Party's Parliamentary Press Officer, was alleged to have done some leaking himself. So much for our attempt to maintain any kind of Party discipline.

274

The Prime Minister was also embroiled in a rather bitter legal battle at this time with our European partners over our attempts to withdraw from the European Launcher Development Organisation. But dominating his work and absorbing most of his time was the deepening crisis of the seamen's strike. A nine-man union negotiating committee came to see him about a Government subsidy to finance a bigger settlement. Once more they were told that no settlement would be acceptable to the Government if the total cost exceeded that of Lord Pearson's interim report.

On 17 June both sides were summoned to No. 10 for separate meetings, and later in the day the whole union executive council was called in. Later still, in the evening, they met the TUC once again. But all to no avail – indeed, the day of meetings actually worsened the situation when the union announced: 'This is a fight with the Government, not the shipowners.'

By this time the Government (or, more correctly, the Prime Minister) had by now firm evidence that, although no member of the union executive council was a member of the Communist Party, the union was increasingly coming under communist influence throughout the country. Industrial disruption has always been a major communist objective, so this was an important opportunity for them, though they failed to win the support of other unions or international support.

After all the abortive efforts to reach a settlement, particularly during the past weeks, the Prime Minister told me on the Friday afternoon that he had decided to 'spill the beans' about communist involvement in the strike in a statement in the Commons on Monday 20 June. In the statement he said that 'a few individuals have brought pressure to bear on a select few of the executive council of the . . . union . . . who, in turn, have been able to dominate the majority of that otherwise sturdy union.' He went on to describe three individuals as 'a tightly knit group of politically motivated men who, as the last General Election showed, utterly failed to secure acceptance of their views by the British electorate.' There was no mention of communists, but the reference to the General Election put his meaning beyond doubt. He also announced that we would be asking the House to renew the Government's emergency powers, which would otherwise shortly expire – although, so far, it had not been necessary to use them.

Ted Heath, for once, made an initial supportive response, but immediate support for the seamen came from a number of our own backbenchers. Eric Heffer said we were 'creating greater problems in relation to the dispute and not solving them by the actions which the Government have taken.' As we all expected, one of our Members, John Hynd, asked if the evidence for the Prime Minister's allegations would be made public, and was told that it would – at the right time.

Later, the Leader of the Opposition asked to see the Prime Minister privately and was given all the background facts. But this did not inhibit him from shortly afterwards demanding in the House that Parliament should be given more information to justify the allegations. His behaviour on this matter was in stark contrast to that of Harold Wilson as the Leader of the Opposition, when Harold Macmillan and the head of MI6 put him fully in the picture on the Kim Philby affair.

In the few days following the statement, there were strong condemnations of the Prime Minister in left-wing speeches throughout the country and, of course, the Tory press saw in them a heaven-sent opportunity to widen what they believed was a major breach in the ranks of Government supporters. With one voice they demanded the evidence, believing there was none apart from snippets of gossip which they themselves had unearthed and published. As the demands for information built up, Harold told me he had decided to tell all in the debate on the emergency powers on 28 June. And this he did, with a vengeance – naming names and disclosing such details as whose flat two members of the NUS Executive Council had used on their visits to London during the strike and who had visited them there. The like of it had never been heard before from the mouth of a Prime Minister during an industrial dispute.

But many of our backbenchers told me, and some said in the debate, that his evidence amounted to nothing more than the imputation of guilt by association – a procedure which is not necessarily ineffective, though it is always condemned in Parliament. Ted Heath followed by demanding a tribunal of inquiry into the allegations.

One of the first backbench speakers was Ian Mikardo, on the left, but a resolute anti-communist. He was highly critical of the Prime Minister who, he felt, was overrating communist influence. Eric Heffer, an ex-communist but now also firmly anti-communist, was again extremely critical of the Government's handling of the strike: 'the acme of ineptitude', he called it, and once more appealed to the Government to lean on the shipowners and, if they did not respond, to 'take over the shipping industry and run it on behalf of the nation, and make certain the seamen got a square deal.'

Michael Foot accused the Government of neglecting to take many measures which could have averted the strike which, he went on, 'makes it all the worse that they should have resorted to the kind of accusations which we now see have precious little foundation.'

The Prime Minister, whose opening speech had lasted fifty-two minutes, wound up the debate with a thirty-four-minute speech. I never knew how he had found the time to prepare long speeches of this kind in the turmoil of the past few weeks, when every minute of his waking day seemed to be occupied with one troublesome problem after another. Yet, when he stood up at the despatch box, he always produced a carefully constructed and typed speech.

The emergency regulations were approved without a division, but the day's debate left me and all my colleagues in the Whips' Office acutely unhappy about the spectacle of a deeply divided Party. We had suffered internal dissent about Government action – or inaction – in the last Parliament, but nothing approaching the degree of condemnation by such Members as Eric Heffer and Michael Foot in this one.

I felt that I was failing in my job but, I wondered, could the Archangel Gabriel have been any more successful in a party such as ours, when faced with the cumulative effects of the seamen's strike, our ambivalent attitude to the United States in Vietnam, our continued delay in withdrawing from military commitments east of Suez, the highly divisive selective employment tax proposals and the promised legislation on prices and incomes – striking, as it threatened, at the basic function of the trade unions. But there were some signs that Harold, who since October 1964 had always given me complete support in all I did, was beginning to believe that my views on Party loyalty, unity and discipline were no longer appropriate in a Parliament where we had a considerable majority and many new Members – and that maybe the Whips' handling of a series of difficult situations was to blame for the growing disarray.

There were many doubts in the Party about whether Harold's unprecedented revelations would shorten the strike. Most Members, I believe, thought he had exacerbated the problem. The Leader of the Opposition said they could lengthen the dispute – but he would, wouldn't he?

However, events very quickly proved that his remarkable political instinct had not failed him. Four days later, on 2 July, the seven-week strike ended in spite of all the prophesies of gloom and disaster from the Opposition, from our own left wing and from the press.

Looking back over the whole dismal episode, I asked myself how much substance there was in the strictures of such Members as Eric Heffer, Michael Foot and others about the Government's handling of the strike. I had two doubts. With the benefit of hindsight, I doubted whether Ray Gunter, who had personal problems at this time, had either the ability or the flexibility to deal with it. In fact, towards the end, the Prime Minister rather than his Minister of Labour handled the whole situation. Again with the benefit of hindsight, I doubted whether Harold's television broadcast on the first day of the strike was wise, making it a strike against the Government from the start, though at the time I fully supported it.

The consequences of the strike for the union were not unlike those for the National Union of Mineworkers after their recent strike. Membership fell catastrophically from 120,000 to 55,000 and, according to the *Economist*, their finances were in a parlous state. But worse than this, they found themselves without industrial muscle. In the past they had all too often been a willing, or an apathetic, tool of the employers. Now they had no option – they were a weakling among unions.

But the damage to the economy, which had been so painstakingly nursed back to health over the preceding eighteen months, was appalling. It was not so much the effect on our export performance, though that was bad enough, as the speculation against our currency. The Central Banks had co-operated early in the strike to stabilise the situation to some extent but, when the figures came out on 4 July, they revealed a steep and continuing fall in our reserves. The publication of the figures itself precipitated further considerable speculation against the pound. A report in the *Financial Times* from French Government sources that the United Kingdom might have to devalue before entry into the EEC gave a further impetus to the speculators – as did reports from anti-Government sources in the City of London, which can always be relied upon to put the boot in when a Labour Government is in difficulties. Harold said subsequently that the seamen's strike had blown us off course. To mix his nautical metaphor, it did so by precipitating an enormous avalanche in our path.

In my view, it was a tragic turning point for the Labour Government, which up to this time had been achieving a considerable degree of success and winning not only credibility but admiration. How otherwise could the General Election results be interpreted? Had the seamen's strike not occurred, the result of the 1970 General Election might have been very different. The Labour Party owes its existence, and much more, to the trade unions, but all too often individual unions have been its worse enemies.

For the Parliamentary Labour Party the strike was extremely divisive. The waters were muddied and took long to clear. The old friendly and productive tension between right, left and centre had become soured and counterproductive.

The fates themselves appeared to be conspiring to make life difficult for us in the early summer of 1966. A few hours after the bitter debate on the renewal of emergency powers, the United States bombed Hanoi and Haiphong in North Vietnam. The Prime Minister had told a special military envoy from President Johnson earlier in the week that if the bombing of the North was resumed, we would publicly dissociate ourselves from the American action. After warning the Foreign Office that they must not issue any statement, as they had done to the anger and dismay of the entire Party the previous January, Harold made statements both to the press and in the House. These were carefully worded, so as to dissociate ourselves from the bombing in a way which was not too condemnatory, while leaving intact our general support for American objectives in Vietnam. Ted Heath's critical reaction to the Prime Minister was entirely predictable, as was that of our own left wing, who were disappointed at our limited disapproval.

As well as being lashed by the Party's fury over the bombing, which many genuinely felt could escalate into war with China, I also had on my hands a near revolt of a different kind from our new Members. But, time-consuming though it was, this was a rebellion I welcomed. They were a lively group and much younger on average than the Party in the previous Parliament. Many had come from occupations where they had enjoyed modern office accommodation and equipment and they were appalled at the lack of the most basic facilities for doing their job efficiently at Westminster. Although we had improved MPs' salaries by implementing the Lawrence Report, the problem was, as always at Westminster, that though the salary was adequate for the dormant Members – and there were some – even after our improvements it was inadequate for the more active ones. Activity by an MP always results in a larger postbag and more invitations to speak at functions – all of which cost a great deal in postage and secretarial assistance. And most of our new Members were active, some hyperactive and ambitious.

But their grievances were not confined to finance. They thought it ludicrous that an MP should have to sit in a draughty corridor to dictate his letters or interview a constituent, that he should not have a desk, a filing cabinet or a telephone to call his own, that he should have to pay a charge imposed by the Serjeant-at-Arms whenever he photocopied a letter, that all his phone calls on behalf of his constituents and all his postage should have to be paid out of his 'salary' – not to mention his living expenses in London. In my view their anger was fully justified. It gave me a head of steam in demanding the resources from the Treasury to do something about it.

Herbert Bowden and I had a number of meetings with Members and listened to all their demands (and that is what they were!) and promised what really amounted to a planned campaign to revolutionise their working conditions. Taking over the control of the Palace of Westminster from the Lord Great Chamberlain had made this possible; indeed, in many respects it was already under way. Before the takeover, the whole building had been run by and, we often believed largely for, the officers and officials of the House. MPs had been made to feel they were there on sufferance – or at any rate that they had to keep within tightly confined limits. This state of affairs, which had developed and ossified over the centuries, was in effect the residual power of the Crown keeping the representatives of the people in their place. I always felt it was unfortunate that Parliament had ever met in a royal palace. Our new MPs were not prepared to tolerate these restrictions, which to them struck at the heart of a free, democratic Parliament.

A small group, led by Gwyneth Dunwoody, demanded that I take them on a tour of those parts of the building which MPs had hitherto never seen. They refused to believe that in this enormous building there was not sufficient space to give each MP an office of his own – as in most other western parliaments. We found huge rooms beautifully furnished, carpeted and curtained, each occupied by one official. We penetrated into the large amount of virtually unused space above the Speaker's inordinately vast accommodation, and found that his secretary had three rooms for his own personal use. In the same area we discovered a fine, well-proportioned room which, as it was open to the elements, had obviously provided a haven for the pigeons for many years and been forgotten by everyone. We found a room above St Stephen's Entrance which was

281

labelled 'National Liberal Chief Whip'. This was 1966, and none of the younger Members even knew what a National Liberal was.

We promised to ask the Minister of Public Buildings and Works, who had already had rooms built for the Shadow Cabinet, to carry out a thorough survey of the Palace and begin a long-term programme of creating office accommodation for Members, by reorganising existing space where that was possible and by building in the many interstices where this could be done. Thanks to this programme, two decades later every MP has his own place of work at Westminster.

On Monday 27 June I had heard on the Downing Street grapevine that Frank Cousins was once more pressing to resign from the Government. I saw him twice early in that week to try to dissuade him, but by this time his mind was made up. He said he would feel a traitor to the trade union movement if he remained a member of a government which introduced legislation to interfere with free, collective bargaining between unions and employers. Even though he had always resolutely opposed it inside the Cabinet, the doctrine of collective Cabinet responsibility would prevent him from expressing any public disagreement with the Government, and he would find this situation intolerable. The legislation had been promised in the Queen's Speech in November 1965 and again in April 1966 and, he said, must now be imminent. It was time for him to go.

I was extremely sorry that he had reached this decision. I had always enjoyed working with him and admired his transparent honesty – though I frequently disagreed with him. But, more important, the presence of one of the most senior and respected trade union leaders gave our Government a dimension in industrial and economic matters which was of crucial importance, as the seamen's strike had shown. Of course we had other ministers, such as Douglas Houghton and Ray Gunter, who had been senior trade union officials, but none had Frank Cousins' authority and influence in the unions.

I met Herbert Bowden in the corridor outside the Cabinet Room on the Wednesday morning, and he staggered me by telling me that I was to be the beneficiary from Frank's

282

resignation. I told him that I had, in fact, spent a good deal of time in the past few days trying to prevent his resignation. The plan was, he told me, that Anthony Wedgwood Benn was to become Minister of Technology – an office only very recently enhanced by important new powers for the oversight of both the engineering and shipbuilding industries – and that I was to follow him at the Post Office. This explained a remark Harold had made to me two days earlier. He had said, in that enigmatic way of his, that he wanted to see me on Friday afternoon. Now, Harold had two enigmatic ways of saying things. One was accompanied by a thunderous glower, which was the nearest he ever came to administering a rebuke to one of his ministers; and the other was accompanied by his most puckish smile. In my case, it had been the latter, so I had assumed he wanted to see me about something pleasant.

When he offered me the Post Office, of course I expressed surprise – though I had had two days to think about it. Had he offered to make me Postmaster General after the General Election, I should probably have refused it – as I did the Ministry of Public Buildings and Works – but after two months of this new Parliament, I was so thoroughly sick of trying to hold our enlarged Party together that I accepted without hesitation, but not without some misgivings about taking over a highly technical department. However, my two years at the Post Office turned out to be the happiest and most productive in the whole of my public life, largely because of the staunch and expert support and advice I had from such dedicated Post Office officials as Sir Roland German, the Director General, and Bill Ryland and Ian Wolstonecraft, his two deputies.

I told him about my efforts to persuade Frank Cousins not to resign and I said I thought his going would weaken the Government. But, always the supreme rationaliser, Harold said it would be good for sterling. (In this the next few weeks proved him quite wrong. We were heading for a major sterling crisis, and Frank's resignation, if it had any effect whatever, presumably hastened it.)

He then, rather touchingly, told me he was to have a press conference at the weekend to announce the Government

283

changes and, in case anyone thought I was getting the sack, he would say he had intended to give me a department in October anyhow, but was doing so now as an opportunity had arisen. This remark seemed to me the clearest indication that, in his mind, I *was* getting the sack – though I doubt whether anyone else would have seen it in that way.

I was rather saddened to be going with this whiff of failure in the air, even though it was probably confined to Harold's conscience. But, I consoled myself, that is the lot of all ministers, even of Prime Ministers. Their going is rarely without some sense of failure.

John Silkin was to follow me as Chief Whip. To him would fall the unenviable task of getting the prices and incomes legislation through the House and persuading a mainly hostile Party to support it. And the best of luck to him, I thought.

One of the daunting aspects of being a minister is that you are sitting at your desk one day dictating letters, making decisions and being advised by Civil Servants whom you have come to know and like, and the next day you are either out on the street or, if you are fortunate, sitting at another desk in a different department dictating different letters, making different decisions and being advised by Civil Servants who are strangers to you.

I had to be at Post Office Headquarters at St Martins-le-Grand, behind St Paul's, on the Monday morning, and so I had to spend most of the weekend clearing out my papers and other belongings from No. 12. In the twenty months I had been there I had accumulated thousands of letters – each with a copy of the reply I had sent pinned to it. Many were angry reactions to some Government action – or inaction; others were effusive and fulsome in their praise of the Government – a fair number written, no doubt, with the honours list in mind!; but the vast majority were between these two extremes. This was an episode in my life which had ended, and I had always thought it was a conceit on the part of politicians to accumulate their 'papers' and eventually bequeath them to a library or university. Apart from the Churchills and Lloyd Georges, few of these collections are ever likely to be of sufficient historical significance to justify storage, let alone cataloguing. I decided to destroy them all, except one short letter, which I had received by hand at breakfast-time one morning during the summer of 1965 after a very difficult night in the House. It read:

10 Downing Street
11.15 p.m.

My dear Ted,
    Heartiest congratulations to you, Sydney, to John Silkin and to all your Whips on this great result.
    I will say no more than this: between you, you have saved the Labour Government and all we are able to do, in all the years we remain, will be due to your efforts at this testing time.
    It cannot have been easy, and we who have been remote from your efforts, can have little idea of the organisation and dedication which lay behind the result.
    On behalf of this Labour Movement and everyone here and overseas who may be depending on us – thank you for what you have done.
                                    Yours ever
                                    HAROLD

At least, I thought, I have this – the accolade of having saved the Government. Nothing can take it away. And it was all I ever wanted from my time as Whip to Wilson.

INDEX

287

290